FLY FISHING IN SALT WATER
Lefty Kreh

Fully Illustrated

Introduction by Frank Woolner

CROWN PUBLISHERS, INC., NEW YORK

This book is dedicated to my wife,
EVELYN,
who gave me the time and encouragement
to gather the information and experiences
needed to do such a work

Library of Congress Catalog Card Number: 73-82957

Manufactured in the United States of America
Published simultaneously in Canada by General Publish-
ing Company Limited
ISBN: 0-517-506130

10 9 8 7 6 5 4 3 2

CONTENTS

INTRODUCTION / iv

PART ONE •
THE LURE AND TACKLE OF SALTWATER FLY FISHING / 1

1 • The Lure of Saltwater Fly Fishing / 2
2 • Saltwater vs. Freshwater Fly Fishing / 5
3 • Tides / 10
4 • Tackle / 14
5 • Knots and Leaders / 35
6 • Flies / 61

PART TWO •
TECHNIQUES / 89

7 • Saltwater Fly Casting / 90
8 • Angling Techniques / 106

PART THREE •
INSHORE AND DEEP-WATER
SPECIES AND STRATEGIES / 143

9 • Inshore Fishing / 144
10 • Deep-Water Fishing / 204
11 • Boats / 234
12 • SWFRA—The Saltwater Fly Fisherman's Home / 246

Index / 251

Introduction

When I met Lefty Kreh, a lot of years ago at Barnegat Bay, New Jersey, satanic friends arranged an elaborate put-on. "You'll be fishing with a beginner," they said, "so don't cast too far. Make him look good."

Because I am a natural patsy, my throws were limited to 40 or 50 feet. We caught a few striped bass on popping bugs and I noted—with furrowed brow—that my "beginner" seemed very capable.

Presently I saw him stripping all of the fly line off his reel, plus an astounding amount of backing. *This dude has to be out of his mind,* I thought, but wisely refrained from comment.

He made one false cast and then, still telling me some outrageous tale (Lefty has more ribald stories than anyone in the world), put some muscle into a final effort and dropped his rod into the bow of the boat.

I don't remember the story because I was hypnotized. That line kept going out—and out! Loose coils spiraled off the deck. Loops straightened and reserve backing whistled through the guides like a herd of snakes. Whap! A good 120-foot cast touched down, better by 30 feet than anything I could achieve by grunting and groaning.

So I cursed the man in several languages—grimly, joyously. Friends in a nearby boat laughed so hard they almost fell overboard. I'd been had.

Since that time we've become pretty good friends, and it has been my pleasure. Lefty wears well. If he has detractors—and I haven't met them—then you can figure professional jealousy. He's just very good.

Kreh is, well—Kreh! Physically, he is no mountain of a man, but he is built like a friendly gorilla. They say he can be "Crab-Kreh" on a fishing ground where you can't measure up to his standards. I haven't seen this, but it is true of every great sport fisherman in the world.

He is balding, twinkle-eyed, possessed of steel-trap reflexes. He is the best teacher of fly casting I have ever seen: a ten-minute session with Lefty is better than ten years of trial-and-error experimentation. He is a master of trivia and he knows more shortcuts than anyone in the business. He has fished all over the world, in sweet and salt water, and he is an authority.

Kreh is a showman who can produce the goods. Goggle-eyed, I have watched him double-haul an effortless 100 feet, then do the same thing with no haul at all. To cap the demonstration, he throws 100 feet or better with nothing but the tip section of a fly rod. He is that strange bird, the superb caster who is also a master angler.

Lefty is not a hard-drinking man—in fact he is very cautious with the sauce—but I like him best in some dim, leather-upholstered sewer where we trade good-natured insults, ridiculous jokes, and tales of great fishing. That's much better than competition—although I am always eager to be instructed. In marine fly casting Kreh can give me aces and spades and beat me with a slice of rye bread. He's just the best, and I offer this appreciation grudgingly because I am an all-out competitor.

I have a feeling that this book must become a primer for the big league saltwater fly caster, both beginner and expert. It is a cornucopia of how-to, ranging from a detailed examination of tackle components up through the high art of playing big fish offshore and inshore. Plus lots more, like an examination of boats suitable for fly casting, chumming, teasing, and—naturally—a comprehensive list of fly patterns the author deems most effective, and why. Lefty knows what he is talking about: he is one of the most exciting fly-rod technicians in America today.

Frank Woolner

PART ONE

THE LURE AND TACKLE OF
SALTWATER FLY FISHING

1 The Lure of Saltwater Fly Fishing

Why would a man want to fly-fish in salt water? There are many reasons, some obvious, others understood only by those who have actually tried this kind of fishing. The sea has always been a fascination to me, and the creatures in it offer the greatest challenge a fly rodder will ever know. The solitude on a mountain brook is a taste of the real solitude of wading along the shore or on a shallow flat in search of trophy fish.

Saltwater fish are much stronger than their freshwater counterparts. The freshwater fly rodder worries that a fish may break his leader—the saltwater man occasionally wonders if he owns enough line to hold the fish streaking through the water with his fly in its mouth. No one can really describe the run of a bonefish, the slugging battle of a jack crevalle, the mighty leap of a tarpon; these things have to be experienced. Once they are, the freshwater angler is never the same.

Anyone who has hooked a tarpon of more than 100 pounds and seen it emerge from the surface like a silver rocket, throwing water like a broken fire hose, appreciates fly fishing at its best. To watch a billfish, enraged because it cannot get the teaser, suddenly charge your fly as it trails in blue water behind the transom will thrill you as no freshwater fishing moment can. I once hooked a 50-pound Allison tuna in 150 feet of water on the Challenger Banks off Bermuda. Nothing, literally *nothing*, has ever stripped line from my reel with the speed of that fish—it was awesome. And when, twenty minutes later, I had that magnificent game fish lying fifteen feet off the transom, exhausted but still beating its tail, I was completely overjoyed. Minutes later the line had somehow tangled in the rudder and the fish was lost; but the memory of that great fish and the battle that it gave was worth the game.

No stocked fish roam the seas. These are fish straight from God's hand, and they are in prime condition. There is little cover in the sea, and since almost every sea creature feeds upon something smaller than itself, the only way the pursued can escape is to go away—fast. Species that did not learn to swim quickly did not endure. When a saltwater fish hits your fly, its speed is evident as it strains your tackle in its natural attempt to escape.

Unlike fresh waters, the sea is wide open to anyone who has a boat or cares to wade. And, while fresh waters are diminishing at an alarming rate, there has been only a slight decrease in the areas good for saltwater fly fishing. In fact, new saltwater fishing areas are being discovered all the time, as adventurous fishermen test new waters.

Saltwater fly fishing often combines the best qualities of hunting and fishing. Such is bonefishing, seeking permit or tarpon, searching for big cruising sharks on the flats, looking for heavy stripers that move up on the mud flats to feed, or trying to stalk a big shark in the shallow water. Sight-fishing is one of the ultimate thrills for the true angler, and many like this type of angling so well that they do no other kind.

Where it is tailored to the fishing, as for dolphin, bonefish, tarpon, and other fish that take flies well, the fly rod is really the most efficient tool for the sport.

As an outdoors writer for more than twenty years, I have fished for everything from giant tuna to bluegills, with anglers who have sampled every area of fishing. I have never met a single fisherman who did not prefer a fly rod to any other type of tackle.

You need not justify the lure of saltwater fly rodding to those who have tried it.

The brown trout may frustrate you, but a permit will drive you mad. Fewer than one hundred of these fish have been taken on a fly rod in all the years they have been pursued. I kissed the first one I caught; it weighed only 5 pounds. The permit is an extremely strong fish, perhaps one of the strongest in the sea. It is endowed with keen eyesight, and it's as wary as a cat in a dog pound, ready to flee at the least disturbance. Permit will rarely take a fly, but enough have done so to encourage us to keep trying. Perhaps someday, someone will discover an effective technique for fishing this wary game; until that time, the permit will remain the supreme challenge for a fly rodder.

A 10-pound striped bass offers little resistance on a rugged surf-spinning stick, but that same fish on a light fly rod and leader is another experience. Somehow, a sea fish caught on fly tackle is that much more rewarding.

There is a bonus thrill, too: fishing over huge schools of feeding fish. Anyone who has ever approached a school of savage bluefish or jacks tearing into frantic baitfish, and tossed a fly into the carnage, wants to keep repeating this experience forever. The excitement of the chase—getting there before the school goes down, and then catching as many fish as you can—is difficult to describe.

Mark Sosin casts his fly to a big Bahama bonefish near Grand Cay.

2 Saltwater vs. Freshwater Fly Fishing

Nearly three-quarters of the earth is covered by salt water, most of it relatively unexplored by fly fishermen. Naturally, the high seas are not considered fly-fishing waters, even though many anglers do fish with flies many miles from shore. But somewhere, at any time of the year, saltwater fishing is at its peak. Bluefishing on the northeast coast is at its best in late summer; Florida bluefishermen like the winter period. The angler who can travel can find his sport somewhere whenever he can get away.

Much of the potential of saltwater angling is yet to be discovered. Central America, South America, Africa, and perhaps much of Asia offer fishing better than most of us have ever experienced. I've waded flats in Central America where I've seen more bonefish in a week than I do in a year in Florida, and the fish were just about as wary as those in Florida.

As new areas open to pioneering anglers, tackle is improved, and better techniques are developed, we will find the fishing even more exciting. Whereas freshwater angling has few real physical frontiers anymore (but plenty of room for refinement in technique), saltwater fly fishing is still in its infancy, and there are a lot of "growing" years ahead.

The various areas of the oceans are vastly different in terms of their underwater geography, and of the fish species that inhabit them. The fish in northern coastal waters eat different foods and live in a different environment from their cousins in tropical waters—and require different fly-fishing approaches and techniques.

No significant insect hatches occur on the seas as they do on fresh waters. The saltwater fishes exist primarily on smaller fishes, crustaceans, and other bottom life. Exact imitation is relatively unimportant, except in a few cases.

Freshwater fishes are minor league swimmers compared to the wahoo, the kingfish, and the barracuda. To the uninitiated, the ferocity of a barracuda's strike, its prodigious leaping, and its sheer strength will be startling. Gene Utech, a great trout fisherman, hooked a 20-pound barracuda the first time he went fly fishing in salt water with me. The cuda proceeded to jump over a small mangrove bush on its first run, breaking the leader in the process; the expression on Gene's face was something to behold.

Saltwater fish are, with a few exceptions, much stronger than freshwater fish. We all like to think of the bass and the trout as real battlers, but we scale our tackle down to give the fish a chance. An albacore or a jack crevalle needs no handicap—they can slug it out on any tackle you can find. Fishing near the Dry Tortugas with Jim Gilford several years ago, I located a school of permit on a wreck in shallow water. Jim had hooked several fish, but they had repeatedly broken his line. Finally, determined that he would land one, Jim locked the drag on a heavy-duty trolling reel loaded with 50-pound monofilament. He cast to a school of 30-pounders, and they swarmed to the surface. Jim sat down in the front of the boat, and waited for one of the fish to take the crab. He felt the line come tight and struck; the rod bent like a question mark. Straining, neither Jim nor his drag would yield; the big permit began to beat its sickle tail in an effort to get back to the wreck below and safety. Slowly, very slowly, Jim was pulled from the boat seat to his knees. Then the fish dragged Jim and the rod the entire length of the boat. When he came up against the fish locker at the back of the boat, the rod bent even deeper.

Jim is a husky guy, and he hung on.

Suddenly, like a firecracker exploding, the 50-pound monofilament broke, and Jim fell into the bottom of the boat. The fish had escaped. No 30-pound freshwater fish can drag a man the length of an 18-foot boat and break a 50-pound line in the process. Saltwater species are tough, and the fly rodder new to this fishing will learn quickly to appreciate their strength.

Saltwater tackle must receive extreme care. Guides must be securely attached; the rod must have casting *and* lifting power. When a 100-plus-pound tarpon is lying eight feet below the boat, the angler must often forcibly lift the fish with his own muscle and the latent power

The lifting power of a rod required to bring up a big tarpon like this one that Captain Cal Cochran is gaffing for Bob Stearns, is clearly demonstrated here. Note that Bob has lifted the 100-pound tarpon to the surface with a reserve of bending power still in the lower portion of the rod.

appeared an amberjack, cobia, or large grouper that simply inhaled the hooked fish. Teasing a big amberjack or sailfish with live bait right at boatside, then throwing a large popping bug or streamer fly at the fish, which takes it with a splash that fills your face with salt water, is a tremendous thrill.

Fishing salt water is different in many ways, perhaps the greatest being the fact that you can often tangle with what appear to be unlimited numbers of fish—and opponents so powerful that unless you follow a careful plan, the fish will win, and even destroy a certain part of your tackle.

Much of your inshore fishing will be done from a poled boat, the active fisherman standing near the bow, hunting the fish. Other methods of fishing shallow water include wading, drifting, and using an electric motor on a boat.

3 Tides

Perhaps the greatest adjustment a freshwater angler will have to make is learning to fish with the tides. In freshwater angling, temperature and clarity of the water are the two most important factors. If water temperatures are acceptable to the trout, and the streams are not roiled by rains, the angler can usually fish successfully. That is not true in salt water.

Temperature is important, of course, but turbidity in salt water is rarely a factor. Sometimes water will muddy from wind or wave action, and bottom-feeding fish like mullet and bonefish create mud, but these waters will clear with the next tide.

The tide especially influences inshore fishing, though it also affects some offshore angling. Since most fly fishing is conducted in the shallows, it is vital for the angler to have a basic understanding of the tides.

Few people who fish really understand much about tides and what they do to fishing conditions and how they affect angler success. Thus an angler not familiar with a specific area should either hire a guide or at least inform himself about tidal effects on local waters.

The tide causes many changes. One, important to the angler, is a temperature change. Shallow water that has lain under a hot summer sun will become too uncomfortable for fish; but as the tide rises, it brings in cooler water from deeper areas, and with this come larger fish. The tide has an enormous effect upon water clarity. It can sweep all muddied water from an area, exchanging it for clear water; and it can carry away all debris and floating grass which during the previous tide had made it impossible to retrieve a fly.

Rising tide can cause fish to move into a specific area or to be widely scattered. Low tides can cause fish to concentrate in scattered deep pools in the shallows, for safety. Common sense helps in analyzing tidal effects: if there are wide shallow flats with a deep, narrow channel cutting through them, on low stages of the tide you would certainly expect most fish to be in the channels. Another basic tidal situation that any fly fisherman can easily understand and take advantage of is an inland bay or lagoon. If such a body of water is tide-drained through a narrow creek, fish will obviously feed on the bait swept through such a funnel-like arrangement. The place to fish is at the downtide side of the mouth of the creek.

River mouths are in most cases best fished on a falling tide. Some rivers have bars at the mouth where feeding stations occur on rising tides. But as the tide rises, moving inland, the baitfish will seek shelter in the shallows. When the water falls, the predator fish know that the baitfish will be swept from the shallows, and will wait at any drainage area to intercept them.

Much of the striped bass fly rodding in the New England area is done as shown here. Howard Laws works the shoreline near Shelter Island, New York. The tides are critical!

So the most important fact for fishermen to know about tides is that tidal currents carry the small baitfish to and fro. These tiny fishes can't swim against the tide, so they must drift with it. Larger fish know this and take up their feeding positions accordingly.

Even people with some understanding of the tides mistakenly think they are caused entirely by the gravitational pull of the moon. The National Oceanic and Atmospheric Administration (NOAA) employs thirty-seven variables in figuring its tidal predictions. The word is *predictions,* because they are not always borne out.

The wind is an important factor in relation to tides. For example, on the West Coast when the prediction is for a high tide at 6:00 P.M. but there is an exceptionally strong west wind blowing against the shore, high tide will occur a little earlier, and it will certainly be higher than was predicted. The warming of northern seas in the summer can cause higher tides at that time of year. Barometric pressure can affect the tide's height. Even a flexing of the earth's surface can affect the tide.

But the moon and the sun cause the major effects. If the angler has some basic understanding of these two bodies, he can better relate his fishing to the tides. It takes twenty-eight days (scientists say the time is a little less), or roughly a month, for the moon to travel around the earth; it does not move in a perfect circle. At points in its orbit the moon is farther away, and this reduces its tidal effect. The moon exerts nearly two and a half times as much gravitational pull on the earth as does the sun. As the moon moves around the earth the water is pulled toward it. Naturally, the "bulge" in the earth's water is always behind the moon as it orbits the earth. During the month, as the moon completes one circle of our planet, there is a seven-day period when it is closer to us than at any other time during that twenty-eight-day period. And the sun and the moon are in nearly a direct line with the earth. When this positioning of the three bodies occurs, the tides rise higher and fall lower than at any other time during the month. These are called spring tides. At this time the moon is said to be in perigee (usually indicated on tidal charts).

The moon will continue to circle the earth, and during the next seven-day period there will be only a slight rise and fall in the tide. When minimal tides occur, they are referred to as "nip" tides, properly called neap tides. During the next seven days there will be another set of spring tides, but they will not range quite as high or low as the first set of spring tides. Following this will be a week of nip tides. Then the cycle is repeated.

Broken down into a simple pattern, what the fisherman can expect during a twenty-eight-day period is a week of spring tides, a week of nip tides, another week of spring tides, and finally, a second week of nip tides.

How can you quickly determine which kind of tide is occurring in your local area? Simple: if you see a full moon or a new moon (no moon or a very small sickle) there is a spring tide condition. If the moon is in one of the quarters, there will be a nip tide.

There is another fact about tidal effects that inshore fishermen should understand. The moon is not only in an elliptical path around the earth, but it is alternately north or south of the equator. Naturally, in North America the tidal effects will be greater when the moon is above the equator.

On both the Atlantic and Pacific coasts the tide rises and falls twice in a twenty-four-hour period. Let's say you are fishing San Francisco Bay around the pilings and take big stripers on a spring tide. Note the day and the hour when the fish are biting well. Suppose it's two o'clock in the afternoon on the tenth day of the month. If you come back on the twenty-fourth at exactly two o'clock and weather conditions are approximately the same, you can reasonably expect stripers to be feeding well again since tides repeat themselves roughly every two weeks.

Just as important is to be aware that reverse tides occur exactly a week apart. If you had great fishing in Nantucket Bay last Saturday, where a rising tide was carrying baitfish across a bar, don't go back there next Saturday at the same time—the tide will be exactly opposite.

Remember, too, that tides occur roughly one hour later each day. So, if today tarpon were riding up on the bank along a certain shallows at eleven in the morning, you can expect them to show about noon tomorrow—assuming weather conditions are about the same. Fish respond to weather as well as tide, and if a radical weather change occurs, they will react to it, *regardless of the tide*.

How can you determine what kind of tides will occur in your area? There are a number of ways. Local newspapers along the coast usually carry tide tables. Regional magazines often carry them, too. Two books published by the National Oceanic and Atmospheric Administration give the tides throughout the Western Hemisphere. These books are available for $2.00 each from NOAA, U.S. Department of Commerce, Washington, D.C., or from major marine stores. The titles of the two books are *Tide Tables—High and Low Water Predictions* (specify year) *for the East Coast of North and South America* and *Tide Tables—High and Low*

Water Predictions for the West Coast of North and South America (including *the Hawaiian Islands*).

Remember a very important point about reading a tide table: the listed time is for a specific area. If you want to know the tidal conditions some distance from that point, you must look for a tidal "correction." Here is an example: if the tide begins to rise at the mouth of Barnegat Bay, New Jersey, naturally it will be higher at the inlet before it reaches the same stage farther up the bay at Tom's River. And as the tide falls, it will reach the lower stage first nearer the inlet. The tidal correction tables will indicate that there is perhaps a three-hour difference between high tide at the inlet and high tide at Tom's River. Therefore, if high tide is to occur at noon at the inlet, you know that it is due at about 3:00 P.M. at Tom's River.

The charts show water depths, and although the depths are indicated in a slightly different manner on East and West Coast charts, the figures are reliable. Unlike maps, which tell you where to go, most of the time these charts indicate where you should *not* go.

There are some areas, like the Gulf of Mexico, where only one tide occurs daily. And in some parts of the Gulf there is practically no rise and fall. Pensacola, Florida, sees practically no tidal effect! If two persons move up and down on a seesaw, they rise and fall considerably, but the center of the board remains at one point. Pensacola is in a position comparable to the center of the seesaw.

The fly fisherman who goes fishing in the salt must learn some of the basics about tides—or hire a good guide—if he is to succeed.

4 Tackle

FLY LINES

Any discussion of fly-casting tackle must begin with the line. Most anglers buy what they feel is the correct rod, then find a line to match it. Wrong!

The fly line transports the fly to the target. If you're casting large, bulky, wind-resistant flies, then it is vital that the line be able to overcome all handicaps. If you are fishing on a bonefish flat with calm water, a perfectly matched heavy rod and line will not do. The resounding crash of the heavy line on the water will frighten your quarry.

Since you are going to select the line first, you should know something about the various tapers. There are four basic ones: level, double-taper, weight-forward, and single-taper (called shooting taper). Saltwater fly fishermen should be concerned only with weight-forward and single-taper lines; levels and double-tapers have little application in saltwater fishing.

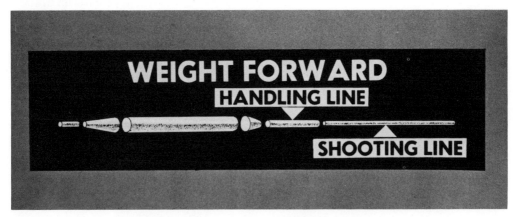

Weight-forward line, showing component parts; leader is attached to left end of line.

Weight-forward means that most of the line's weight is concentrated in the first 30 or so feet from the tip; behind this large portion is a thin running line. The angler will work the heavier portion outside the guides, then make a forward cast. At the end of the stroke he releases the running line, which is easily dragged through the guides by the heavier portion. Weight-forward lines allow the angler to fish the fly toward him until only the weight-for-ward section of the line remains outside the guides. Then, with a quick backcast and a forward cast, he can shoot the fly back to the target and begin his retrieve.

This part of the line with a larger diameter is called the *belly*. The belly section length differs with various manufacturers, but most of them make a belly approximately 20 feet long, with a 10-foot taper in front and 2 or 3 feet tapering to the rear to meet the running line.

When sight-fishing for tarpon, bonefish, and other species, the angler can hold the fly and part of the weight-forward line in his hand until he sees a fish; a special weight-forward taper, called a saltwater taper, has been designed for this type of fishing.

This taper is approximately 5 feet shorter than the standard weight-forward, allowing the angler to hold much of the belly section outside the rod guides. Thus, when he sees a fish, the angler can throw the belly section into the air, and with one false cast, shoot the fly to the target.

The saltwater taper has another advantage. It was designed to give a positive turn-over with big flies and bugs, due to its short, stubby front taper. While most people feel that this specific design does aid in casting heavy, bulky flies, I'd like to emphasize that it is also valuable where speed-casting is vital. In most saltwater fly fishing situations, particularly for striped bass and bluefish, the saltwater taper does not cast as well, form as good a loop, or present the fly as nicely as a standard weight-forward.

The standard weight-forward, with the weight distributed over a longer portion of the line, forms a much smoother loop, and certainly does not "dump" a lighter fly at the end of the presentation. Saltwater tapers, being larger in diameter, also increase air resistance, so that long, into-the-wind casts are more difficult.

When casting with a weight-forward taper, of any design, the angler should start with the weight-forward section outside the rod tip, and make as few false casts as possible there-after, before shooting the line. An efficient caster usually will not bring any portion of the weight-forward section inside the rod guides. This he can pick up, and with a single back-and-forward cast shoot line a reasonable distance. Knowing just where to make the pickup with the belly section outside the rod tip took experience. Scientific Anglers solved the problem for those not quite expert by installing a "bump" in the running line, called a "Tele-Cast." The angler, stripping on his retrieve, can feel the bump as it hits his fingers; he then picks up the fly and makes a backcast, and then shoots to the target.

Aside from the two basic designs, weight-forward lines come in different types. Most popular is the floating weight-forward: all of the line floats. This is one line that all fishermen should carry in their box. The floating line is extremely versatile, its greatest asset being that it can be lifted from the water for a backcast at any point during the retrieve. Some lines that have a portion which lies under water require that the angler bring the fly close to the rod tip before making a backcast.

There are variations of the floating line. The intermediate-density is a very slow-sinking line—like a silk line—if it isn't dressed with flotant. It *will* float (again, like a silk line) poorly, if dressed. The intermediate-density is growing in popularity among fishermen seeking giant tarpon.

The sinking tip is a line that, except for the first 10 feet, also floats. This is a valuable line for fishing in relatively shallow water where you want the fly to sink quickly; because most of the line floats, it is fairly easy to lift a lot of line from the water and make a quick backcast to a cruising fish.

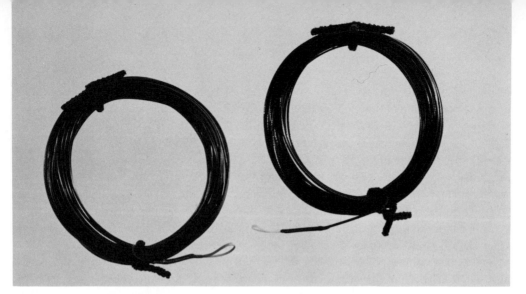

Several shooting tapers, leaders already connected. These lines in different weights of sinking characteristics can be carried in the angler's pocket and quickly substituted for the line in use.

Another useful variety of floating weight-forward line is the sinking head: the entire head sinks. This is an especially valuable line when the angler is fishing in four to six feet of water and wants to "bomb" the fly toward the bottom, but also wants the advantages of casting a floating line. It is excellent for fishing big tarpon.

Weight-forward lines are also made in slow-sinking designs. Often used in the same place as an intermediate-density, this line has great application to specific problems. Tarpon fishermen love it, and bonefish in two to three feet of water are better fished with such a line. However, if a tarpon should turn off course, most of the line will have to be stripped back to the angler before he can pick up and make a backcast and shoot the fly again.

Northern anglers are plagued with floating grasses, and the intermediate-density and slow-sinking lines will settle through the grass and ride under water. Floating lines stay on top during the retrieve and funnel the grass down to the hook.

Fast-sinking lines are sometimes preferred over the slow-sinking variety. Extra-fast-sinking lines, of which Scientific Anglers' Hi-D is the almost universal choice, sink extremely well, so you can fish the bottom in twenty feet of water if there isn't a strong current. Being thinner in diameter, the line will cast better in the wind. But there are disadvantages, too; the running line is rather limp and breeds tangles on long casts. In addition, the line must be brought to within twenty feet of the boat and a high roll cast made to lift the line from beneath the surface before a forward cast can be made. Most anglers agree that the floating line is infinitely more pleasurable to use, but many stick with the extra-fast-sinking line simply because it is the correct one for the job.

There is still another type of line worth considering, for it allows the angler to cast longer distances and fish deeper, if he desires, than with conventional line tapers. The *shooting taper* (called *single taper* by the manufacturers) has reached a zenith of popularity on the West Coast, though it has surprisingly few adherents on the East Coast. A shooting taper is 30 feet, or less, of weight-forward line, to which is connected some very thin running line, usually 100 feet in length. The idea here is that the angler can make a backcast with the relatively heavy 30-foot section, and when he releases the extra-thin running line at the end of his forward cast, the larger taper will drag the lighter line easily through the guides.

You can make a floating or sinking shooting taper by cutting the first 30 feet from a standard double-taper line. Then make a connecting loop of Dacron on the rear of the line, and tie your extra-thin running line to it. Of course, the other end of the double taper can be used in the same manner. Some anglers like to remove one foot from the tip section of a 30-foot head, claiming that this lends superior casting qualities to the line.

Since a double taper, a single or shooting taper, and a weight-forward taper all have almost identical tapers for the first 30 feet, you can also make a shooting taper from the front portion of a weight-forward line; however, you will lose the advantage of getting another shooting taper from the rear end, as you would with a double taper.

Originally, monofilament was used as the extra-thin material for the running line that connected to the shooting taper. Of the many kinds of monofilament, two types have emerged as the most popular. One is the oval design monofilament, which tends to spiral and twist under hard use. There is another type of monofilament, very soft, which, when stretched, releases the coils that were acquired under storage. This line is marketed as Maxima; most freshwater anglers prefer the 20-pound-test, but for several reasons the 30-pound-test is recommended for hard use in salt water. It is less likely to tangle, seems to blow around the boat less, and, being larger in diameter, it is easier to grasp.

Another type of line is rapidly replacing the use of monofilament. This is a super-thin fly line, about size level 3; both Cortland the Scientific Anglers market this line. Scientific Anglers makes it in bright orange, and this coloration will help you keep the fly under surveillance.

There are other advantages to using the shooting fly line over monofilament. Monofilament comes off the spool in coils, and of course shooting line does not. Shooting line is easier to grasp. (Of course, you can make monofilament float by adding fly dressing to it, but a shooting line floats without dressing.) Very little distance is sacrificed. The amount of overhang (distance between the rear of the shooting taper and the rod tip) is much less critical with a shooting line than it is with monofilament. Being able to see the orange (or other bright color) shooting line in flight allows some anglers to apply "English" to the cast, to correct its flight. And the line does not blow around the boat or the water surface as easily as monofilament. When using monofilament or shooting line and a shooting taper you can easily hit 120 feet on a cast, which will result in a lot of line lying all over the floor, ready to tangle. One way of preventing this is with a shooting basket, described in detail later. Another way is to place a garbage can, with a block of ice in the bottom, in the boat near the caster. The ice serves several purposes. It prevents the can from overturning, as the ice quickly conforms to the can bottom. It is cold and wet; the coldness stiffens the shooting line or monofilament, and the water lubricates it, allowing much better casting.

Shooting tapers come in the five types already described in the discussion of weight-forward lines: floating, intermediate-density, slow-sinking, fast-sinking, and extra-fast-sinking. You can attach the monofilament to the rear of the shooting taper with a clinch knot, or better,

Shooting taper, leader connected to left end; shooting line is connected to backing on fly reel.

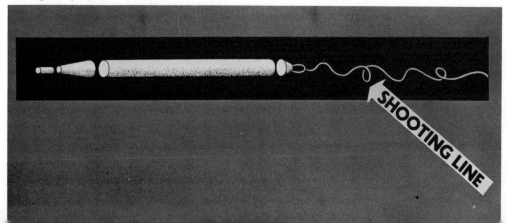

a needle knot. Some people like to build a loop in the shooting line and another in the shooting taper, allowing them to interchange various tapers with the same shooting line.

Floating shooting heads are very effective when you're wading shallow beaches and blind casting, where long casts are necessary. The angler wading for stripers on the northeast coast can double his effective casting area with a shooting taper.

Fast-sinking and extra-fast-sinking shooting tapers have great application for deepwater fishing. An extra-fast-sinking conventional fly line often cannot get to the bottom in swift current; there is too much drag against the line. The extra-fast-sinking head, with very thin shooting line, offers less water resistance, and so allows you to fish much deeper with the same fly.

There is a very specialized type of shooting taper available, called a lead-core head. Lead-core trolling line is used in place of the conventional shooting taper; the lead builds up incredible speed during a cast and you can throw a fly to distances that will astound you. It can also nearly make you jump from a boat if the lead-core head strikes you in the back on the forward cast. It's dangerous, so handle it with care.

One lead-core line is by far the best choice for our purpose: the Gladding Mark Five, made by the Gladding Company. This is a conventional lead-core line with an outer coating of clear plastic, which makes the line much easier to handle. It comes in connected 100-yard spools. The lead core is soft lead, and it is the same diameter in all sizes. That is, if you buy a 60-pound-test line and a 30-pound-test line, you will have two lines with the identical lead-core size, but the outer braided line will have more strength. Therefore, it is recommended that you purchase line that does not exceed 30-pound-test, since you increase resistance in the air and water if you increase the line size.

Start with 30 feet of lead-core line if your rod handles a number 10 or 11 line. If you find that it overloads the rod, cut off a foot of the lead-core line at a time, testing to see which amount of line suits you.

Most anglers attach the lead-core line to the running line with an Albright Special knot.

One great advantage of the shooting taper over conventional lines is that you can carry one reel, loaded with shooting line and backing. In your pocket you should carry several types of heads, kept in place with pipe cleaners. When you require a certain head, untwist the pipe cleaners and loop the head on the rig. If you decide later to change heads, you can simply unloop the one in use, wrap it up, replace the pipe cleaners around it, and install the new head.

It's appropriate to mention here that whenever you make an extended trip, you should carry spare lines or shooting tapers. I have frequently had lines ruined by being cut on a sharp rock, a barnacle, or an obstruction.

Conventional fly lines range from 90 to 115 feet in length. Shooting heads are about 130 feet, if you count shooting line and shooting taper. That's not nearly enough line to subdue a free-running king mackerel, sailfish, large striper, or bonefish. You need to have backing attached to the fly line.

Backing is a fighting strategy tool. It allows the fish to run a great distance, at great expense of its energy, and still be connected to your reel. Backing must be strong enough to battle the fish, yet take up little room on the spool. For general saltwater fly fishing, where you do not expect to encounter monsters, 18-pound-test Dacron or Micron is recommended. If larger fish are to be fought over an extended period, then approximately 30-pound-test Dacron or Micron is more desirable.

Monofilament spinning line should only be used on very special occasions. Monofilament stretches under strain, afterward returning to its original shape. If you fight a strong fish with monofilament backing, stretching the line, it will later attempt to return to its original shape, and may ruin the reel spool.

But there's an even more important reason for using Dacron or Micron instead of monofilament. Because the monofilament came onto the reel during the battle under varying degrees of pressure, some portion will be lightly placed on the reel, forming a soft bed. On top of that may come some very tightly stretched line, which tends to burrow into the softer bedding. When a long-running fish takes off, the line will, of course, peel smoothly from the reel until it hits the buried spot. There will be a definite lurch, and often the line will snap. And remember, when fighting any big fish, it is usually the sharp jolt that breaks the line, not steady pressure.

Dacron or Micron is relatively nonstretchable compared to monofilament. It is important, however, when you first spool the line on the reel, to establish a good firm bedding.

Squidding line, a special type of braided Dacron, is essentially coreless. Squidding line will serve almost as well as Dacron or Micron as backing material. Chapter 5, on knots and leaders, shows how to attach Dacron or squidding line backing to the fly line.

Many anglers often cut back on the running line to obtain more space for backing. Most of the good tarpon anglers I know fish with a conventional fly line that has had at least 10 feet removed from the rear portion. When fishing for fast-running fishes, like tuna, king mackerel, and the billfishes, you will find it helpful to shorten the line to reduce water friction against the fly line. If you fish with a 6-pound tippet, you'll quickly discover that fast-running fish can break the tippet because of the fly line's resistance. Billy Pate, who with his wife Laura caught world-record black marlin on 6-, 10-, 12-, and 15-pound-test tippets in Australia, found he had to cut his fly line to a total length of 18 feet and use 100 feet of 20-pound-test monofilament in front of the backing when using 6-pound-test tippet. Special situations will require unique answers.

The color of the line can often affect fly-fishing success. Bright, flashy lines, especially white, reflect light while the line is in flight, and the reflections often cause a nervous bonefish, tarpon, or permit to flee. I have seen bonefish flush from a false cast that was still some distance from them. The color that has won the widest acceptance among shallow-water anglers is dove gray. One manufacturer now tints his saltwater-taper lines this color. If you already have a line and want to change the color, you can use RIT dye, available at any supermarket, and just follow the directions on the box.

In fly casting, the line itself comprises the weight that is cast. Add a fly that is too heavy for the line and the line simply won't be able to transport it to the target. Anything placed on the fly-line end will somewhat impede the cast. The weight of the line must correctly match the power of the rod, too. Fortunately, almost all glass fiber rods today are made to handle a specific line best, and do a respectable job with a line one size lighter or heavier than the proper size.

Years ago lines were made differently, and you ordered a certain line by designating several combinations of letters, such as GAF or HCH. With the advent of plastics, line construction changed radically. Today all fly lines carry a standard braided core, over which is built a smooth plastic covering. These innovations threw the former line designations into chaos.

So the American Fishing Tackle Manufacturers' Association (AFTMA) established new guidelines. Each fly line is numbered according to size. In the case of tapered lines the AFTMA specifications call for the weighing of the first 30 feet of any fly line after all of the level tip section is removed. Now, no matter what manufacturer you buy your line from, if it is a number 10 line, it will be acceptably close to any other company's number 10, whether it is a sinking or a floating line.

The following table lists the differences between line sizes and the weight tolerances allowed by the AFTMA.

LINE SIZE	WEIGHT (grains/30')	TOLERANCE
1	60	Plus or minus 6 grains
2	80	Plus or minus 6 grains
3	100	Plus or minus 6 grains
4	120	Plus or minus 6 grains
5	140	Plus or minus 6 grains
6	160	Plus or minus 8 grains
7	185	Plus or minus 8 grains
8	210	Plus or minus 8 grains
9	240	Plus or minus 10 grains
10	280	Plus or minus 10 grains
11	330	Plus or minus 12 grains
12	380	Plus or minus 12 grains

As we have seen, not only do lines have weight, but they possess other characteristics such as taper, and floating or sinking qualities. With this in mind, AFTMA came up with a simple lettering system, so that by adding the relevant letters to the line number, you can see at a glance what line you have. We will not cover all the code letters used, only those more important to saltwater fly fishing.

F stands for floating; S means *sinking;* L tells you the line is *level* throughout; WF means *weight-forward;* DT indicates that it's a *double taper;* and of course ST means *single taper,* although it is usually referred to as shooting taper.

If you want to purchase a weight-forward line in size 8 that floats, the label will read WF-8-F. If you want a number 10 shooting taper that will sink, you order a ST-10-S; if you want a double-taper 6 floating line, you order a DT-6-F.

For practical saltwater work, fly lines of less than number 8 are infrequently used, and the most popular sizes are 9 through 11. However, there definitely are times when a number 12 fly line is a great asset. You may need this heavy line to flex the powerful rod used to battle giant tarpon, amberjack, or billfishes. A number 12 fly line, because of its enormous weight, will drag a popping bug with a face the size of a silver dollar—or a Lefty's Deceiver carrying 20 saddle hackles surrounding a number 7/0 hook—to a large fish forty feet away. Fish such as very large striped bass, more than 40 pounds in weight, are not going to be taken consistently with small flies. It will take a big feather duster to interest such fish, and a large, heavy fly line and rod to propel the fly to the fish.

RODS

It is vital that the line be selected for the particular fishing conditions anticipated. But if the rod is not properly matched to the line weight, the game will be no fun to play, and may be lost. Fishing is supposed to be fun, but it won't be with mismatched equipment.

It's true that many good anglers can cast sixty or more feet of fly line with a rod tip—but they certainly wouldn't fish with it. You need a rod that creates as few casting problems as possible, does not tire you, and stands up well to the elements.

Fly rods are made from either bamboo or fiberglass. Bamboo is the classic material, and while it casts well, it has never been accepted by the majority of serious saltwater fly fishermen. There are several difficulties with bamboo rods, including the selling price, which can exceed $150. Also, saltwater fly rods must handle lines on the upper limits of weights, from size 8 through 12; it takes a really stout, heavy bamboo rod to work a number 11 line. But there is another even more important reason for the general preference for glass fiber rods over bamboo in the salt: glass is infinitely tougher. Many large fish are fought and beaten under stress conditions that are marginal for bamboo, but the real crisis arises when a beaten fish, quite heavy, lies beneath the boat. The fish must be literally *lifted* by the rod and angler. Bamboo just won't do it, and every year you hear about bamboo rods that have failed in this critical situation.

Impregnated bamboo requires little upkeep, but rods without this protection are vulnerable to ruin in the salt if not well cared for. This evaluation of bamboo applies only to saltwater fly fishing; many fine bamboo rods, handling the smaller lines, and battling smaller freshwater fish, give superb service.

But glass rods are light, strong, and durable; they need little care, and, in my opinion, cast as well as, and often better than, good big bamboo rods. Many people share that opinion.

The various manufacturers construct rods with different tapers, or actions. A rod's action is difficult to describe; it is a thing you must feel. Correct rod action makes casting a delight; a poor rod can spoil your cast and your day.

All fly rods have a quality known as recovery; this is simply the number of vibrations made by a rod tip after a cast has been made. Well-designed rods will vibrate two or three times at the end of the forward power thrust, then the tip will stabilize as the running line pours through on the way to the target. If you observe the line on a good rod outside the tip top, you will see that the line flows smoothly, almost straight. Poorly designed rods, with a lot of shock in the tip section, will continue to vibrate after the power thrust and cause a series of rolling line waves or humps, which radically increase air resistance.

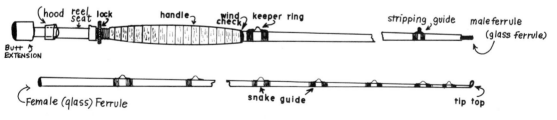

Rod nomenclature.

You can easily check a rod's recovery. Hold the rod in front of you and snap your wrist sideways, causing the rod to vibrate rapidly; then squeeze the rod handle. After you have squeezed the rod, the vibrations should stop almost immediately. If you get more than three or four vibrations after you have squeezed the rod, you are holding a rod with poor recovery.

There are three basic rod-action designs: fast-tip, progressive-taper, and slow-taper. Most of the fast-tip rod is very stiff and unyielding, the line being cast with little more than the upper fourth of the rod. An expert caster can throw a good line with almost any fly rod by making subtle adjustments in his casting technique, but the average angler will have considerable trouble trying to correct the faults of fast-tip rod action. Since only the tip section moves, the rod develops a very small, narrow loop that will often tangle toward the end of the cast. Timing is crucial throughout the cast. Lifting the line from the water is more difficult, and there may be trouble in striking a fish, since the tip tends to collapse.

The slow taper, also a poor choice, bends deeply down to the handle, even on a short cast. It tends to flex throughout its length whenever any stress is exerted against it. Slow rods rarely develop enough power for long casts. They slow down the angler who is trying to lift line from the water quickly to reach an escaping fish; and because they are so slow, they make it difficult for many people to time their cast properly.

A rod with a progressive taper and good recovery is the most desirable. Progressive taper means that the rod bends easily at the tip, gradually stiffening as more power is applied on the cast; it is a compromise between the other two rods.

If you could cast a number of rods you could probably tell quickly which ones you liked, and what their tapers were like. But unfortunately, most anglers must purchase a rod right from the store. With the snap test you can determine quickly whether the rod has good recovery, and there is a simple guide that will help establish whether a rod has a progressive or a fast taper. Hold the rod handle at eye level, extending the tip to the floor in front of you. Press the thumb and forefinger down on the rod handle and watch the tip. A good progressive-taper rod will rarely have more than 3 or 4 inches of the tip lying flat on the floor when gentle pressure is applied. If more than 6 inches touches the floor, eliminate the rod from your selections.

The length of the rod must be considered. For saltwater fly fishing you'll rarely want a rod of less than 8 feet. There is no question, however, about the fact that a shorter rod is superior for fighting fish. The most deadly fish-battling rod I have ever used was a 7½-footer. It was a heavy-duty spinning rod, and I used it on the reef line for groupers, amberjack, and other husky fish.

I got the idea of converting it to a fly rod after realizing that I had never seen a long offshore-trolling rod used against marlin and other huge fishes. These short boat rods are fighting tools. I converted the spinning stick to a fly rod, and I later landed a 100-pound tarpon in twelve minutes, and then a 28-pound amberjack in fourteen minutes. It was astounding what a short rod would do to a fish. When you moved the rod you moved the fish.

As in all things, however, there had to be compromise. The short stiff rod required an exceptionally heavy line to get any flexing from the rod shaft. More important, the timing required was too critical. I was fine in the backyard, casting flawlessly to 90 feet. But when a big fish appeared near the boat the whole cast often fell apart. I finally reconverted the rod back to spinning again, where it rightfully belonged.

A rod of 8 to 9½ feet is just right. This length allows the angler to pick line smoothly from the water, and he can hold it high above the line-cutting growths on a shallow flat, when a fish is running. The man who wades will also find a rod of about 9 feet helpful in keeping his backcast off the water. Long rods will allow you to manipulate the lure better, too.

Be sure to get the proper line weight for your rod. As mentioned before, a line that is too light won't carry the fly, and requires that you cast the rod rapidly to keep the line moving. A line that is too heavy will overload the rod, interrupt your timing, and generate too much line speed, tightening the loop too much, often dumping the cast. Almost all modern rods have the proper line size marked somewhere on the shaft. Scientific Anglers, the world's largest fly line manufacturer, has established a chart that suggests the proper line for most fly rods made today. You can get a free copy by writing to Scientific Anglers, P.O. Box 2001, Midland, Michigan 48640, requesting the latest line recommendation chart. Please enclose a self-addressed, stamped envelope.

You may think rod color is unimportant, and for much of saltwater fly fishing that's true. However, for fishing in the shallows for very wary species, dark-colored rods are preferable. A white or brightly colored rod may reflect light during the cast, and flush the fish.

The hardware on a saltwater fly rod is extremely important. It must stand the strain of fighting really strong fish; and it must resist saltwater corrosion. Look over carefully any rod that you intend to use in the salt. Many fly rods have a butt extension—a short section projecting toward the angler from the base of the reel seat; when you are fighting a fish it can be pushed against the body, putting the reel several inches away from entangling clothing. Though the butt extension does make reeling easier during fish-fighting periods, it will often catch the running line on a cast. Some organizations forbid a butt extension longer than 2 inches from the rear of the reel seat. (The Salt Water Fly Rodders of America, who compile the recognized world records, prohibit a butt extension more than 6 inches long). Anglers who build their own rods get additional legal inches to that extension when fishing under these rules by reversing the reel seat, so the threaded end is toward the angler.

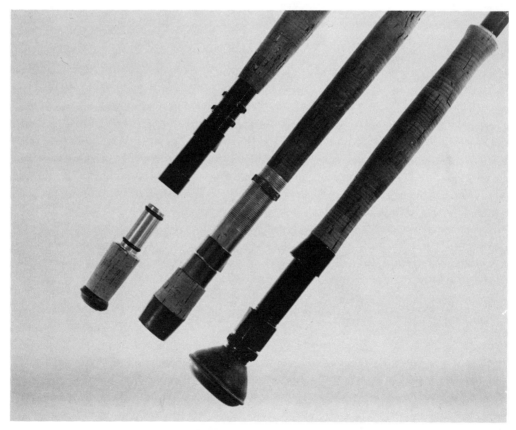

Three styles of extension butts: left to right, removable butt, permanently installed butt, and another installed butt.

If you purchase a rod with a butt extension, avoid extensions that have sharp corners or are constructed of very hard materials. Having such extensions positioned against the body for any length of time (as while fighting a fish), can really be painful. Look for extensions that are rounded and rather soft but firm, and that feel comfortable. Some rods have removable extensions, and these are desirable on smaller rods, since extensions can be inserted when needed, but can be removed for normal use.

In front of the butt extension is the reel seat, the device that holds the reel onto the handle. It should be made of either chrome on brass or high-grade anodized aluminum. Inexpensive rods carry one locking ring to retain the reel on the seat, but you should purchase a rod that carries two locking rings. Try the rings in the store; some are so thin you can't apply proper pressure to tighten them.

Almost all good saltwater fly reels have a foot 2½ inches long between the locking rings. One very popular reel has a foot 2⅜ inches long; some reel seats will not accommodate this size foot. The 2¼ inches is shorter than the reel foot, but by inserting the reel foot under the front hood first and then slipping it under the rear hood, you can make them fit.

A good rod handle should be made from fine-grain cork, firm and *almost* unyielding to the fingers. Grasp the handle to see if it is comfortable; some manufacturers make their reel handles so slim that they are tiring to cast. The handle should be full size and offer a comfortable grip. The proper position of the casting hand on the handle is with the thumb on top. When you deliver the final power stroke on the forward cast, the half-wells type of grip furnishes the thumb a resisting base. Rods with handles that taper away from the thumb defeat this purpose.

Just in front of the rod handle is a tiny guide called a ring-keeper. Saltwater fly rodders do not need or use this ring-keeper. Often the saltwater fly rodder must get into action in a hurry, when a fish is sighted and the rod lies in the boat. To obtain more line in the ready position outside the guides, the angler will take the leader, bring it down around the outside base of the fly reel, and then carry the hook up and slip it inside a guide on the forward section of the rod; then, when a fish is sighted, he slips the leader from around the reel base, shakes the fly loose, and has 11 to 13 feet of fly line outside the tip enabling him to make a rapid cast.

With 100-plus-pound tarpon, large amberjack, billfish, and other such fighters, the battle may rage for extended periods of time, and a foregrip will be welcome. This is a cork grip approximately 6 inches long, located in front of the rod handle. The angler can wind line onto the reel with one hand and support the rod during the fight by grasping the foregrip. It enables him to pump a fish while fighting it. Foregrips of necessity have to be thin, so they should be constructed from the best, densest cork. The foregrip should be within easy reach. If it is positioned too far forward, it will be very uncomfortable to grasp for long periods.

The number of guides on a rod is important; inexpensive rods usually have too few. There should be enough guides to support the line along the rod's length during a cast, preventing sagging between the guides. The guides must support the line along the rod's length when it is in a deep flex during a fight. How many guides should you expect? Roughly, there should be a tip top and 8 guides on an 8½-foot rod. Or, you should have a guide, including a tip top, for every foot of rod length. The butt section of your rod will usually carry two guides, either flex-foot or bridge. I prefer bridge guides, since they sit closer to the rod and are less likely to be bent or damaged in the boat. The two butt guides should be made from chrome on brass. Carbide guides will never wear, but a chalky dust builds up from a reaction with salt water; unless kept scrupulously clean and the chalky material removed, carbide guides can pit and erode a fly line. Chrome-plated guides wear for years and never lose their good looks. The new aluminum oxide guides are also excellent.

The first guide nearest the reel should be a minimum of 12 mm in size; 14 or 16 mm is even better. The second guide can be the same, or one size smaller. The guides on the tip section are almost always made with the snake guides. They should be of hard stainless steel or very high-grade chrome on brass. Most saltwater fly rods carry guides that are too small. Frequently, when a fast-running fish has struck and streaks away, the line, leaping from the deck and streaking through the guides, will pick up a tangle or a knot. If the guides are too small for the tangle to pass through, the fish will be lost. Large guides reduce this probability.

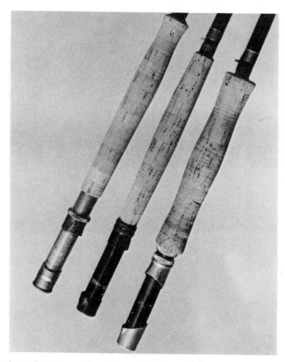

Three basic styles of rod handles exist. From left to right: half wells, cigar shape, and full wells.

For the same reason the tip top should be as large as the last snake guide on the rod tip. Since the tip top receives the most wear, the coating on the tip should be inspected frequently.

Guides should be anchored securely to the rod. Don't be impressed by the heavy coarse thread used by some manufacturers; this is the wrong type. Heavy thread cannot be drawn as tightly against the rod as thinner thread, and there are more wraps with thinner thread. A good epoxy covering should be given to all wraps. Fortunately, today most better rods have an excellent finish. If you make your own rod, there are several things you can do to help your guides stay on the rod better. Use smaller thread, wrap it under the most tension possible, and just before you position the guide on the rod, place a drop of Pliobond under the foot and on the rod where the guide foot will be positioned.

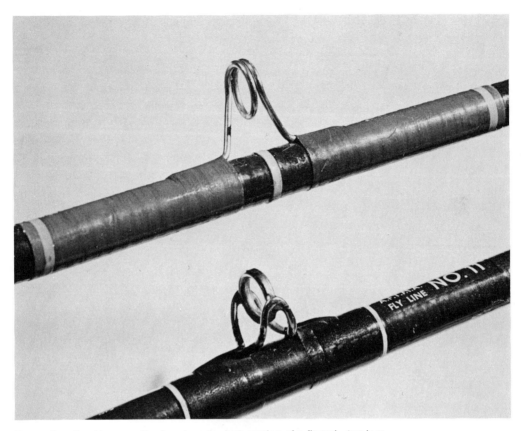

Two styles of guides, usually placed on the butt section of a fly rod—top is a flexible foot guide of hardened wire, bottom a bridge guide.

The chart below is a guide to selecting the proper line and rod for various saltwater species.

Fish	Line Size	Type of Line
Albacore	#9—11	ST, WF-S
Amberjack	#10—12	SWT-F
Barracuda	#8—10	SWT-F, WF-S
Channel bass	#8—11	WF-F, ST-S, WF-S
Kelp bass	#8, 9	WF-S, ST-S
Striped bass	#8—11	WF-F, WF-S (wet-tip), ST-S, ST-F
Bluefish	#8—11	WF-S, WF-F
Bonefish	#7—10	SWT-F, WF-F (wet-tip)
Bonito	#9—11	WF-S, ST-S
Cobia	#9—11	SWT-F, WF-F
Corbina	#9—11	ST-S, WF-S

Fish	Line Size	Type of Line
Dolphin	# 9, 10	WF-S
Flounder	# 9, 10	WF-S
Halibut (Pacific)	# 9 — 11	WF-F, WF-S
Jack crevalle	# 8 — 11	WF-F, WF-S
Ladyfish	# 7 — 8	WF-S, WF-F
Mackerel (all types)	# 8 — 10	ST-S, WF-S
Permit	# 9 — 11	WF-F, SWT-F
Roosterfish	# 9 — 11	WF-S, WF-F
Shark	# 9 — 11	SWT-F, WF-S
Snook	# 9 — 11	SWT-F, WF-S
Tarpon (baby)	# 7 — 10	SWT-F, WF-I (wet-tip)
Tarpon (over 80 lbs.)	# 9 — 12	SWT-F, WF-I (wet-tip)
Tuna	# 10, 11	ST-S, WF-S
Weakfish (all types)	# 9 — 11	ST-S, WF-S
Yellowtail	# 9 — 11	ST-S, WF-S

Naturally, these are rough guidelines and some adjustments will have to be made for specific situations; but in the interest of fun and sport, try to use the lightest rod and line possible.

REELS

Freshwater anglers generally agree that the fly reel is simply a storage compartment; but a saltwater reel is a different tool entirely. It is perhaps your single most important piece of equipment, for if it fails or malfunctions during a fight, you will probably lose your fish. Three types of fly reels exist: automatic, single action, and multiplying.

The automatic has almost no use in salt water. True, it will keep fly line off the floor when you are fishing, and if you walk a shoreline the device is certainly a good way to get rid of loose line. But it has too many drawbacks. Because the reel has many parts subject to corrosion, and is difficult to keep free from salt, it has a short life by the sea. Automatic reels have horrible drags, and so little line capacity as to be worthless for battling many saltwater species. You also have little control over your fish when using an automatic. You must clamp on the lever to retrieve line, or hope the fish doesn't strip you on a long run—betweentimes you can wind up the reel.

The single-action reel is the most widely used type. Such a reel turns the spool one complete revolution each time the handle makes a full circle. Reliability is of prime concern on the ocean, and the single-action reel has it. There are few working parts, and they are easy to repair; line capacity in most models is ample. Most important, the drag on a single-action reel designed specifically for the salt is usually good.

The multiplying reel is constructed like the single-action, except that the spool revolves at a higher ratio per turn. Most of them revolve about two and a half times for every complete turn of the reel handle. Although some organizations and tournaments forbid the use of the multiplying reel (reasoning that it takes advantage of the fish) the Salt Water Fly Rodders of America allow it.

The very best saltwater fly reels are made from anodized aluminum, with a solid spool, usually of one piece for maximum strength. Reel pillars and the foot should be made from chrome-on-brass or stainless steel. The spools are not too wide, usually one inch across. If the spool is much wider than that, the angler can experience trouble trying to evenly lay the line retrieved on the spool while fighting a fish. A buildup of line on one side occurs and then suddenly collapses, causing a fatal tangle.

The drag should be fairly large, and capable of reducing heat buildup—and it should be smooth; teflon and cork composition seem to be the best materials now in use.

You can check to determine if your drag is operating smoothly: thread the fly line through the guides of your rod, adjust the drag for about one pound of pressure, then have someone take the line end and run down the street. The rod tip should dip one or two times, then quickly settle and remain steady as the line flows through the tip top—if the drag is a good one. If the drag is poorly made the tip will bounce around like a conductor's baton. In fish-fighting with light tackle, it is the sudden jerk that usually breaks the line, not steady pressure. A bouncing rod tip indicates a poor drag.

Sometimes you can smooth the drag by setting it at about one-half pound, tying the line end to a car, and having the driver drive away for 100 yards at 10 miles per hour; this will fre-

Some reels, like the Scientific Anglers model, allow you to control drag pressure by pressing the outside of the spool frame (which revolves during the run) against the shirt.

quently remove the rough spots from the drag. Replacing defective washers may also be necessary.

Some of the best reels, like the SeaMaster and the Fin-Nor, have drags that will last for years. These big cork composition rings need only a little neat's-foot oil compound rubbed into them every once in a while. *To maintain any good drag you must remove all pressure adjusted to the drag when finished fishing for the day.*

It is a matter of personal choice whether you prefer a click on your reel. Some people do; others hate to hear that raspy sound; most better-quality saltwater reels do not have a click device.

Good saltwater reels are expensive; many cost close to or more than $100. If you expect to fight a big fish for a long period of time, tape the reel foot to the rod seat; many rod-retaining rings tend to work loose during a long fight. I have seen some good trophies lost this way.

There are several reels that have successfully met the challenge of time and fishing. Some have limitations. The following comments are based on the experience of myself and many other anglers who have tested them. They are offered as a guide, to enable the saltwater novice to make his own choice.

SeaMaster—Capacity, 250 yards of 30-pound-test Dacron backing and a SWT-11-F line. Perhaps the finest saltwater fly reel made. A larger model (Marlin) is available, too.

Fin-Nor—Capacity, 250 yards of 30-pound-test Dacron backing and a SWT-11-F line. Superbly made. Two models in three sizes.

Shakespeare Model 1898—Capacity, about 250 yards of 30-pound-test Dacron backing and a SWT-11-F line. Fair drag, well made, with click.

Pflueger 578—Capacity, about 250 yards of 30-pound-test Dacon backing and SWT-11-F line. Excellent drag, well made, solid spool, capable of taking very large fish. Side frame is painted.

Pflueger 577—Capacity, about 280 yards of 20-pound-test Dacron backing and SWT-9-F line. This is a smaller version of the 578 model.

Scientific Anglers (System 10 and 11 reels)—Capacity, about 250 yards of 30-pound-test Dacron and a SWT-11-F line. This is a well-made English reel. The drag is adjusted by manual pressure against the outer edge of the spool. It requires a little more skill than conventional reels, but is infinitely more fun. The reel has a click. Scientific Anglers sells these reels in sizes to match rods from number 4 through 11, and each number reel is designed to match the rod of the same number.

Pflueger Medalist (1498 Model)—Capacity, nearly 300 yards of 30-pound-test Dacron backing and a SWT-11-F line. This reel is perhaps the most popular ever used in salt water. It is inexpensive and, for light saltwater fishing, entirely ample. For use in bonefishing, a counter-balance should be installed on the spool opposite the single handle to reduce vibrations when the fish is making a long, fast run. A reel with a single handle performs much like an out-of-balance tire under a high-speed run.

Valentine Model 375—Capacity, about 200 yards of 20-pound-test Dacron backing and a SWT-9-F line. This is an excellent reel for use when a large capacity of line is not necessary. Good workmanship, nice drag and appearance. The reel is a multiplying type (about 2½ to 1).

All of the above reels have met and passed severe tests on salt water. With the exception of the SeaMaster and the Fin-Nor, all reels come with easily changed spools.

A collection of the most frequently used acceptable saltwater fishing reels: top row, left to right: Shakespeare 1898 EC, Scientific Anglers System 11, Pflueger Supreme #578, Pflueger Medalist #1498. Bottom row, left to right: Seamaster, Valentine 375 and Fin-Nor #3.

CARE OF TACKLE

Since salt water is corrosive, proper care of your equipment is extremely important.

Lines

Modern floating lines will indeed float, providing they are kept clean and free of materials that break the surface tension. The line is constructed of a braided core, with an outer casing of plastic. Within the plastic are imbedded millions of tiny glass bubbles, resembling on a tiny scale the round glass balls used by deep-sea fishermen to support their nets. If the line is not worn out and is clean, those bubbles will successfully keep the line on the surface.

Lines *must* be kept clean, and there are several ways to clean them. One company sells a special cleaner, a disposable moistened cloth that comes in a plastic envelope. There are some other cleaners with a greaselike base; these are not truly cleaners, and will only accumulate more dirt.

If you use the moistened pads, be careful. All fly lines have a chemical in them, called a "relaxer," to make them flexible. It is the same kind of thing that you feel in a plastic worm. Relaxers have a chemical property that leads them to distribute themselves evenly. The moistened pad not only removes the grime and dirt, but will take some of the relaxer from the fly line—which doesn't hurt the line, unless you use the cleaner too frequently. Under most fishing conditions you need clean your line only once or twice a year.

Another method of getting algae and slime from a fly line is to use warm, not hot, water, with a little liquid detergent added to it. Run the line through a soft sponge that is immersed in the soapy water. WARNING: when finished cleaning, you must rid the line of all traces of detergent, or the soap will break the surface tension and sink your line. A liberal washing in cold water is recommended.

A fly-line cleaner that has proved itself over the years is Lava soap. Merely moisten a rag and rub some Lava on it. Draw the line through the soapy rag until the rag no longer picks up a dirt stain, then rinse the line in cold water.

Fine grit will not only wear a fly line, but also ruin your guides. Double-hauling a line coated with grit is like running sandpaper through the guides. You can clean grit from the line with one of the three above-mentioned methods; one method of preventing grit from getting on the line is to clean the deck before you drop a fly line on it.

The plastic coating of a fly line can be ruined if certain solvents are allowed to come in contact with it. One line-destroying solvent not generally recognized is contained in insect sprays. Be careful when using these repellents; keep them off your hands.

Never kick or roll a fly line under your foot on the deck. This will put a permanent twist in the line that will really impede your casting.

Knots can deteriorate and so should be checked occasionally. The nail knot and the needle knot are buried deep in the plastic finish of the fly line and flex millions of times during a season's casting: be sure the knot is in good shape.

Reels

Check the knots on the backing and look at the backing itself to see if it's worn. If the backing has been drawn through the water while you were fighting a number of fish, it will have soaked up a lot of salt. This trapped salt can eventually corrode even the best reel; wash your backing occasionally in warm, soapy water. If the backing is frayed it should be replaced.

Reels should be sponged off with warm soapy water after each trip. Many people take a garden hose and spray heavily against the reels; this only carries the salt particles deep within the reel.

After a reel has been properly sponged clean and dried, it should receive some protective coating. The best I know of is hard paste wax; be sure the reel is both dry and clean before applying the wax. I first began using wax back in the forties, when duck hunting, to protect my gun barrels from the corrosive effect of Chesapeake Bay. The water would roll off in tiny beads. I prefer paste wax to all other lubes, and a good coating will last a long time.

The greatest problem in maintaining a reel in the salt is keeping clean the areas where the pillars join the reel sides, and around the base of the reel foot. These two areas entrap salt and it's difficult to get at—the best bet is to use a toothbrush for such work.

Remove your reel from the rod after each trip.

Release the drag adjusted tension after each day's fishing. Good drags are always made from alternating soft and hard materials. Leave a drag set under pressure for a long time and it will deform the washers, giving you a very poorly operating drag.

If your reel handle can be unscrewed, do unscrew it occasionally and lubricate and lightly grease the shaft. Fighting a fish with an immobile handle is hell.

A wonderful way to carry extra reel spools is in a heavy sock, each spool separated from the others by a heavy rubber band.

Never lay a reel down on sand or a dirty boat deck, or anywhere it can pick up grit. Don't let your reel become immersed, either. The water, besides transporting salt, will carry grit inside.

Saltwater fly reels are generally expensive, and they deserve the best of care.

Rods

Fiber-glass rods are tough—so tough that many people abuse them without realizing they can actually be permanently damaged. When not in use a rod belongs in its case. But never store a rod that is damp in an airtight case: it can ruin the finish. The moisture, coupled with the heated air in the container, can blister the tough finish right off the rod. Thoroughly dry any rod before putting it in a case.

When removing a rod from a case for fishing, check all the guides. The tip top should get first attention since it receives the most wear. The chrome plating is sometimes worn on either the tip top or the guides, and it will strip the plastic finish from a fly line. It's a good idea to carry a piece of ferrule cement and extra tip tops in your tackle bag or box. You can quickly check your guides by running a section of nylon stocking through them. Any woman can tell you how quickly a nylon stocking snags, and the stocking will catch any imperfection in a guide.

Many of today's better-grade fiber-glass rods don't have a metal ferrule; instead, one section of glass slips into the other. You might think this would solve all problems. It doesn't. Paraffin wax should be rubbed on both ferrule joints to prevent sticking. If all lubricant is removed through heavy use, the rod may become stuck. If it does, an excellent way to get it apart is to have someone hold the butt section firmly while you grasp the other part, after wrapping a thin section of rubber around it. Then twist the sections in opposite directions. I have never seen a stubborn rod that did not yield to this technique.

Many anglers using fiber-glass rods have made a cast only to see their rod tip go flying away in front of them. Some fiber-glass rods must be put together with a one-quarter twist; if they are not put together properly they'll loosen during the day. Other fiber-glass rods are aligned and put together in the same way as metal ferrules—by a straight push. The rod should be taken apart in the same way as it is put together. If a twist is needed to install the ferrule, a twist in the opposite direction will be required to loosen it.

If your rod carries metal ferrules and one begins wearing so that you're afraid it may slip out while you're fishing, there's a simple way to get another year or two of use from it. Place the male end of the ferrule in a drill chuck and tighten it. This squeezes three equal humps out from the rounded shaft. Try it in your rod; if it does not fit tight enough, repeat the chuck operation until you have a snug fit.

Many anglers who use a fly rod have special holders for them in the boat. That's where rods belong. Never lay a fly rod down on the boat deck where someone could step on it. On an offshore boat you can often lean the fly rod vertically against a support, where it is quickly available. But be sure that wind and wave motion won't throw the rod to the deck. Rods easily suffer hidden damage from sharp blows, so take extreme care to keep this from happening. One of the most common ways this occurs is when small-boat fishermen lay a rod so the tip section rests on the sharp edge of a boat seat and then run the boat through choppy water,

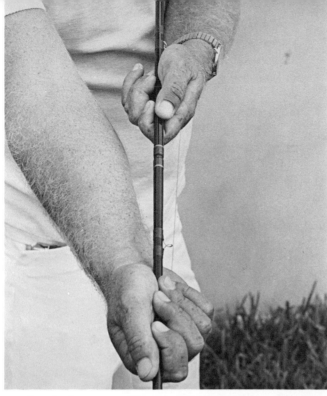

A straight pull or push is needed to disjoin or put together many fiber glass and all metal ferrule rods. Some glass rods are designed to be joined with a quarter twist motion.

causing the boat to act like a jackhammer. The rod repeatedly flies up and down, striking the sharp corner of the seat. Almost certain structural damage to the rod will result. If you must lay a rod on a boat seat, place a towel, raingear, a boat cushion, or any other soft object beneath it.

Don't store your fiber-glass rods in a bent position for long periods. They may take a set, which will ruin the casting characteristics of the rod.

After returning home from a trip, you should take certain precautions. Simply spraying cold water on a rod will remove very little accumulated salt. You can easily check this statement by spraying cold water on your boat, letting it dry, and then running your hand over it. You'll feel the salt crystals. It takes *detergent* and water, preferably warm, to get rid of salt—not just plain water. A simple and fast method of cleaning your rods is to hold the portion that is being scrubbed over a bucket of warm soapy water. Then dip a sponge into the warm water and wash the part. The excess water will fall back into the bucket and the soap and water will drive all salt from the rod. Rinse the entire rod in cold water when done.

Slimy rod handles can lose you fish. Clean them with the detergent and a rough rag, being sure to rid the handle of the soap when finished.

Never store a reel on a rod. The reel foot nestles inside the rod seat hoods, entrapping salt, which soon begins its dirty work. Remove the reel, and clean inside the hoods and threading.

Another method of ensuring an even pull when disjoining a rod with a sticky ferrule.

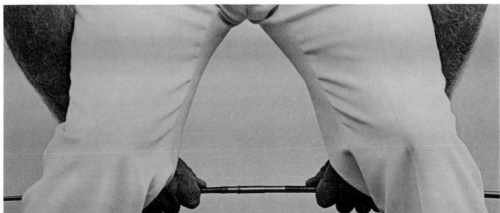

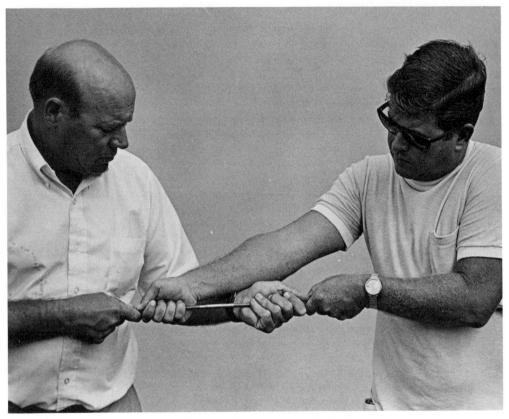

One method of taking apart a rod with a stuck ferrule. Be sure that both anglers pull with the same pressure.

Flies

Flies made on hooks constructed of any metal other than stainless steel are impractical for saltwater use because they demand too much care, although some people are concerned about a fish that escapes with a stainless hook impaled in its mouth.

Small plastic envelopes can be used to store each fly individually. There are some boxes on the market with a spongelike floor; this allows you to position the flies for instant use. If you throw flies loosely into a plastic box the wings may deform; if some feathers dressed onto the flies are not colorfast, the dyes may bleed onto other flies.

It's helpful to carry a plastic bucket of fresh water in the boat. As a fly is used and discarded for the day, it can be dropped into the bucket.

Each fly hook should be sharpened before use.

5 Knots and Leaders

One of the smallest elements of your fly-fishing tackle is the most strategic—your knots. The finest reel, the best rod, the most seductive fly, are all for naught if the knots won't stand the strain of battling a fish.

Freshwater anglers who have been getting by with poorly designed and tied knots suddenly realize that in salt water they will have to master some knots if they expect to participate. Fortunately, only a few knots are required for most saltwater fly fishing, and with a few more you will be able to meet any fishing situation.

Even an excellent knot will fail if not properly tied. It behooves the angler to master the knots he needs *before* he goes fishing. Trying to tie a Bimini Twist or a good Albright in four-foot seas with fish crashing bait twenty yards away is impossible unless you have spent some time learning how to tie the knot well—and quickly. The DuPont Company, which has probably done more testing of knots than any other manufacturer, always has the person who is going to tie for testing purposes practice a knot for one half hour before any tests are made. He already knows how to tie the knot, but they want him in peak form for his performance. That ought to be a hint.

There are good and bad knots. A bad knot is one that is not suited to the situation, is improperly drawn tight, is incorrectly trimmed, or is just inefficient. A good knot is designed to meet the particular fishing condition; it is properly drawn and trimmed correctly.

Understanding what a knot is, its functions, and how it might fail are important. Almost any knot that is put into line is weaker than the main line itself, although there are exceptions. The ideal fly leader has only knots that are stronger than the tippet. This *is* possible.

Most knots are actually some form of a clinch knot; the blood knot, for example, is simply two clinch knots joined together. Knots never break until they slip—perhaps the most important point you can learn about a knot. If you can build a slip-proof knot, you have one that will be roughly as strong as the line you have constructed it from. That means that knots should be drawn as tight as possible. With monofilament, the knot can be tightened best if it is lubricated in your mouth before final drawing takes place. Lines larger than 15-pound-test cannot properly be tightened with bare hands.

The size of a knot is important. Obviously, a bulky connection between the monofilament butt section and the fly-line end would gather grass and debris in many fishing areas; a neat but strong knot is required here.

A blood knot that has been improperly trimmed. It will catch the leader on a
turn-over, snag in the grass, and is of poor workmanship.

The same knot properly trimmed.

The function of the knot is important, too. You can connect your 12-pound tippet section to the butt of the leader in several ways, but a quick change loop-to-loop is the smartest
method, for it allows you more flexibility.

There are five materials that concern the fly fisherman, as far as knots are concerned.
They are braided wire, solid trolling wire, monofilament, Dacron or Micron (for backing),
and fly line. Connections must be made to each of these components, and so it is necessary to
learn at least several knots.

Braided wire is composed of a number of filaments of relatively soft wire which have
been braided together to form a single strand. It is a mini-cable. Two types exist: plain braided
wire, and braided wire with a coating or shell of clear nylon. Most anglers prefer the latter;
braided wire is easy to tie and is flexible. Numbers of fish can be caught on braided wire, and it
will remain kink-free. It can be purchased in coils that are easy to carry and store. Braided
wire is rustproof, and the best type is that which has been heat-treated. It does have two disadvantages. It is much larger in comparative size to solid wire (nylon-coated braided wire is
almost twice the diameter of solid wire); and sharp-toothed fishes will often tear the nylon
coating loose. This shredded nylon hangs in dangling strands, and often causes fish to refuse
the fly.

Solid trolling wire is another material used in fly fishing for fish with sharp teeth, like
barracuda, bluefish, and king mackerel. Solid wire is stronger, it will remain at the same
strength throughout a fight. If you plan to fish for sharks, for example, braided wire will often
fail. During a long fight the shark's teeth will slowly cut through one strand after another,
until the wire breaks. Solid wire has a smaller diameter for the same line strength. Draw-

Insert braided wire through hook eye and form knot as shown. Then draw knot tight. Upper fly shows the Figure 8 Knot . . . lower fly shows a Homer Rhode Loop Knot in braided wire.

backs to solid wire are that making good knots in it takes longer, and that it kinks easily, often necessitating a change to a new shock tippet.

When faced with the problem of angling for a fish with sharp, line-cutting teeth, you will probably have to use wire. Which type you choose is really a matter of personal preference, but one good rule is to use the shortest wire shock leader you can.

38 •

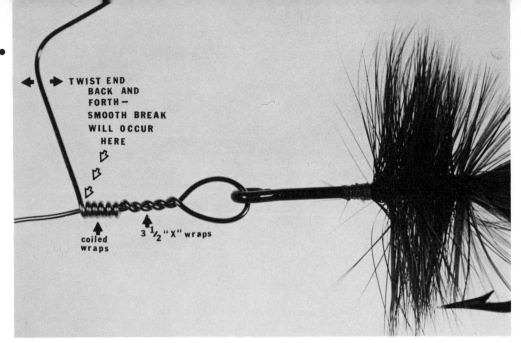

TWIST END
BACK AND
FORTH—
SMOOTH BREAK
WILL OCCUR
HERE

coiled
wraps

3 1/2 "X" wraps

The Haywire Loop is easy to make—but it is important to remember that you must make at least 3½ "X" wraps before spiraling the wire coil-fashion around the main strands. It is the "X" wraps that furnish strength. This knot is used in solid strand trolling wire.

SOLID TROLLING WIRE

WIRE NUMBER	DIAMETER INCHES	POUND-TEST
2	.011	28
3	.012	32
4	.013	39
5	.014	54
6	.016	61
7	.018	72
8	.020	88
9	.022	108
10	.024	127

Nylon monofilament changed the whole fly-fishing game, in both fresh and salt water. Formerly, strands of animal gut were used; they had to be soaked before use and tied with care. Size limitations and, often, unavailability, plagued the angler. Then monofilament arrived. This clear plastic material required no soaking, could be stored for long periods of time, and was uniform in diameter. But it too had a disadvantage. The hardness of monofilament rendered useless most of the knots used with natural gut. New knots had to be devised.

Monofilament has a uniform strength, varying little in the same strand. For years the erroneous notion that 80 percent of the monofilament's strength was in the outer 10 percent of the line was accepted as fact. This is not the case.

When building some knots, you will find that you often change the shape of the line as well. Tying a Bimini Twist, for example, you'll notice the line appears to deform. But it still has the same mass, and repeated tests on my line-testing machines have convinced me that line that deforms during the tying of a knot does not diminish in strength.

A nick, however, will radically reduce monofilament's strength. To demonstrate this fact, take a garden hose, have two people pull on either end of a short piece, then slice a small nick

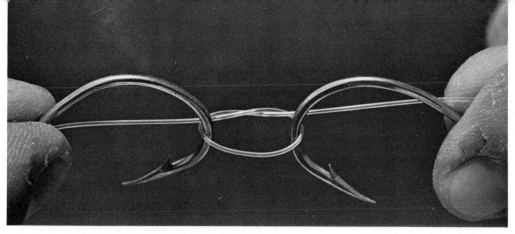

A wind knot (overhand knot) occurs frequently in anglers' leaders. A simple way to remove such knots is with two hooks, as shown.

in the hose. The nick combined with the strain will run through the hose, causing it to separate completely. This is just what happens to monofilament; anytime you can feel a nick in a leader, replace it!

The wind knot that anglers get during casting is an overhand knot that appears in the leader, usually in the tippet section. Wind knots can reduce the line strength by as much as 60 percent; check your leaders constantly to be sure wind knots have not formed. One way of removing a wind knot, if it is not too tight, is with two fish hooks. If you cannot remove the knot, replace the leader.

Monofilament comes in many colors, ranging from bright orange, black, gold, blue, green, and nearly clear to clear. I prefer the clearest monofilament I can get, although I must confess I have caught some very spooky fish on blue, green, and bright yellow. I do think that a shock leader of 60 or more pounds in strength should definitely be clear in color, for the most strikes. As far as butt sections are concerned, coloration of the monofilament has little effect.

Monofilament should be protected from the sun, since ultraviolet rays will harm it. Store any unused monofilament in a dark place. Very dry air will make the line become brittle. Leaders that have been made up and stored for long periods, even in a cool moist place, will lose as much as 5 percent of line strength. I suggest that you make up new leaders each year if you desire maximum strength from them. Oil is tough on monofilament. Keep service spools in your tackle boxes in packaging which will prevent the line from being nicked by other objects in the box.

Monofilament can be stretched repeatedly without harm, below the extreme upper limits of the line's strength.

Monofilament comes in various degrees of stiffness from very stiff to exceedingly limp; each has certain characteristics that should be noted. Limp monofilament is the poorest choice for knots and leaders; the limp materials tend to slip and crawl in a knot under pressure, insuring that it will break well below the line's strength.

Hard or stiff monofilament is more difficult to tie properly, since it resists being drawn tight. It does not slip as quickly as limp material, but the very fact that it is so hard encourages slipping.

Medium-stiff monofilament is the best choice.

There are a number of reasons for this selection. There is no question in my mind but that medium-stiff monofilament will turn a leader over better than hard or stiff monofilament. For years it was thought that a stiff monofilament leader, with a softer tippet, was the ideal combination. The idea was that the stiffer monofilament would flip the leader over better and the limp tippet would allow the fly greater freedom on the retrieve. But I have thoroughly determined to my satisfaction that medium-stiff monofilament will turn a fly over much better than the stiffer material. (This is also true for freshwater trout leaders.) Spinning-line material, like Stren, Maxima, Mason, and others, is my first choice to build the complete leader. I foresee the time when no one will use stiff monofilament in any portion of a tapered leader.

Though there is some room for discussion on this point, I feel that medium-stiff monofilament does not abrade as quickly as does the harder monofilament. Softer monofilament tends to move away from the fish's raspy mouth, or roll with the punch, so to speak. Harder monofilament is less yielding and so will wear faster. Abrasion characteristics are obviously important in the shock tippet of the leader, but the smaller-diameter tippet section is often rubbed against the surface of the fish, so abrasion is really a problem throughout the leader.

Most anglers assume when they buy a spool of line designated as 10 pounds in strength that it is exactly 10 pounds. That's not true; the manufacturer is saying that the line is *at least* 10 pounds in test. Most lines exceed the line test by at least 15 percent. More expensive lines generally adhere closer to the actual stated line test, but anyone who is considering taking a record fish should either buy tournament-tested line (pretested line guaranteed to be of the stated line test) or should check the line personally beforehand.

There is an easy method of checking monofilament. Select a 6-foot sample of the line, and tie a Bimini Twist in either end. Attach the doubled section to the handle of a bucket, wrap the other doubled end around a support, and hold the bucket several inches off the floor. Add water (sand is better) to the bucket until the line breaks. Then weigh the bucket and its contents on a grocery scale, or any accurate scale. Subtract 12 percent (lines lose about that much when wet [for an initial period]) and you will have the accurate test-strength of the line.

You must learn to tie knots well, but there are times, too, when it is vital to be able to tie them well—and *quickly*. If you break off a schoolfish during a fight, and others are still around the boat, you may get another chance if you can tie on another fly fast enough.

Know the knots you need for your fishing. Obviously, if you fish in an area with no sharp-toothed fish, you may not need to learn the knots for wire. But once you have mastered those you need for your immediate fishing, learn the others, too. You never know when you may have a chance to fish somewhere else. And *don't trust the other person's knots*—learn to tie your own properly.

BACKING

The basic fly line is about 90 feet long, but if you are to fight long-running fish, you'll need more line than that. So, backing is attached to the rear end of the fly line. It is usually made of Dacron or Micron, both registered trade names for synthetic lines that are soft, have few stretch characteristics, and lie flat on the reel spool.

These lines are generally attached to the fly line by one of two methods: a nail knot is used, or a loop is whipped in the fly line, and then a loop is made in the Dacron; then the two lines are joined by the connecting loops. I prefer the loop-to-loop connection for several reasons: this connection cannot entangle in the rod guides, it allows the angler to substitute or exchange lines to the backing with ease, and it is extremely strong if properly connected.

The nail knot is connected in the same way as the butt section is attached to the front end of the fly line. However, the nail knot leaves a stub projecting where the fly line ends that can catch in the guides—and I have seen nail knots tied from backing to fly line slip under pressure. I suggest putting Pliobond glue on the joint to both strengthen and smooth the connection.

NEEDLE KNOT (to connect butt leader to fly line)

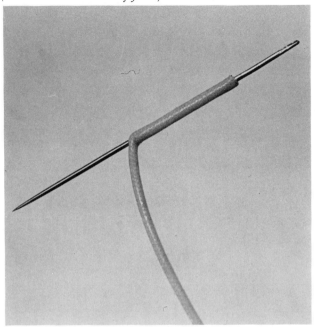

Insert the *smallest needle* that you can find into the end of the fly line as shown.

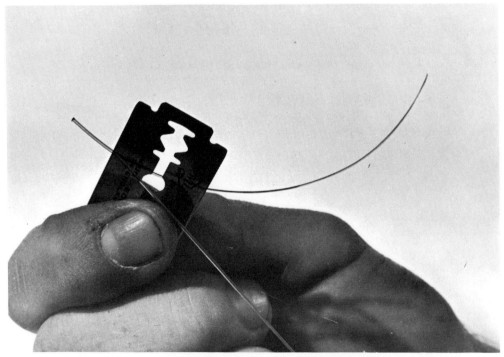

Using a *new* razor blade, slice the monofilament end of the butt section with several cuts until you have it tapered to a fine tip.

Insert the tapered end of the butt section into the eye of the needle.

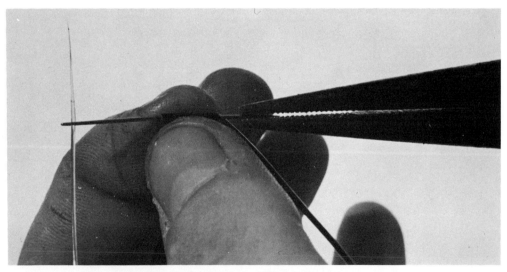

Pinch the fly-line end between thumb and first finger, then, grasping the needle with a pair of pliers, pull the needle toward you, withdrawing it from the fly line.

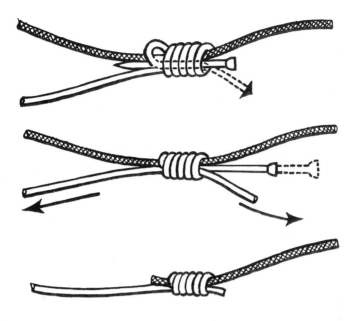

NAIL KNOT, used to connect butt section to fly line.

Butt section of leader will come through as shown.

To make a loop in the Dacron or Micron is simple—just tie a Bimini Twist or Spider Hitch in the line. I then prefer to double this line end and make a double surgeon's loop, so that the final loop to connect to the fly line is made from four strands of Micron or Dacron.

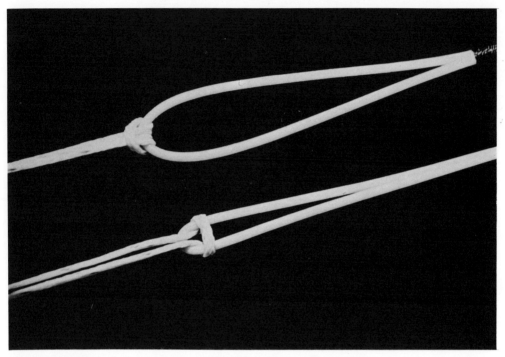

Upper line shows the fly line, to right, and the Dacron loop improperly positioned to the fly line. This connection will cut through under stress.
Lower connection is proper way to make a loop-to-loop knot.

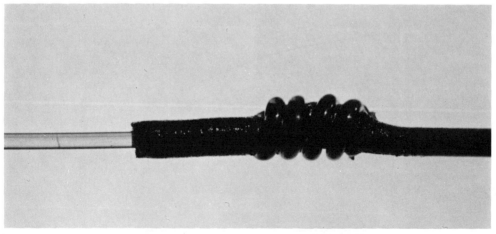

Tie a conventional nail knot in leader end and you have the result shown here, where the leader actually comes out of the center of the fly line and cannot hang up in the guides.

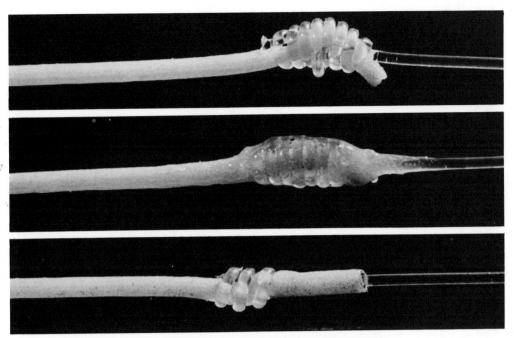

Top view shows butt section tied with conventional nail knot. Notice that projecting stubs extend from line and could catch in guides. *Middle line* shows the same knot, properly trimmed and with several coatings of Pliobond rubber-based glue, which forms a "football" shaped joint that feeds through the guides easily. *Lower line* shows how needle knot looks after it is complete.

FLY LINES

You could really get by with two knots as far as the fly line is concerned. A nail knot at the front will connect the monofilament butt section to the fly line; a whipped loop on the other end will suffice to connect the backing to the fly line. I much prefer the needle knot to connect the monofilament butt leader to the fly line. It is stronger and cannot catch in the rod guides, and it is really easy to tie.

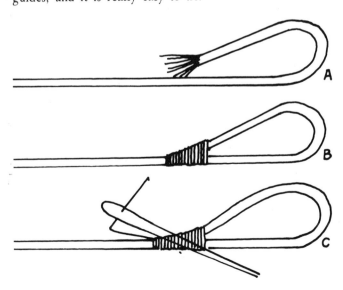

A—Fray about one-quarter inch of fly line and fold it over as shown.

B—Wrap size "A" nylon tying thread over the wrap as tightly as possible.

C—Lay a piece of 6 to 12-pound test monofilament loop along the wrap and make at least ten to twelve wraps over the monofilament; put through the monofilament loop, as shown. Then, draw the monofilament from the wraps, which carries the thread through, finishing the whip. Coat this with a little Pliobond. Make an additional wrap the length shown on the bottom drawing, so it overlaps the first whipping. This is insurance, in case the first wrap wears through while you are fighting a fish.

LEADERS

A leader is a connection between fly line and fly. In fresh water the approach is to build a tapered leader that turns over well, presents the fly with a minimum of disturbance, and is invisible enough to deceive the fish into taking the offering.

Most freshwater leader principles do not carry over to the salt. First, the conventional tapered 9 to 12 foot freshwater leader is appropriate for only a few saltwater fish, such as bonefish, permit, mutton snapper, and a striped bass. Most saltwater species couldn't care less what the fly is attached to.

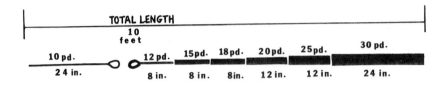

TAPERED MONOFILAMENT LEADER

To make a good tapered leader of any length it is recommended that 60 per cent of the rear portion of the leader sections be large, as shown here (six feet), 20 per cent be the mid section (the three 8-inch strands), and that the tippet comprise the remaining 20 per cent. Using the 60-20-20 formula, you can make any length leader you desire. Medium-soft monofilament makes better leaders than does hard or stiff mono.

Tapered leaders are used for some saltwater species, but for most your leader should be composed of three parts: a butt section, a tippet, and a shock leader. The butt section is a heavy piece of 30- to 40-pound monofilament, tied to the fly line. Modern butt section leaders are attached to the fly line with either a needle knot (preferable) or a nail knot. If you use a nail knot, it's a good idea to apply several coats of Pliobond to the knot to form a sort of "football connection" that will not catch in the rod guides. Tie a doubled surgeon's loop on the other end of the modern butt section leader.

The tippet is the weakest section of the leader. If you fish according to the standards set by the Salt Water Fly Rodders of America, you will use one of four line strengths for the tippet: 6, 10, 12, or 15 pounds. You can construct tippets in the following manner: select approximately 4 feet (2 extra feet for 6-pound tippets) of line. Tie either a Spider Hitch or a Bimini Twist in one end, and the same knot in the other, so that the single strand between the knots is about 18 inches long.

Let's assume you are building a 12-pound-test leader tippet. You now have approximately 18 inches of 12-pound line with a Spider Hitch or Bimini Twist in each end, forming a loop. Take one loop and make a doubled surgeon's loop from the two strands. Connect it to the butt section by slipping one loop through the other. The leader now consists of a butt section to which is attached 12-pound-test monofilament leader by a doubled loop. Take the other end and attach your shock leader with a proper knot. If the shock leader is 60-pound monofilament or less, I prefer to use the surgeon's knot; it is fast, small, and strong, and it can be trimmed very close. If the shock leader is 80- or 100-pound monofilament I recommend the Albright. If braided wire is being used, the surgeon's knot is again the best; for attaching solid wire use two knots. A haywire loop is formed in the wire, then an Albright is used to tie the doubled 12-pound section to the loop. If you merely bend the wire in a **U** and make an Albright, the knot will often creep out under fighting pressure.

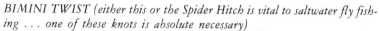

BIMINI TWIST (either this or the Spider Hitch is vital to saltwater fly fishing . . . one of these knots is absolute necessary)

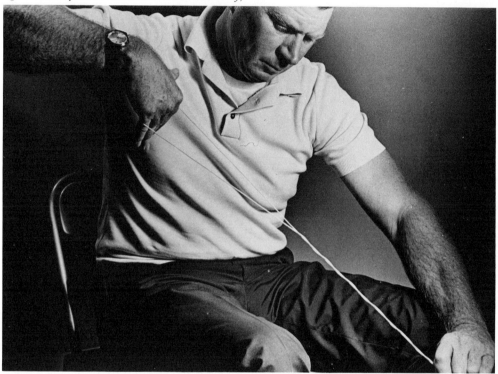

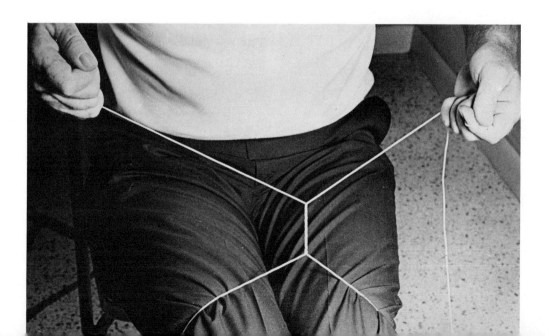

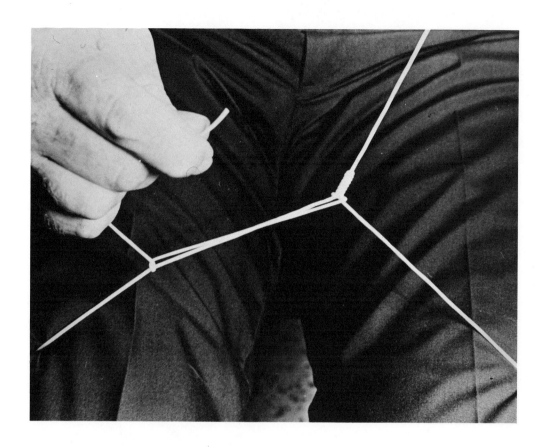

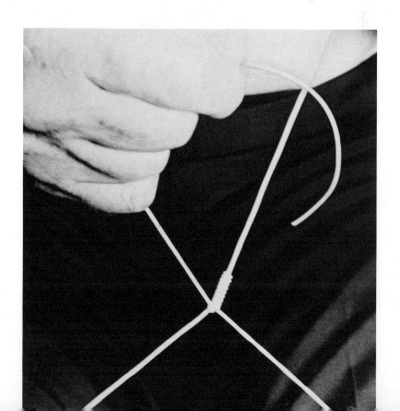

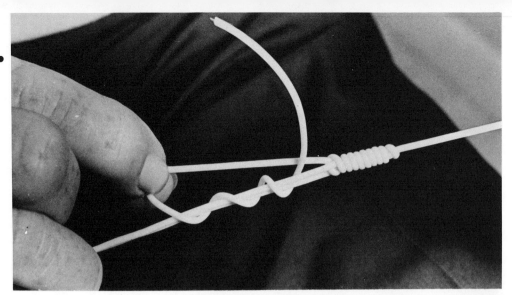

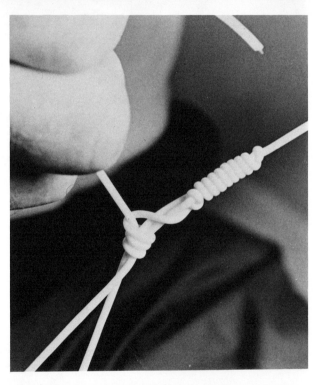

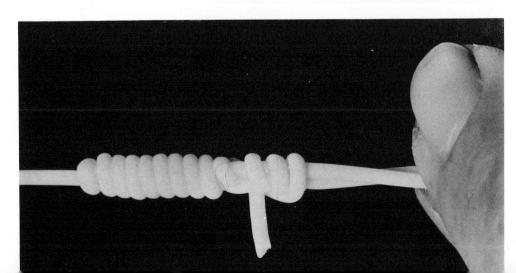

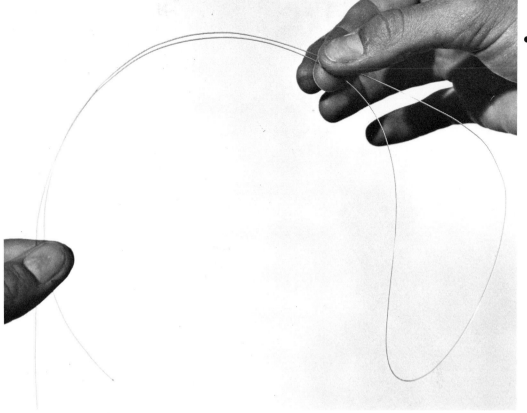

SPIDER HITCH

The Spider Hitch is a fair substitute for the Bimini Twist. The loop they both form allows you to use two strands, or *double* the line strength, to tie connections. The Bimini Twist is a better knot, but one or the other is vital to the salt-water man who fights big fish on light tackle.

The instructions here are easy to follow. First make five wraps around the thumb. After you have pulled all loops from around your thumb and before you draw the knot completely tight, make sure the two loops are the same; if not pull on either the line end or the tippet to adjust before final tightening.

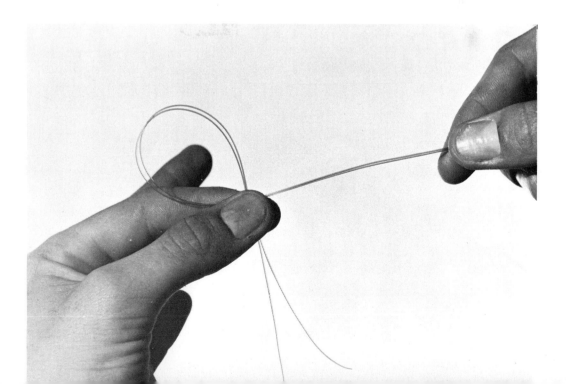

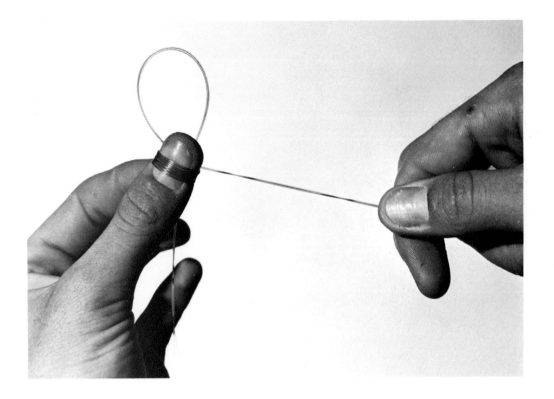

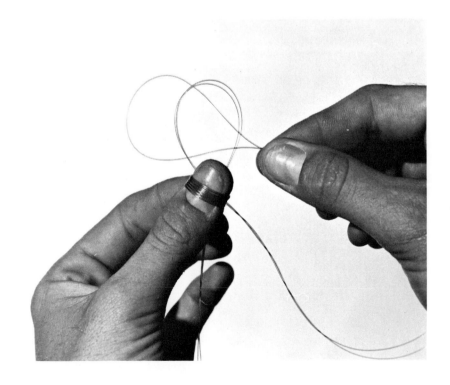

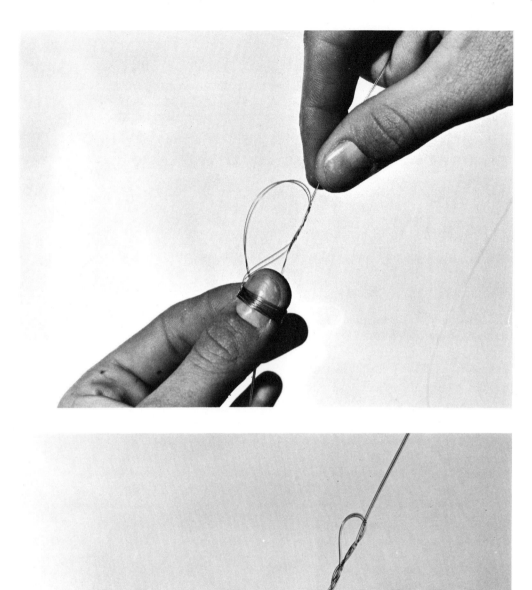

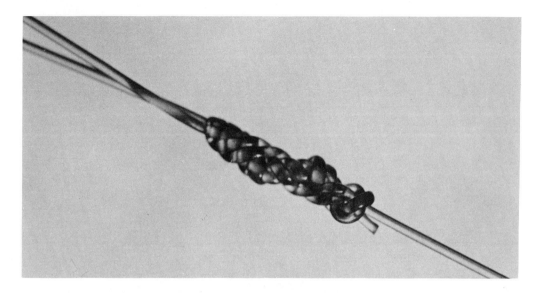

One more knot is essential to the modern saltwater leader, and that is the one used to attach the shock leader to the fly. For braided wire, and monofilament of 25 to 100 pounds, many anglers like the Homer Rhode loop knot, a free-swinging loop which allows the fly to maneuver in the water. This knot is only about 50 percent of the strength of the line, and should not be used in shock leaders testing much under 25 pounds.

Some very fine anglers do not like to use a loop knot attached to the fly when using 80- or 100-pound monofilament. They prefer, instead, to tie the fly to the heavy strand with a three-and-a-half-turn clinch knot. This makes the fly ride straight, but you must constantly check the knot to be sure that it has not slipped to one side of the hook eye, causing the fly to come through the water unnaturally. (This same knot is used to attach level shooting line to the head.)

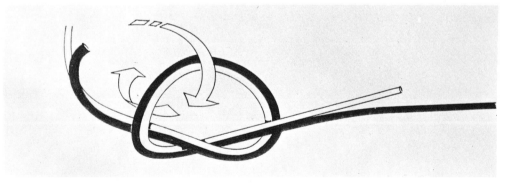

SURGEON'S KNOT (used to connect large and small strands)

Perhaps one of the four or five most important knots that a serious saltwater fly rodder can learn is the Surgeon's Knot. It can be used to tie braided wire to monofilament, or tie monofilament to itself. It is the best knot I know for connecting monofilament shock leaders, up to 60 pounds, with the Bimini Twist or Spider Hitch. The knot is really simple, although the drawing may not look it. Actually it is a double overhand knot. Simply lay the two strands alongside each other and bring the right two through, forming an overhand knot; then bring the two strands through again and draw tight. Trim close.

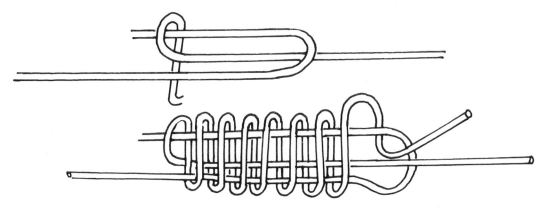

ALBRIGHT KNOT (To connect very large shock leader material, wire or mono, to the tippet)

The Albright is the best knot to connect a very large wire or monofilament strand to the smaller diametered monofilament. If you use solid wire, make a haywire loop in the wire first, or it will "snake" through the knot under pressure. The knot is simple to make. To tie an Albright simply fold the heavier strand as shown, then bring the smaller monofilament in and make at *least* 12 *wraps*, before tucking it through the bend. Draw tight on *both* strands until knot is firm. Be sure to trim the larger stub on a slant, so it will not project.

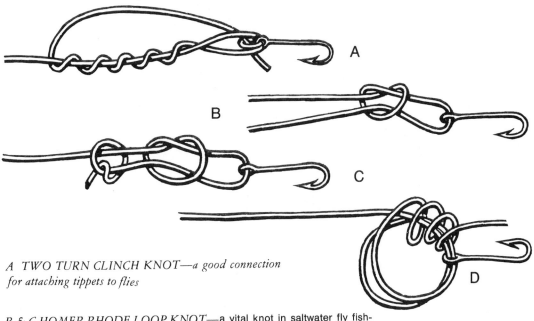

A TWO TURN CLINCH KNOT—a good connection for attaching tippets to flies

B & C HOMER RHODE LOOP KNOT—a vital knot in saltwater fly fishing. It is used to tie a large strand of shock leader (either braided wire or monofilament) to the fly. Make an overhand knot *before* you insert the line end into the eye of the hook, then bring the line end back and through the overhand knot. Now tie another overhand knot around both strands. Draw tight and you have a free-swinging loop that gives the fly more action. *Caution*—this knot is only about 50 per cent when tied properly, so do not use this knot in small tippets, only in larger shock tippets.

D JANSIK SPECIAL—a superb knot for attaching a fragile leader tippet to a fly. Pass the tippet end through the hook eye twice, then make three turns around the two coils as shown. Be sure to draw tight.

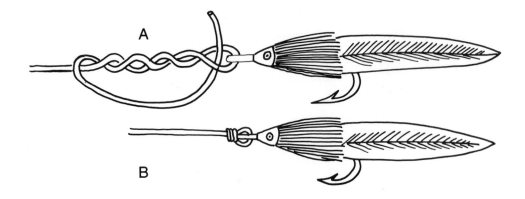

3½ TURN CLINCH KNOT (used to connect large shock leader tippet to fly or running line to shooting head)

Some anglers do not like a free-swinging loop, but prefer that a large shock tippet hold the fly steady as it comes through the water. The 3½ Turn Clinch Knot does this, but be sure, if you use this knot, to check it occasionally, for it sometimes gets off center and comes through the water improperly. Simply pass the heavy monofilament shock leader through the hook eye, make three and a half turns, insert end back through line loop at hook eye, and draw tight. You should use a pair of pliers and wrap a handkerchief around your hand holding the monofilament. It has been determined that you cannot properly tighten monofilament knots with the bare hand if the strands exceed 20 pounds in test.

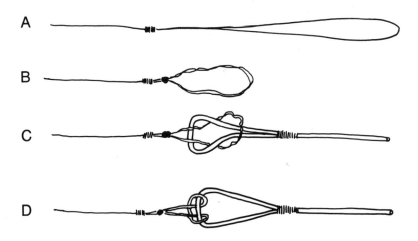

Using Bimini Twist or Spider Hitch to Connect Leader to Shock Tippet

"A" shows a Spider Hitch or Bimini Twist formed in leader tippet end. Take this loop and double it, then tie another loop so you have two strands to each side for greater strength. Then, loop the doubled strands of the tippet to the shock leader as shown in "C."

The total length of the leader is generally unimportant for most saltwater fishes. I am convinced that, especially on sinking lines, a leader need not have a total length of more than 3 or 4 feet. Many clubs have special requirements, however, and the Salt Water Fly Rodders of America dictates that your shock leader cannot exceed 12 inches in length—and that includes all knots. The tippet section must also be at least 12 inches long, although no maximum length is required.

Where a tapered leader is called for, as in fishing for bonefish, striped bass, permit, and other fish that require you to present the fly delicately and with as invisible a connection as possible, the 10-foot leader is often the best choice. For most fishing of this kind a tippet section, 2 feet long, of either 12- or 10-pound test, is adequate. Experienced anglers may want to go lighter for the sport of it. In the diagram of a basic 10-foot leader, note that the tippet section is attached to the next strongest piece of monofilament with a double surgeon's loop; this allows you to change tippets at will. Where waters are especially calm or shallow, or the fish are spooky, you may go to an even longer leader; I like a 16-footer for tough bonefishing situations. You can easily build one that will turn over well, using medium-stiff monofilament.

Charles Ritz, the great French fly fisherman, devised a simple formula that works extremely well in building tapered leaders of any length. His formula is 60:20:20. This means that 60 percent of the back section of a leader is constructed of the largest diameters. Each foot in a 10-foot leader represents 10 percent of the whole leader. The butt section can be composed of 4 feet of 30-pound and 1 foot each of 25- and 20-pound, which is a total of 6 feet—or 60 percent of the leader. The middle section (sometimes called the hinge) can then be composed of three 8-inch parts of 20-, 18-, and 15-pound test, for a total length of 2 feet, or 20 percent of the leader. The tippet is 2 feet of 10-pound test—the final 20 percent of the leader.

Joe Zimmer, a Baltimore angler, has devised a neat system for building tapered leaders. Joe carries nine small spools of leader, ranging from 40- to 6-pound test, on a loop of old fly line. The spools are threaded onto the fly line in numerical order. A snap swivel completes the loop, allowing him to open the snap and replace any spools used. Joe has a clip that allows him to snap the loop of leader spools to his wading jacket or himself; a pair of nail clippers completes the leader kit.

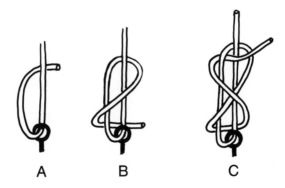

A   B   C

MAXIMA OR CRAWFORD KNOT

This is perhaps the best, easiest to tie, and certainly easiest to learn knot for tying small tippets to a fly. The knot is almost 100 per cent if tied as shown.

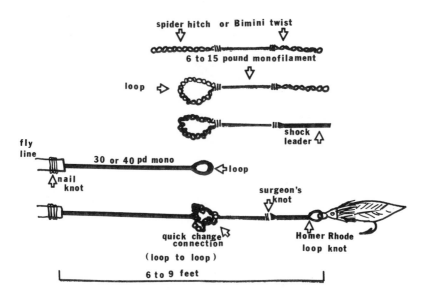

spider hitch   or Bimini twist

6 to 15 pound monofilament

loop

shock
leader

fly
line

30 or 40 pd mono ⟵ loop

nail
knot

surgeon's
knot

quick change
connection
(loop to loop)

Homer Rhode
loop knot

6 to 9 feet

Modern Saltwater Fly Leader That is Not Tapered

How to make a modern quick-change fly leader, where broken tippets are easily removed and replaced. Take a six-foot strand of 6 to 15 pound test monofilament line, form a Spider Hitch or Bimini Twist at either end and then make the doubled loop on one end. Attach a heavy shock leader to the other end with either a Surgeon's or Albright knot. Slip the loop in the tippet through the loop on the butt section and draw connection properly tight. Should you break the tippet, if you have pre-rigged some tippets, you need only unloop the broken strand and quickly replace it.

Joe Zimmer carries a series of medium-soft monofilament leader spools on a piece of fly line. The spools are arranged on the loop in numerical order. A snap swivel allows him to replace any used spools, and the nail clip is permanently attached to the spools, too.

When anglers first use the heavier monofilaments for their shock leaders, problems may arise. Trying to straighten a piece of 100-pound-test monofilament can be difficult. If you are building shock leaders in monofilament 60 pounds in test or larger, you can use several methods to straighten the leader. One of the simplest is to tie the fly to the leader with the knot you desire, then have a companion hold the hook with his pliers while you stretch the shock leader taut. Then rub along the length of the leader with your hand (careful—it gets hot), or use a piece of oiled rubber, to straighten it out.

Another method, however, is to place a long length of the heavy monofilament in a pan of hot (not boiling) water and let it sit for at least a minute. Remove the monofilament, and, while it is still warm, stretch it very tight; this will remove all kinks and coils. If you do not remove the coil characteristics from the leader it will cast badly, and cause the fly to ride unnaturally through the water.

The smart angler will build his leaders *before* he goes on a trip. There are two quick methods. Bob Stearns, an excellent fly rodder, realized that the time-consuming part of making saltwater fly leaders is building the two Bimini Twists or Spider Hitches in the tippet portion. So, at home, Bob builds a series of 6-, 10-, 12-, and 15-pound-test monofilament tippets, and he ties the Bimini Twist in each end of the single strands. Then he loops one after another onto a small leader spool. When he is fishing and his leader breaks, he needs only to remove the broken tippet, loop on one of his premade tippets, and quickly tie to that the desired shock leader. Another way that is more work and takes up more room but gives you instant readiness with your leaders is the method used by Captain Cochran of Marathon, Florida. He has a tackle box rigged to hold complete leaders, so the 100-pound monofilament remains straight.

Captain Cal Cochran has developed a method of keeping the 100-pound shock tippet straight on rigged leaders. He makes his quick-change leaders, coils the lighter test, and places it in the left side of the box. Then he clips the clothespin to one end of the 100-pound material, and the hook is inserted in some elastic cord at the other end of the box. Under such tension the leader remains straight. The arrows point to the taut 100-pound shock leader.

Perhaps the neatest leader trick I've seen the past few years was developed by Harry Kime of Orange, California. Harry places some lead dust in a shot glass, and adds enough Plio-bond rubber-base glue to it to half fill the glass. Then he adds enough methylethylketone (MEK), which can be purchased at any local chemical supply house and at some paint stores, to the Pliobond to make a thin glue. The lead dust settles to the bottom of the shot glass. Harry stirs the mixture with a small camel's-hair brush until the lead dust is well distributed. Then he paints the lead-glue mixture on his leader *butt section;* the mixture must be stirred well before each application. Using this technique he can add lead dust in any amount he desires to the leader butt. I have tested this method; it works well, sinks the butt section like a bomb, and has no effect on leader strength.

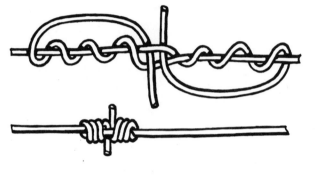

BLOOD KNOT (used to connect various sizes of monofilament for making tapered leaders)

The Blood Knot is a good knot if it is tied *properly.* Monofilament knot strength is reduced sharply as the number of turns is decreased. In 10-pound monofilament a four-turn knot will break at about 8½ pounds. Three turns will further reduce it to about 7 pounds. To be sure of getting good strength in blood knots, it is advisable to tie the smaller strand with at least five turns—naturally, the larger strands near the butt section do not need their maximum strength. The five turns holds true for the smaller section of a tapered leader near the tippet.

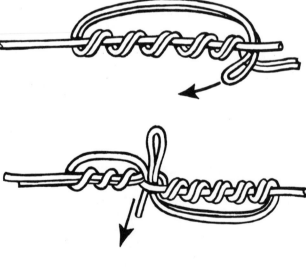

IMPROVED BLOOD KNOT

Several years ago, while doing an assignment for *Sports Afield,* I discovered that almost always the knot that breaks in a tapered leader system is not the one tied to the fly—but the knot used to connect the leader tippet to the next larger size in the taper. Therefore, it is recommended that the Improved Blood Knot be used, which when properly tied will give 100 per cent strength.

Several colors and sizes of Lefty's Deceiver

Joe Brooks's Blonde

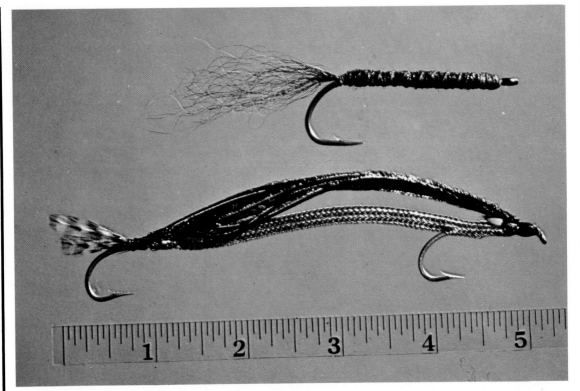

Top: Lou Tabori's Sand Eel   *Bottom:* Bub Church's Sand Launce

White Whistler

Gallasch White Bomber

Left: Stu Apte Tarpon Fly

Right: Cockroach Tarpon Fly

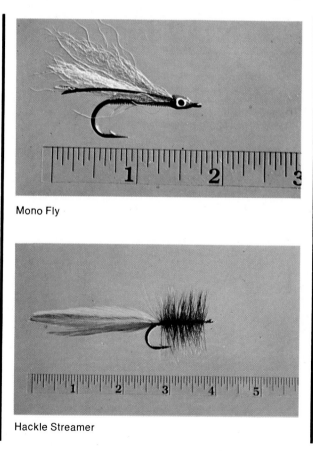

Mono Fly

Hackle Streamer

Top: Blue Tail Fly
Bottom left: Frankie Belle
Bottom right: The Horror

Left: Connecticut Shad Fly
Right: Irv Swope's Shad Fly

6 Flies

Saltwater fly rodders are continually searching for patterns that will enable them to tempt fish into striking.

I get letters constantly asking for specific tying instructions. The writers are anglers, usually adept at dressing trout flies, who want to put their skills to this new kind of fishing. They want to know about exact dressings, blends of furs used—the whole gamut of tricks that go with properly tying *trout* imitations. And there lies the problem.

The sea hatches few insects as we know them in fresh water. Mayflies, caddis, and stoneflies, or their counterparts, just don't exist, so exact imitation is almost beside the point. I say almost, because there are exceptions. If fish are definitely feeding upon a specific species of baitfish that is, say, greenish on the back, silvery on the sides, and about three inches long—then an exact imitation of this might be advisable. But even then it might turn out that the largest fish caught took something very much larger than the imitation.

Most imitations are constructed to resemble baitfish, or sometimes a crustacean. In southern parts of the country, and in tropical waters, there exists such a confusion of fish foods of all sorts and sizes, shapes, and colors that you simply would not know what to imitate. They range from small gaudily colored tropical fishes to nearly colorless squids. In northern waters there is a reduction in this prolific variety of marine life, and imitation of particular baitfish is more effective.

Most freshwater fly patterns have tail, body, ribbing, beard, wing, hackle, and head components. Saltwater flies are simple by comparison; most of them have just a wing and a head. Saltwater flies often have to be large, on the other hand, in order to entice fish to strike. That means that the body must be constructed of a nonabsorbent material, or the angler won't be able to lift the fly from the water. And the fly must not be bulky either, or the angler will never overcome air resistance and get it to his target.

But perhaps the single most important principle of tying saltwater flies is size: the fly must be the correct size for the specific species of fish for which it is intended. A husky 50-pound amberjack is not going to notice a 3-inch streamer, no matter how beautifully it is tied. I am convinced that to get the big stripers consistently, you have to use flies 8 inches or larger.

I do not mean to imply that large flies are the whole ticket. In fact, I feel fishermen have been misguided by some outdoor writers, who have implied that bigger flies are the answer; they aren't.

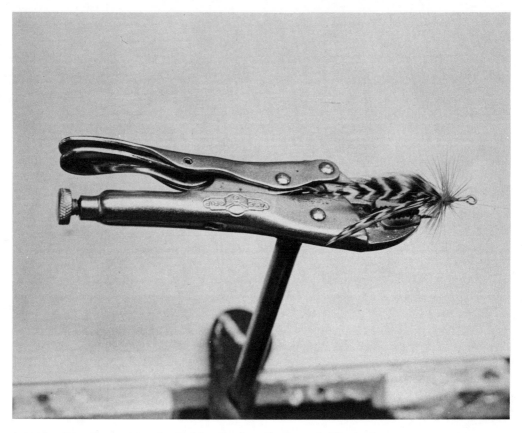

A Jr. Vise-Grip pliers makes a fine fly-tying vise for saltwater work. The vise is instantly adjustable for hook sizes from 8 to 8/0.

I once measured the mouth of a 10-pound bonefish. When it was stretched taut, the maximum distance I measured was 2¼ inches. That means that flies larger than 3 inches in length are not going to appeal to bonefish; in fact, most good bonefish patterns range between 1 and 2 inches. The same is true of snapper and small tarpon. They simply are not attracted to a large fly. Pan-sized striped bass are among the most size-selective fish I've ever taken; sometimes a half-inch difference in flies spells success. I fished one day near Herald Harbor, Maryland, with Sandy Sanderson, one of the state's fishery biologists. Chesapeake Bay was like glass, and the October weather had the stripers breaking all over the surface. I threw flies into boiling masses of stripers time and again with almost no luck; Sandy kept catching one fish after another on a little jig. Finally, I looked at his lure: the jig was about 2 inches long. I was fishing a white streamer with a green top that was perhaps three-quarters of an inch longer; I cut my fly back to the same size as his jig, and began to take fish consistently. Apparently the baitfish the stripers were feeding on were about 2 inches long.

Sailfish can be teased easily to boatside with a 10-inch belly bait, and sometimes with a foot-long plastic squid. If you take out the teaser and throw a 5-inch streamer in its place, you're wasting your time. But toss a big, noise-making popping bug or a large streamer to the same aroused fish and you'll probably get an instant strike.

So if you know you are into fish and they have refused the lure a number of times, the first change in tactics should be to alter the size of your fly.

But if fish are deep, a beautiful imitation of their food—even the correct size—is not going to do any good if you can't get it down to them. Among the most important fly characteristics is something we call "sink rate."

Saltwater fishes are almost constantly moving. Some species swim continually to stay alive; if they stop, they die. When the freshwater angler locates a fish, he can test it with several patterns and sizes. If he gets a refusal, he can walk up the bank and get advice from a friend, or even tie a new fly to accommodate the situation—and then return to cast and catch the fish. No such luxury exists for the saltwater fly rodder. If you cannot complete a cast in less than 6 seconds after you have seen the fish, it is generally too late: your fly must not be too bulky to cast, and it must sink to the proper level at once. There are few second chances.

Remember, you should be holding the fly in your hand when you stalk many saltwater fishes. Using specially designed saltwater taper lines, the angler can hold most of the belly section of the line outside the rod tip; upon sighting the fish, he should make a rapid backcast, a forward cast, another backcast, and then shoot the line to the fish. Experts can often perform the task with a single back and forward cast, shooting the line perhaps 70 or 80 feet.

The fluffy patterns with palmer-wound hackles and big "breather flies" that made the scene in saltwater fly fishing years ago are out. Today's angler mostly uses sleek flies that offer little resistance as they are picked from the water or moved through the air, and they have a specific sink-rate.

Let me cite an example of how these characteristics are combined in a fly that has gained wide acceptance among tarpon anglers. To my knowledge, Stu Apte of Miami first conceived this tarpon streamer, but after several years of researching the sport I wonder how anyone can claim to have discovered anything in fishing. I wouldn't be surprised if someday archaeologists opened an Egyptian tomb and found on the wall a painting of a fisherman using a fiber-glass rod.

Years ago, Stu was guiding and fishing in the Big Pine Key area of the Florida Keys where in the spring and early summer giant tarpon came in from the ocean to roam over the shallow banks and flats. Some of these monsters were encountered in two or three feet of water, slowly cruising along. Others were found in schools, traveling along a channel edge or even in a deep channel, like a pack of drifting green logs.

A fly pattern had to be developed that would interest these large fish. The fly also had to be castable, for Stu guided many anglers who were new to the business of standing on a casting platform defying a giant tarpon in its own ring. And, since the fish were encountered swimming in waters of various depths, the fly would have to be sunk to the depth of the tarpon; tarpon will rarely see or go to a fly that sinks beneath them on the retrieve. They often will not rise to take one, either; when possible, the fly should arrive on a collision course. Then, at the right moment, the fly must have some action and color appeal for the tarpon.

Apte came up with a fly that looks like an uncompleted freshwater pattern. He tied several orange hackles onto the rear of the hook, then several bright yellow ones onto the outsides of the orange ones. Generally, a total of two orange and four yellow ones were used. One or two turns with an orange and yellow hackle were made around the hook shank directly in front of the saddle hackles. Everything was tied into the rear of the hook shank, leaving the entire straight portion exposed. Some claimed that this blending of orange and yellow created a color quite similar to a shrimp, and that the swimming motion of the fly also resembled a shrimp's.

Here was a fly for giant tarpon whose length did not exceed 4 inches, and could be scaled down further for smaller fish. With all feathers attached at the rear, it hardly ever fouled during the cast. Since many change-of-direction and long casts are necessary in salt water, this nonfouling characteristic is vital.

The sleek, sparse dressing allowed the fly to sink quickly. When the fish was sighted, the angler would gauge how far ahead of the fish to cast, then make a hasty presentation. Flies can be *too* sleek—a bare look casts terribly—but Stu had done considerable experimentation, and achieved the right balance.

This fly has become a standard among tarpon anglers. There are some areas, like the Ten Thousand Islands, where large, 7-inch flies are best for big tarpon, but in most places I've fished for them, this small fly of less than 4 inches has greater appeal to the silvery giant.

However, we found that in some clear waters this bright fly would flush fish. So John Emery, a superb light-tackle angler from Miami, popularized a fly pattern originally developed by Norman Duncan, another excellent fly fisherman. It had 6 barred rock saddles tied in at the rear, then laid down along the hook shank was some deer hair from the top of the tail. John named it the Cockroach.

This pattern did not have many of the standard components of a freshwater pattern; it had a wing (attached to the rear instead of the front of the hook) and a collar. That's all. To fishermen, it seems a drab, unappealing fly. But I am convinced that, armed with this and the tie Stu conceived, you can successfully fish tarpon in most places in the world.

The point to be made here is that many effective saltwater patterns are incredibly simple in construction, but they still appeal to fish and meet conditions.

If I had to choose a single fly to carry with me for fishing all types of saltwater situations, it would be a fly I developed myself while fishing Chesapeake Bay. Stripers are among the most finicky of fish. Today they may want a small fly, tomorrow a large one, the day after a medium-sized one. Really big stripers want a mouthful almost anytime. So I wanted to be able to alter size at whim, and to change color combinations if I desired. I needed a fly that would cast well in the almost ever-present wind, and one that would sink quickly.

The Lefty's Deceiver has all these qualities.

Few flies are simpler to tie. Six to eight saddle hackles are attached (nonflaring) straight along the top of the hook shank at the rear; this prevents fouling on the cast. A body of Mylar (or tinsel) is wrapped to within one-quarter inch of the eye. I clip some hair a little longer than the hook shank from either polar bear, calf tail, or bucktail, and tie it at the eye so it encircles the hook shank. This gives the impression of bulk but adds no weight. It flows symmetrically to the wings at the rear, forming the shape of a baitfish. I consider it important that you use saddle hackles instead of neck hackles for the wing. Neck hackles are stiff; saddles undulate and look like a swimming fish. When lifted from the water, the fly collapses into the shape of a knife blade.

Since I first designed the fly an important new material has come on the fishing scene—Mylar. Now I add 3 or 4 silver strips to each side. I prefer the 1/64-inch Mylar, but will reluctantly use up to 1/8-inch if I have to. Topping can be added for more realism. I use peacock herl, dark bucktail, or horsehair. But most of the time I tie it all white.

For some fish, especially dolphin, I tie the Lefty's Deceiver with a red collar and yellow saddle hackles, with Mylar of either gold or silver.

Here is a fly, with the shock leader and tippet rigged on it, carried in a plastic envelope ready for instant use.

Following this procedure you can make any fly pattern weedless. Tie your basic fly, as shown here. . .

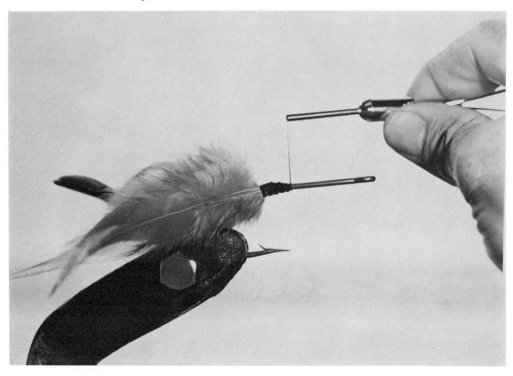

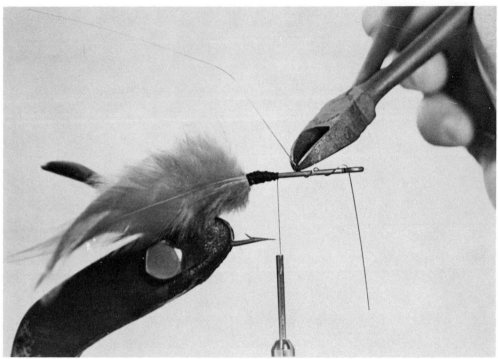

Run a piece of number 7 solid trolling wire through the hook eye and bend as shown; clip away end with pliers.

Wrap thread firmly over the wire, bend the wire under the hook to the indicated position, and the weedless fly is finished.

I have tied this fly in many lengths, from 2½ inches to more than a foot in length; it has taken many sailfish. Larry Kreh, my son, tied this in an oversized version for Lee Wulff, who took his record striped marlin with it.

Everything from Allison tuna to tiny bluefish have struck at this fly. I think it is the single most useful fly—providing the size is varied—I know.

Mylar is an important material in most saltwater flies; the majority of the working anglers I know use it in all but a very few patterns.

According to Dupont, Mylar is a synthetic: it is a very stiff, clear plastic film. Chemically, it's a polyester and is similar to Dacron polyester fiber. Mylar is often "metalized"—a very thin coating of metal is applied to one side of the plastic. Since the Mylar itself is transparent, the composition looks like a strip of metal. It comes in many colors—blue, green, red, silver, gold, yellow.

To a fly tyer, Mylar looks like tinsel, but the resemblance stops at appearances. Tinsel is thick and hard to work with; it corrodes easily, and shreds away when abraded by sharp-toothed fish. Mylar has the shiny appearance of tinsel, but does not corrode, is super-thin (making dressing the fly easier) and very tough, undulates in the water, and requires no further protective treatment. Mylar does almost all the jobs formerly performed in fly tying by tinsel.

When Mylar first appeared, it came in wide sheets, which could be trimmed to a width of 3/16 to 1/4 inch and placed on the side of the fly. It looked good in the vise, but was a poor performer in the water. The wide strips or panels would flutter badly in the air and impeded the cast. They gave off surprisingly little flash in the water, too. It is important to realize that most of the reflective flashes come not from the long strip or panel of Mylar, but from the flopping end. A mirror is a total reflector, but it does little flashing when held still. It has to be moved back and forth to give off flashes; the same applies to Mylar. Mylar strands attached to a fly need only be long enough to allow them to undulate in the water, and should be no longer, since the stuff is so thin and supple that the extra-long strands have a tendency to foul on the hook.

What really helped push Mylar as a favorite new weapon of the fly tyer was the appearance of ribbons of Mylar resembling fly-tying tinsel. After much testing, many good fishermen determined that Mylar ribbons wider than 1/8 inch were too wide; 1/32 inch is better, and most of us consider 1/64 inch best. Three or four strands to a side of a fly are sufficient; you can overwhelm a fly with too much Mylar. There are some rare situations in which an all-Mylar fly, made of multiple strands, will take certain fishes, but most of the time it should be used to create a subtle flash.

For a long time it was difficult to obtain Mylar ribbon, and it took a lot of looking and knowing the right people to get a good supply. Today a number of the larger fly-tying firms retail it to customers, although the selections they offer are usually limited.

Almost all flies used in salt water become better fish attractors with the addition of Mylar. And I have satisfied myself that for minnow imitations, Mylar will improve a bass or trout fly.

If you want to obtain Mylar strands in your own locality, go to a sewing-supply store. Almost all of them carry Mylar piping. This piping resembles a braided rope, with a core of cotton strands and an outer shell of Mylar. It's very inexpensive, something like a few cents a foot.

There are all sizes of piping, but the 1/8 O.D. (outside diameter) piping works fine for hooks 2, 4, 6, and 8. For most other uses in salt water the 3/8 O.D. will accommodate you.

There are several ways you can use piping to make flies. One is to cut off the appropriate length, remove the cotton strand core, then tease apart the many strands of Mylar. You'll have enough strands to place on the sides of several flies. The material is crimped and crinkled, but the fish don't seem to mind.

Another method is to make a section of piping slightly longer than the straight portion of the hook shank. Build a wool or yarn body on the hook shank, slip the Mylar tube over the built-up body and tie it down on both ends. You will discover that the fly body has the most realistic scale finish of any fly you've tied.

Do the same thing, but leave a series of the Mylar strands extended beyond the body to the rear, and you have multiple reflective ribbons of Mylar that further improve the fly.

Many of us who fish a great deal have felt that Mylar should not be used for bonefish, permit, and tarpon. We still do not use it for permit, but we have determined that just two or three strands to a side often give a fly extra strike appeal for tarpon.

Captain Bill Curtis, of the Key Biscayne Yacht Club, is in many people's opinion the most productive bonefish guide in the country—perhaps the world. His success ratio is astounding. During one year Bill was booked on 256 days; this included days when frontal systems passed through the area and turned Biscayne Bay into a light-colored soup; it also included guiding women in high-heeled shoes, and men who had never seen a bonefish. Yet, of those 256 days, Bill managed to put fish in the boat for his clients on 252. On one of the remaining days the clients hooked five, and on another, two. If anyone else has even approached that record, I am unaware of it.

One day Bill fished with Kay Brodney, who was a national ladies' casting champion; Kay fishes everywhere with a fly rod, and is on the advisory board of the Salt Water Fly Rodders of America. She brought along with her a fly new to Bill, called a Russian River Shad Fly. (The Russian is one of the West Coast rivers that see a spring migration of shad.) It certainly did not look like a bonefish fly, but Kay insisted on using it, and took several bones under tough conditions; Bill was highly impressed. The fly had one hackle wrapped palmer style at the head, with a collar of purple chenille right behind it, and, of all things, a Mylar-wrapped body and a few strands of Mylar for a tail.

After considerable experimentation with this pattern Bill has arrived at a design that has taken an astounding number of fish for him in Biscayne Bay; I have found it to be effective in British Honduras, Mexico, and the Bahamas. He later made a slight variation in the pattern, so he now uses two different flies. But most of the customers Bill takes out use his fly—the Blue Tail Fly, or the Golden Getter. They are simple flies, similar to Kay's. The Blue Tail Fly has a blue tail of 4 to 6 strands of 1/32-inch Mylar, a body fully wrapped of gold Mylar, a yellow collar of 2 turns of 1/8-inch yellow chenille, and 2 turns of yellow hackle at the front—that's all. His Golden Getter Fly is the same tie, except that the tail is of gold Mylar, rather than blue. Bill dresses the fly on a number 2 regular shank hook. He prefers the offset point on the hook, but it seems to work with the standard round-bend Model Perfect, too.

The fly sinks well and casts like a dream, and the little reflective flashes attract bonefish. Bonefish feed on small minnows, and I feel that the Blue Tail and Golden Getter flies give that minnowlike sparkle. That same flash allows you to keep an eye on the fly as it is retrieved. I have also tied this fly on Keel hooks, and teased it along the bottom with great success. The fly appeals to snapper, small barracudas, jacks, and little tarpon. This fly works best when chumming bonefish.

The Frankee-Belle is another fly that has stood years of testing; it was popularized by Joe Brooks, and designed by the wives of two of his friends. Both women were excellent fishermen, who fished extensively for bonefish. Many close imitations of this fly have also produced well. The original pattern is listed and shown with other great flies at the end of this chapter.

Since Pete Perinchief introduced me to Bermuda fly fishing I've never been the same. Offshore fishing there—standing in the back of a charter boat anchored on one of the deep-water banks, watching the many fantastic game fish lying back in the chum slick—is one of my greatest angling thrills. One afternoon while anchored off Challenger Bank I saw five black-fin tuna, an Allison tuna, three wahoo, and at least a dozen almaco jacks lunching in the chum. I knew I would get a taker from among them, and I did.

The most challenging fish in Bermuda are the bonefish that ghost over the incredibly clear waters of the white sand flats of this really beautiful island. They are as easily frightened as permit in the clear water, and so require long casts most of the time. It's some of the toughest and most rewarding fishing I've ever done for bones; in three days of trying, I hooked three and landed one. Pete has developed a fly, based on a concept that I've found exists among many good bonefishermen, wherever they live and fish.

He calls his fly The Horror and it fits the description. In fact, it is so sparsely dressed and of such an ugly color that a salmon fisherman might apologize to any bonefish he hooked on it. But it sure takes bonefish. The fly is tied with a small brown bucktail wing and some yellow chenille for a short collar. The bare hook shank remains exposed. Pete also ties the wing on the bottom of the hook at about a 40-degree angle (see section on fly photos and dressings) so that the hook rides inverted in the water. The fly hardly ever snags on the bottom, which is where bonefish feed. The brown color is a close imitation of many crustaceans that bonefish feed on; what the yellow color is for I don't know—maybe Pete was ashamed of the fly and tried to dress it up a bit.

His method of reverse tying a fly to get the hook point to ride up is a universally accepted bonefisherman's trick now. A great many of the best flies are tied in this manner, since working a fly on the bottom draws the most strikes from bones.

Lou Tabory, from Connecticut, is one of the very best fly casters I have ever known, and a rabid fisher for blues and striped bass. He has developed a fly that has the appearance of being unfinished, but he claims unusual success with it.

Sand eel, often called sand launce and launce-fish, are one of the favorite foods of stripers. These little fish resemble eels, but have a continuous dorsal and anal fin. They live close to the bottom in sandy areas and quickly burrow beneath the sand when pursued or frightened.

Lou's fly is incredibly simple, but effective. On a 2/0 3XL hook he dresses tightly wound black wool, to a diameter of 3/16 inch, the length of the shank. A tail, 1½ inches long, of brown bucktail completes the tie. It sinks quickly, casts well, and gets fish—that's all you can ask.

There are occasions when a sinking fly is a disadvantage. When redfish are moving over the foot-deep clear waters of the flats, a fly must be fished in shallow water, but you need to keep it from snagging on the bottom. One fly, which we call the hackle streamer, almost floats in the water, and when given a twitch it wiggles and undulates in a manner most attractive to fish. The fly is also simple to tie. Six to eight saddle hackles (neck hackles are too stiff) are tied at the rear of the hook. Then a series of saddle hackles are wound as closely as possible the length of the hook shank to make the fly look like a multilegged caterpillar. The hundreds of hackles support the fly in the water so that it sinks ever so slowly. The saddle hackles tied in at the tail move back and forth and tantalize the fish. You can skim such a fly over a bottom in six inches of water, getting an enormous amount of action from the fly with slow movement.

Several color combinations have proven effective and popular: red and white; yellow and red; all-yellow; orange and red; and all-brown. The many hackles on the fly also make the fly semiweedless.

Joe Brooks, whose famed Blonde series is well known and has taken many species of fish, created a fly that every serious fly fisherman should have when trying for saltwater fishes. It's a simple tie: a short wing, usually of bucktail, is tied at the rear of the straight portion of the shank; then tinsel or Mylar is wound to within 3/8 inch of the front. Here, another wing, similar in length, is tied. The wings do not foul on the cast and the fly offers very little air resistance. You can make the rear wing a light color and the front wing, which acts almost as topping, darker. Many color combinations are used, but all-white and all-yellow are the most popular.

Whenever the angler is forced to fish where there is excessive floating grass, or where the bottom will snag the fly, he should consider dressing his fly patterns on Keel hooks. These are hooks bent in such a shape that they are almost impossible to foul. When Bing McClellan, of Burke Flex-Products, first gave me some to try, I walked into my front yard and cast one over a tree. I slowly retrieved the fly back to me with no hang-ups. I repeated the operation a number of times; only the leader knots caught.

The next morning I worked one of them in front of a tarpon at Flamingo, deep in the Everglades area. The tarpon swirled, took the fly, leaped and spit it out. That's not too unusual; I've been used to such humiliating treatment from tarpon for years. But after six more hook-ups I began to suspect something. I had two strikes from redfish during this time, and lost one that appeared to gobble the fly. I took a pair of pliers and opened the point a little, being careful not to offset the bend. That made a difference. Since that time I, and others I fish with who use Keel hooks, open the bend of the hook a little. Most standard patterns can be dressed on Keel hooks.

Three types of popping bugs are used in salt water. The most commonly used type is smaller than a whole peanut shell, and has a tail that works in the water to imitate some small struggling thing on the surface. The allure is the popping noises made by the bug when the line is stripped quickly.

The second type of popping bug is called a slider. It has a sharply tapered front, much like a bullet. On the rear are saddle hackles; occasionally bucktail or capras hair is used. This bug slides and darts around on the surface like a helpless minnow, and is especially effective for fishing under conditions where the quarry is easily alarmed; sometimes a regular popping bug makes so much noise that it actually frightens a large fish. The slider, while not used a great deal, is a very fine lure in that respect.

The third type of saltwater popping bug is the giant of the series, often with a hook as large as 7/0. It has one purpose, to create enough noise and commotion to make a big amberjack, cobia, sailfish, or other husky fish think, "Here is a mouthful!" The 15 to 20 full-length saddle hackles, plus the enormous amount of water-action and noise the big bug generates, have trapped many big fish into thinking just that.

The most important factor in making good popping bugs is that the hook point should extend well beyond the rear of the bug body; this helps insure hooking the fish on the initial strike. There is an exception here insofar as the very large poppers are concerned; usually these fish are so big that they inhale the whole lure.

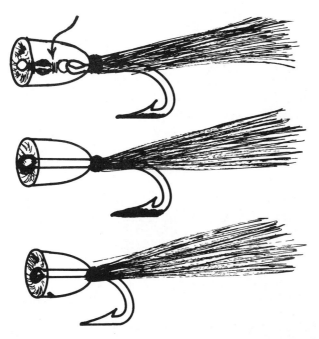

Popping bug design; upper drawing shows hook shank length extended by addition of a connector. Middle drawing shows a well-designed popper with an extra-long hook shank. Lower drawing is of a poorly designed bug; the hook is too short.

Popping bugs are light, are often struck when at rest, and tend to move away from the fish as it approaches it to grab the lure. Therefore, while sharp hooks are always vital to success, the hook must be extra-sharp when using poppers.

Bluefish love a popper, but a popping bug that is constructed on a normal-length shank hook will often fail to get the point into the fish. Use hooks with an extra-long shank.

Freshwater bass fishermen like a lot of flaring hackles on their flies. This is mainly because while the bug is resting the bass may be further enticed into striking if it sees the waving collar of hackles. Most saltwater fly rodding with poppers is done at high speed, and the lure is retrieved rather rapidly, so there is no need for big bushy collars. And, since the average casting distances in salt water are greater, the less air-resistant the bug, the better the caster can perform. Well-designed popping bugs, other than the giants, are sleek, streamlined lures that lift from the water easily.

Balsa wood and cork are the best materials for saltwater poppers—balsa seems a little more durable; cork floats higher. Since the retrieve is fast and the fish hard-mouthed, bugs must be constructed well. Epoxy glue and paint will aid the fly rodder in making lasting bugs. Plastic foam is gaining popularity as bug material.

Finally, when tying flies for salt water you will be using fairly large hooks, and most vises on the market today are designed for smaller hooks. The hooks don't hold well, since these vises are being used for a job they were not designed for. A cheap vise with 1-inch jaws is the best buy. Joe MaCathron, of Trumbull, Connecticut, improvised a simple vise, made for a few dollars, that will accommodate any hook from size ten to 10/0. Joe welds a Jr. Vise-Grip pair of pliers to a round shaft, and this shaft can be substituted in the regular clamp on your vise. Or, you can weld a simple **C** clamp to the lower end of the shaft to make a perfect saltwater vise.

BASIC SALTWATER FLY PATTERNS

The following is a list of flies that will allow you to catch fish almost anyplace in the world where the fly rod can be successful. I am convinced that with these patterns you can fish successfully most places, most of the time. Many of these flies have been in use for ten or more years; some have long, successful records already. Dick Splain's Squeteager was used by him and Joe Brooks with great success to fish sea trout in the mid-forties. I feel I must apologize for not listing other equally superb flies, but even with these few patterns you are armed to fish the salt anywhere.

FRANKEE-BELLE BONEFISH FLY

Hackle:	none
Body:	yellow chenille
Wings:	barred rock over white feather, 1½ inches long, one on each side of hook; wing may be reversed
Throat:	white bucktail under hook and going back ½ inch beyond bend of hook
Hook:	1/0 or smaller

BLUE TAIL FLY (bonefish)

Tail:	6 strands of blue Mylar—½ inch long
Body:	gold Mylar to within 3/16 inch of hook eye
Hackle:	soft yellow, 3 turns
Head:	2 turns of ⅛-inch yellow chenille

THE HORROR (bonefish)

Hackle:	none
Body:	yellow chenille, ½ inch long; ⅛-inch of chenille behind the bucktail wing assures an upright wing that covers point of hook
Wings:	brown bucktail, 1½ inches long, coming out from under the chenille body ½ inch from hook eye and protruding ¾ inch beyond bend of hook; when cast and worked, hook point rides up in shallow water

Top, Frankee Belle. *Left,* The Horror. *Right,* Blue Tail Fly.

CONNECTICUT RIVER SHAD FLY

Body: flat silver tinsel of Mylar
Wing: red-dyed duck feathers ¼ inch wide, tied upright at middle of shank
Hook: 1/0 with red bead at front of hook

IRV SWOPE'S SHAD FLY

Body: fluorescent wool (yellow, insect green, brown, claret, or red)
Hook: 6-8 or 10-3XL long
Wing: fluorescent marabou, ¾ inch long, lightly dressed; green, red, claret, yellow, or brown
Tail: fluorescent marabou, same as wing material, but tail should not exceed ½ inch in length

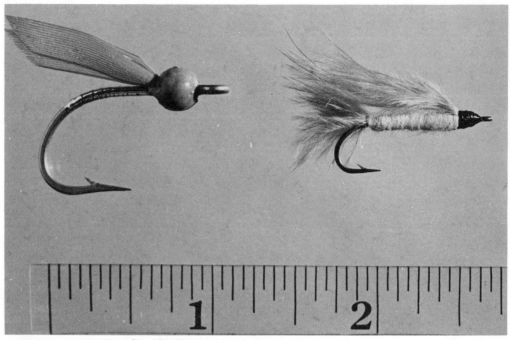

Left, Connecticut River Shad Fly. *Right,* Irv Swope's Shad Fly.

GOLDEN SQUETEAGER

Hook: front hook 1/0, stinger hook to rear is No. 1

Wing: bucktail underneath, 2 white neck hackles over bucktail, one to a side; 2 yellow neck hackles over white ones, one to a side; 2 grizzly hackles dressed similarly over yellow ones

Topping: one large burnt-orange neck hackle the length of the fly; total length of fly is 6 inches

Hackle: burnt-orange 6 turns

Head: orange with large yellow eye
stinger hook is attached to front hook with 30-pound monofilament; hook lies at extreme rear of wing

HACKLE FLY

Tail: 2½ inches of 6 or 8 yellow, white, or brown saddle hackles; Mylar strands can be added to each side if desired
Body: densely wrapped saddle hackles length of fly in red, orange, yellow, or brown
Hook: from 3/0 to size 2

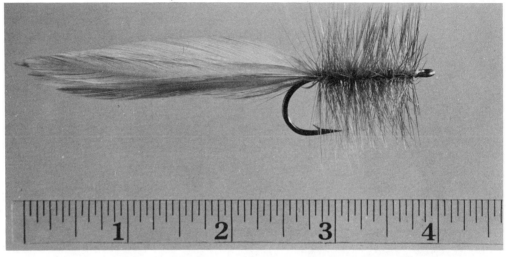

BEAD-HEAD MARABOU

Hook: 1/0
Body: marabou heavily packed on fly in all-white
Head: bead, with spotted eye

KEEL FLY

Body: chenille the length of shank; color of your choice
Wing: bucktail, calf tail, or feather wing 1 inch longer than total hook; color
of your choice

HI-TIE FLY

Hook: from 4/0 to size 2
Wing: approximately 10 separate bucktail wings (⅛ inch in thickness) are
tied on top of the hook shank, one in front of the other
Color: any color
good for many fish; almost nonfouling in flight.

MONO FLY (good imitation of small baitfish)

Body: full length of body wrapped with Mylar or tinsel; 30-pound clear monofilament tied at bend of hook and wound close together to hook eye

Wing: usually green or blue on top and white underneath, of calf tail or bucktail

Hook: from 3/0 to #6

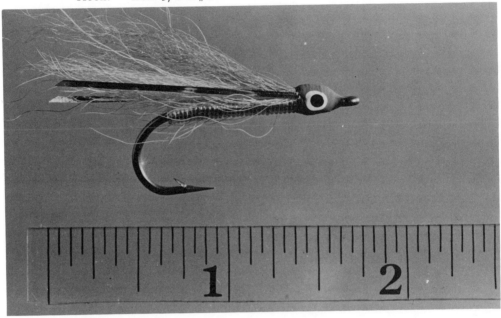

TABORY'S SAND EEL

Hook: 2/0 or 3/0—3XL

Tail: brown bucktail from top of tail, 1½ inches long

Body: black wool tightly wound 3/16 inch thick so body is about the length of hook shank

Head: gray

BUB CHURCH'S SAND LAUNCE

Hook: 2—one at front and one at rear of fly, both size 1

Tail: 2 grizzly hackles 1 inch long

Body: 4 inches of Mylar piping with 30-pound mono attaching from front to back hook inside piping

Wing: peacock herl tied in at head and rear of fly

Head: red

Top, Tabory's Sand Eel. *Bottom,* Bub Church's Sand Launce.

BLONDE FLIES (general-purpose fly)

Hackle: none
Body: silver tinsel or Mylar wrapped on hook shank
Wings: one 3-inch bucktail tied in at rear of fly, another tied in just behind hook eye, both are tied on top of hook shank
Hook: size 4/0 to 1

STU APTE TARPON FLY

Hook: from size 5/0 to 2, depending on size of fish sought

Tail: 2 orange saddle hackles 3 inches long tied at rear of hook shank; on either side of these are tied 2 bright yellow saddle hackles of same length

Hackle: Two to four turns of a mixed orange and yellow saddle

Shank: left bare, or occasionally painted with fluorescent orange paint or wrapped with fluorescent yarn

COCKROACH TARPON FLY

Hook: from size 5/0 to 2, depending on size of fish sought

Wing: 6 grizzly saddle hackles, 3 to each side

Hackle: brown bucktail from top of tail, tied around hook shank at eye so it completely encircles hook

Head: brown

NOTE: red neck hackle is sometimes substituted for the brown bucktail at front of hook

Left, Stu Apte Tarpon Fly. *Right,* Cockroach Tarpon Fly.

LEFTY'S DECEIVER

Hook: from 7/0 to 4

Tail: 6 to 20 saddle hackles (depending on size of hook used) attached at bend; on each side of saddle hackles place 2 to 6 strands of silver or gold Mylar from 1/64 to 1/8 inch in length

Body: wrapped full length of hook shank with Mylar
Head: red or white with eye
Hackle: white polar bear, calf tail or bucktail, laid on hook shank near eye so it encircles hook
NOTE: fly can be made in any length from 2 to 12 inches; dark topping can be placed above saddle hackles

WHITE WHISTLER (Red and Grizzly) West Coast striper fly

Hook: Wright and McGill short-shank 318 model, size 3/0
Wing: white bucktail 4 inches long; 4 grizzly saddle hackles in a north, south, east, west position placed around bucktail wing
Hackle: 3/4 inch of densely wound red hackle, using red thread
Head: large 3/16-inch bead-chain eyes

(see color section)

GIVEN'S BARRED-N-BLACK (West Coast striper fly—especially good at night)

Hook: 3XL size 3/0

Tail: 3 black saddle hackles 4½ inches long, with a good clump of black bucktail 3½ inches long encircling the feathers; alongside bucktail on each side of hook is a single 3-inch grizzly feather

Body: built up to ¼ inch diameter, then wrapped three-quarters of length toward eye with lead fuse wire

Hackle: black bucktail (or black saddle hackles palmered) around hook so ends join beyond end of hook

Head: one 3/16-inch bead-chain eye on either side

REVERSE TIED EEL (West Coast fly)

Hook: regular shank, size 1/0

Tail: 4 slim, sleek black saddle feathers tied at bend of hook

Head: black bucktail 4 inches long; hair is tied at the front with butt's point toward rear of hook; bucktail is folded over and down around hook encircling it, then firmly wrapped around bucktail at hook bend

BILL GALLASCH'S POPPING BUG

Hook: 3XL hump shank bug hook 2/0 size
Tail: several saddle hackles or some bucktail tied along the length of hook shank
Body: cork or balsa wood ⅜ inch diameter and 1⅜ inches long; hook shank is smeared with glue, a hole is drilled lengthwise through center of bug, and hook shoved through and out the front; be sure to clean glue from hook eye: epoxy glue recommended
body painted any color desired

Left, Slider. *Right,* Bill Gallasch's Popping Bug.

GALLASCH'S WHITE BOMBER (for giant fishes . . . amberjack, sailfish, etc.)

Hook: 7/0
Body: dense Styrofoam cut and sanded to round shape 1 to 1½ inches across face of bug; usually white
Hackle: 16 to 20 full-length saddle hackles tied along top of hook shank, then whole shank smeared with two-part epoxy glue; this gluey mess is fitted into previously formed slot in bottom of bug body

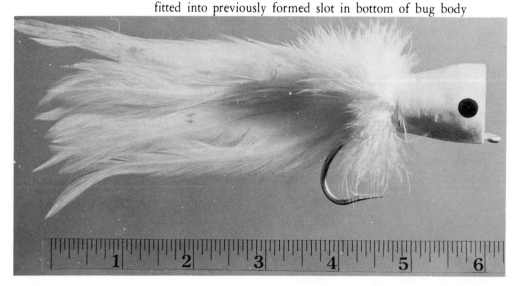

BASIC FLY FOR SMALL STRIPED BASS AND BLUEFISH

Hook: preferably 3XL, but standard length can be used in sizes 2, 1, 1/0, or 2/0

Body: can be built of wool and ribbed with Mylar or tinsel, or made entirely from Mylar or tinsel

Wing: sparse, generally white underwig with top of wing of a darker color

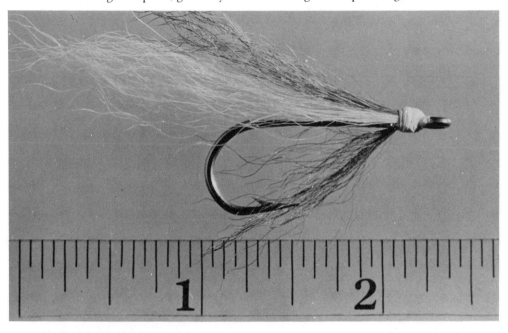

SLIDER (popping bug)

Hook: hump shank 3XL if possible, Wright and McGill's model 66 SS will work, too; size 1/0—3/0

Body: bullet-shaped cork, with pointed end toward hook eye

Hackle: usually saddle hackles are tied along top of hook; caparas or bucktail hair can be substituted; hook is either inserted through bug or fitted into a previously formed slot in bug body; epoxy two-part glue recommended

SEA ARROW SQUID

Hook: Mustad-Viking # 79573 ST, cadmium-plated, 3XL

Tail: 10 white saddle hackles (2 longer than the others)

Cheeks: a few strands of purple bucktail and some short white marabou

Body: large-size chenille over heavily padded base, tapering toward eye

Fin: use 100% Acrylic fiber yarn (sold by Hallmark Co.—called Gift Yarn Tie); yarn is made in 3 strands; use 6 to 9 strands on each side of hook to form fin; start by cutting 4 lengths of yarn about 3 inches long; tie 2 pieces on each side of hook just behind eye; bind yarn in middle so you have 2 ends on each side about 1½ inches long; taking one side of hook at a time, pull two ends of yarn very tight, out and away from hook shank horizontally, and at 90-degree angle to shank; now bind in yarn; this forms one projecting piece; repeat operation on other side.

You are now finished putting material on fly; tie thread off; take scissors and trim yarn on one side with circular motion; yarn will flare to form a perfect half circle; repeat on other side and you'll have shape of squid's frontal fin (this fly developed by Dan Blanton and Bob Edgely).

HOOKS

Only three styles of hooks are used extensively in salt water. Even so, there are several factors that must be considered in selecting the hook.

Perhaps the most important is the hook's holding power. A giant tarpon, cobia, or king mackerel, grabbing a small size 1 or 1/0 hook, is strong enough to crush the point against the hook shank. It takes at least a 3/0 hook to hook such a fish.

The amount of "bite," or grasping capacity, of the hook is also important. A sailfish has a rough outer mouth, rimmed with bone; a small hook cannot grasp enough of the softer meat of the mouth to guarantee ample purchase during a long fight.

But neither should the hook be too large. It is nearly impossible to set a hook larger than 1/0 deep enough with a 6-pound-test tippet; a 10-pound-test tippet's limit is about 3/0 for most fishes. If the cast is not excessive, 12-pound-test tippets can handle up to 5/0 with ease. For short casts, like those thrown at sails and marlin which have been teased right to boatside, a 7/0 can be handled well on 12-pound-test, but the light 10-pound-test leader tippet is marginal.

A hook must be selected for the job at hand. It must have good holding power, ample grasping capacity, and not be too large or too small for penetration.

Hooks come in stainless steel, plain steel, bronzed steel, nickel-plated steel, and cadmium-plated steel.

Plain steel and bronze-coated steel do not resist rust and are almost unknown in saltwater fishing. Nickel-plated steel used to be considered the finest material for fly-fishing hooks. The nickel-plating resisted corrosion, and the tempered steel made for first-class strength. But they were expensive, and the area that was sharpened (removing the nickel-plating) would rust. Because of their cost and the introduction of other metals for making hooks, nickel-plated types are rarely used anymore.

Perhaps the finest sharpening tool for saltwater flies is the Red Devil #15 wood scrapers file, which is 8 inches long and 3/4 inch wide; the fine teeth must be frequently cleaned for best operation. A small brass brush like the one shown here does the job nicely.

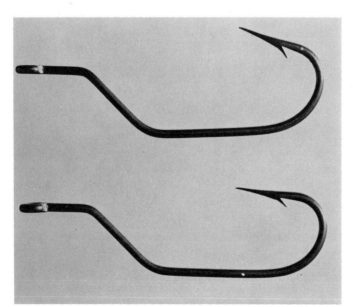

Bottom, a standard keel hook; top, how the hook should appear after it is bent open, ensuring better hook-ups. Be sure not to offset the hook when you bend it.

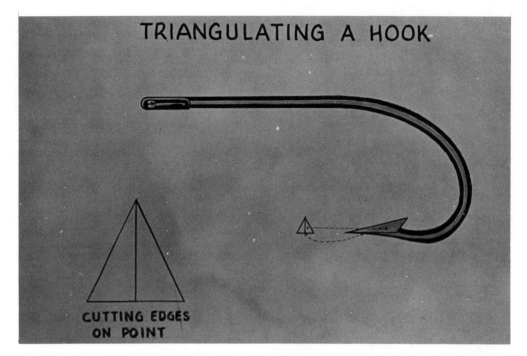

Triangulating a hook. This gives a cutting edge on three sides. The blades are well supported, as is the point.

Cadmium-plated hooks are used extensively, particularly on the West Coast. Many salt-water anglers there prefer the short-shanked, cadmium-plated hooks made by Wright & McGill. Their model 318 is a very short shank hook, originally designed to be buried within a small bait. West Coast fly rodders like this type of hook, claiming that fish will strike at the head of the fly. These short shank hooks also foul the wing less when the fly is in flight.

However, Wright &McGill does not make the model 318 in stainless steel, so you must take care to resharpen the hook continually to keep it from rusting. The other disadvantage is that it is more difficult to get a strong sharp point on this hook than on other styles. The thin, curved point can be well sharpened, but lacks the support of the conventional-style hook.

That leaves us with one hook material that has become almost universally accepted—stainless steel. The word stainless is misleading; not all grades of stainless are truly so, and some of them rust much more quickly than others.

At least three companies now make stainless steel hooks that are first class, and will *not* rust. Perhaps 80 percent of all flies dressed on stainless hooks are constructed on Wright & McGill model 254 SS hooks—excellent stainless steel hooks with the conventional round bend and normal shank length. The earlier 254s were made from a rather soft steel, and the points would often curl on a strike. The company has long since gone to a tougher metal, and that problem has been eliminated.

Another fine hook with the dimension of the 254 SS is produced by Mustad. The hook is model 34007 and comes in a variety of sizes. It is of excellent metal and holds its point on a strike.

The normal shank length does not lend itself to some flies. Many bluefish anglers prefer to dress the fly on the rear portion of a long shank hook, to help prevent cut-offs from the

The file is held against the hook to stroke it for sharpening. The metal should be removed on a 45-degree angle to the center of the outside of the shank.

The operation is repeated on the other side.

sharp teeth of the fish. Some anglers like to make an extra-long, sleek fly; I prefer a long shank hook for my Lefty's Deceiver, if I dress it on hooks larger than 1/0. The two stainless steel hooks mentioned do not lend themselves to this kind of fly as well as one imported by Shakespeare Tackle Company. Its model L-126C is about 2X long, with an excellent point; it comes in sizes from 3/0 through a tiny number 6.

A third type of hook very important to the saltwater fly rodder is the Keel. This hook is a salvation to the bonefisherman, who must drag his fly through the bottom growth for maximum appeal, and a boon to the sea-trout angler who casts among floating grasses. I find the hook to be excellent too whenever there is a likelihood of my fly hanging up on grass, weeds, or debris. Redfish, which take their food on the flats among the oyster bars and grass beds, can be taken with ease with a Keel hook fly; bright orange is a preferred color. When you are using a sinking line on the grassy bottom for sea trout, the Keel hook cannot be beaten.

The Keel hook is made of the finest steel; it is sold by Wright & McGill Company. Even though the hook carries a better-than-average point, it still should be sharpened before use.

I have repeatedly demonstrated to my own satisfaction that conventional hooks are better for fishing for small tarpon. Perhaps it's because of the peculiar way the tarpon closes its mouth: instead of closing normally, the tarpon's lower lip comes to the head in an almost vertical position, and perhaps the fly is shoved away in the process. But for fish other than tarpon, I urge you to have at least some patterns tied on Keel hooks.

Flies stored in individual plastic envelopes on a box like this will be easily available and always in good condition.

PART TWO

TECHNIQUES

7 Saltwater Fly Casting

The freshwater fisherman new to saltwater fly casting will have to alter his approach, learn a few new techniques, adapt himself to slightly heavier tackle, and work in many ways—if he is really to succeed to become a better fly caster. Saltwater fly fishermen must almost always deal with a wind factor. Flies are usually larger; one dressed on a 5/0 hook is not considered really big. The materials on the flies are more intricate; as many as 15 to 20 saddle hackles adorn some hooks. An additional factor not often considered by the freshwater man is the difficulty of casting with a shock-leader tippet. A shock-leader tippet is a heavy wire or monofilament leader (never longer than 12 inches) placed in front of the weakest section in the total leader. Its purpose is to prevent a sharp-toothed or raspy-mouthed fish from biting through the connection to the fly. The shock leader radically increases air resistance, especially if the angler must cast against a breeze.

All of these elements, unfamiliar to freshwater fly fishermen, create casting problems that must be overcome. One solution is to use heavier lines, which will develop more line speed for the angler. Heavier lines, of course, demand stouter rods. Freshwater fly fishing rods take an average line size of from 4 to 8; saltwater lines will average from 8 to 11.

Newcomers to saltwater fly fishing have often been misled by articles playing down the necessity for making long casts. There is an oft-repeated story that most saltwater fish are caught on a fly at a distance of less than fifty feet. Writers have assured readers that they are well armed if they can operate efficiently at that distance.

It's not true!

Most fish are caught at fifty feet simply because most fishermen can't cast any farther.

When I was a year-round resident of Florida, I frequently guided northern anglers; generally, we would go fishing, then call a halt for a casting lesson. Then we resumed fishing.

A recent incident is a perfect example of what occurs all too frequently. A close friend of mine, a bass fisherman, came down to fish with me for three days. He was extremely anxious to take a snook on his favorite fly rod. I knew that a few snook nestled under the mangrove bushes at high tide among certain Florida Bay keys near Flamingo, so we made the forty-eight-mile drive through Everglades Park before dawn, arriving at the dock to be greeted by mosquitoes big enough to romance turkeys. Slapping at them, we quickly slipped the boat into the dark brown waters at the ramp, leaped aboard, and headed for the fishing grounds. I think we lost a pint of blood between us before we got the engine started. I jumped two flats so shallow that the motor prop left a yellow-stained mud trail. We stopped a quarter-mile from a key that showed deep black in the predawn light. I poled into the key, while my buddy stripped line from his reel and made ready to cast.

Big snook lying under the mangroves are the best lure inspectors I know. In fact, I used to think the fish had lockjaw and received nourishment through their scales. But in early morning a quiet approach, and a long cast with a fly that drops silently under the overhanging limbs, will sucker them into striking.

Knowing well where the snook were lying, I pushed the boat within eighty feet of a little ditch with overhanging bushes. I softly stuck the pole in the bottom and tied the bow rope fast to it. I whispered, "Throw the fly under the bush and don't slam the fly line down on the water. Do what I say and you'll get a snook."

He nodded again, gritted his teeth, and after five false casts he shot out the line. The fly fifteen feet short of the bush. He stripped the fly back and made another cast. "That's no good," I whispered. "The fly has to drop *under* the bush—that snook ain't gonna move out to get it. And do it quietly!"

He nodded again, gritted his teeth, and after five false casts, he shot out the line. The fly fell within inches of the previous casts, no more than seventy feet away and ten to fifteen short of the bushes.

"Throw the damn thing *under* the bush," I whispered hoarsely.

"What the hell do you think I'm trying to do?" he grunted as he made another cast that also fell short.

"Push the boat over a little so I can reach it," he urged.

I shook my head, "No use; if we get closer the fish will move out."

After ten minutes of futile casting, and because he became so insistent, I pulled the pole from the soft bottom and shoved the boat with sixty feet of the bushes. Out shot four green fish at least eight pounds apiece. They bolted right by the boat and we could plainly see the black stripe that identified them as snook.

I moved to another key and we repeated the entire operation with the same results. No luck.

I pushed the pole into the muddy bottom at the third key and turned to look at my friend. He shoved the rod toward me. "Here, damn it, I don't think you need to cast from way out here. Prove it to me."

I shrugged my shoulders, quietly moved to the casting platform, and stripped out enough line. I made a long cast, with the loop tilted slightly to the side. The yellow fly came over, and rolled under the limb, dropping into the water with hardly a ripple. The hackles came alive as I made three slow strips with my right hand.

I never saw the fish take, but I felt the line tug, and I struck.

A ten-pound snook came out of the water, gills rattling. It took a few minutes to bring the fish to boatside, where I slipped the fly from its mouth and released it.

"I'll be damned," was all my friend could say.

We drank a cold soft drink and talked about what had happened. My friend explained that he had never used a fly as heavy as a 3/0 with a shock leader tied to it. He figured he could make the necessary cast, since his bass poppers had offered him little trouble up to eighty feet or so.

We had a fifteen-minute casting session and he mastered the technique well enough to gain ten feet over his previous cast. We didn't take a snook at the next key, but he got a seven-pounder at the last place we tried, and I think he was as proud of the cast as he was of the fish.

Long casts have *no* disadvantages. Some anglers have told me that you cannot set a hook beyond sixty feet. Perhaps that is true for big tarpon, which have a mouth resembling the interior of a cinder block. But experienced tarpon fishermen will tell you that it's tough to set the hook at any distance.

Providing you have sharpened the hook, and you strip retrieve by pointing the rod toward the fish and strip with your hand to impart fly action, the fish will hook itself. Distance has little to do with driving that hook into the flesh. Hooks that are properly sharpened will penetrate bone.

I have never lost a fish because I struck it at 60 or even over 100 feet away. Some saltwater fly fishing groups used to practice making a long cast in deep water, then stripping all additional line and considerable backing from the reel, allowing the fly to sink deep in the ocean, then retrieving slowly. This method is deadly, but it takes patience, and in fact is so effective that it has been outlawed by many fishing clubs as not really being fly-casting technique. The point is that no one ever noticed that a long length of line interfered with properly setting the hook. Indeed, it was *too* effective.

There is another vital reason for learning to cast a long line. A fisherman who can throw 100 feet of line downwind can do his casting effortlessly. And, since many, many casts have to be made either into or across the wind, the ability to throw a long line becomes vital; a 100-foot downwind cast might only go 35 feet into a stiff breeze.

I hate to belabor the point, but learning to cast a long distance is the major problem for most freshwater fly fishermen who make the transition to salt water. If you cannot cast well to at least 80 feet, you should always be striving to reach that point—and I consider 100 feet the desirable distance. When you can cast that far, you will be able to meet the demands of most saltwater fly-fishing situations.

The reason most people cannot cast to 100 feet is that they have not *thoroughly* understood good casting techniques.

There are five basic rules in good fly casting. If these are understood and mastered, you can fish anywhere, fresh or salt water, and cope with any casting conditions.

Here are those rules in order of importance:

(1) The fly is not going to move until all slack has been removed from the line;
(2) The smaller the line loop, the more efficient the cast;
(3) Wherever the rod goes, the line will eventually follow;
(4) When you shock the rod you also shock the line;
(5) If you are fly casting and you are working, you are not doing it correctly.

Now let's examine each of the rules in detail.

Rule 1. The fly is not going to move until all slack has been removed from the line. There is no doubt in my mind that this is the single least understood rule, and so the most violated.

As an analogue, consider a garden hose placed on the grass so that it lies in zigzag waves. If one end of the hose is lifted and pulled, the other end will not move until all the curls and waves have been drawn from it. So it is with fly casting; before you can move the fly, you must eliminate all slack. The immediate goal in *every* cast should always be to make that cast with as little slack as possible.

How does slack enter the average fly caster's technique? It actually begins *before* the backcast. The angler usually starts his backcast with his rod pointed at a 45-degree vertical angle. By the time he has lifted all line from the water, loaded the rod, and gotten *ready* for the backcast, his rod tip has passed over his head and begun a downward path behind him. His sharp snap comes at this point, propelling the line to the rear, and the rod tip dips downward, even though the line goes relatively high. As the fly reaches its farthest point behind him, his line has a deep sag in it just off the rod tip.

The angler now begins the forward cast, moving the tip toward the target. The rod comes forward, not moving the fly but lifting the slack line in the deep sag that has appeared. When all the sagging line has been lifted and the line comes tight, only then does the fly begin to move. This usually occurs after the rod tip has passed overhead and begun a downward descent in front of the angler.

Those are the two areas where slack occurs: as the rod is lifted to make the forward cast, and as the rod sweeps forward during the backcast.

Rule 2. If you have ever watched a truly great fly caster, you will note that the line loop he throws is incredibly tight. It is the mark of a superior caster, and the tighter the loop, the better the caster.

The line loop is the bend or curved horizontal **U** that forms as the line unrolls. If the **U** is large, it will have a great deal of air resistance, the smaller the **U** in the loop is, the less air resistance. Look at the diagram and you'll immediately see why.

The size of the line loop is directly controlled by the power stroke. Most anglers make the forward and backward cast with a long, powerful sweep of the whole rod, which creates a large **U**. Instead, the experts lift the rod to load it, then with a sharp movement of the wrist impart an extremely brief snap, with an immediate follow-through. The lifting power-snap and follow-through blend so well into one another that the average fisherman would consider it all a single stroke. It's not!

You can easily demonstrate for yourself how the power stroke controls the line loop. Put out 25 or 30 feet of line and make a backcast and forward cast with long strokes, so that the rod tip nearly touches the ground in front and in back of you. You will note that the loop is so large as not to appear a loop at all. Because of the considerable increase in air resistance, the line will not lay out well at the end of the cast.

Now, lay out the same amount of line and lift the rod a little. Then make a quick snap backward, then a quick snap forward after the line has straightened behind you. You'll note that the loop is extremely tight—sometimes so much so that it may run together.

Rule 3. This rule is closely connected to Rule 2. The longer you make the stroke, the larger the line loop, for the line is in fact attempting to follow the rod's path.

Study your own cast, evaluate it, and correct your own casting faults. Lay out 30 feet of line and then swish the rod back and forth. Note that the line goes back and forth, following the same pattern as the path of the rod: work the rod up and down and you'll see that the same action shows up in the line. With only 20 feet of line outside the rod tip, make big circling motions of the rod in a pattern around your head, with the rod in a vertical position, and as the rod rolls around and around it will form the line into a circle over your head.

Let's apply Rule 3 to a casting situation that occurs all too frequently for many anglers. You have probably noticed wind knots in your leaders from time to time. If this happens a lot, it could be that you are rolling the rod during the cast. Let's examine your cast as it comes to an end over the target. If you noticed that the leader and fly went from right to left and the leader jumped over itself, maybe entangling in the process, you can use Rule 3 to correct your casting fault.

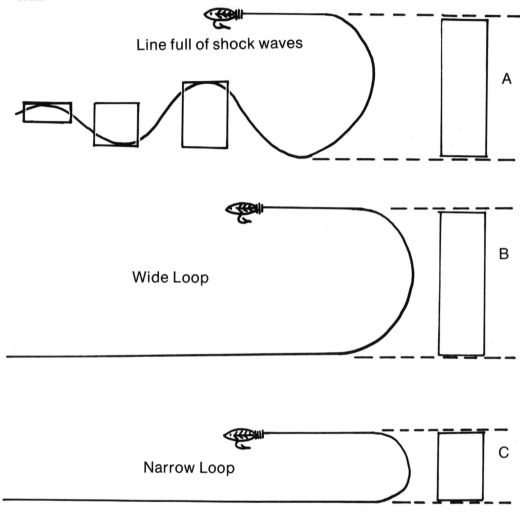

Line full of shock waves

A

Wide Loop

B

Narrow Loop

C

A—A typical large-loop forward cast, with shock waves. The shaded area indicates where air resistance is acting on the line. B—The shock is removed, which radically reduces the wind resistance—but resistance is still substantial. C—The type of line loop that the angler should strive for with both the back and forward cast: no line shock, the loop is tight, and air resistance has been held to a minimum.

You noticed that the leader came from the right and then quickly jumped to the left. That means that during your cast you rolled the rod out to the right, then back to the left. What you need to do is bring the rod back at one angle, and carry it forward at the same angle, thus eliminating the rolling of the line.

Let's take another example of how Rule 3 can aid you in solving your casting problems. Often at the end of the forward cast the angler will see his leader smash into the main portion of the line. Rule 3 says wherever the rod goes, the line will also go. You have made the rod travel straight back and then come straight forward, on the same horizontal plane. It's like running two railroad trains on the same track in opposing directions—they are bound to run into each other.

How do you correct this fault?

You move the rod slightly upward on the backcast and bring it down on the forward cast. The line, following the rod's path, will rise (as the rod did), and the main line will ride under the leader as the rod is lowered.

Rule 4. When you shock the rod you shock the line. Again, this rule is closely tied to the preceding rule. A rod that is shock-free will allow the line to flow from it in a smooth manner. If your rod has a lot of shock (it may be built in, the result of poor construction), the tip will vibrate violently during casting. And when this occurs, Rule 4 comes into play. As the tip rises and falls during the vibrations, the line is sent into a series of **S** waves. These **S** waves radically increase air resistance and make a long or accurate cast almost impossible.

You can take precautions against shock waves in your cast. Buy good quality, well-designed rods. You can easily check a rod to see whether it is relatively shock-free or carries a lot of shock. Hold the rod out from you at belt level and shake it five or six times in short powerful wiggling motions. Then cease the wiggling motions and squeeze the rod handle. If the rod is a good one it will vibrate about four times and stabilize. If it is a poor one it will vibrate many times, which is exactly what causes shock waves during the cast.

Once you have purchased a well-designed rod you can control any shock that may occur during casting. Shock is usually generated by too much force. If you snap back too violently, or use an overly powerful snapping stroke on the forward cast, you will create serious shock waves in both rod and line.

Watch your rod tip. At the end of the backcast and forward cast, the tip should be stationary. When you shoot line to the target, the tip should dip down at the end of the power stroke and, after one or two vibrations, stabilize and remain steady as the line pours through it on its way to the target. Realizing that too much power is the problem, and knowing where to look for indications of this, you can begin to control your own technique and eliminate shock.

Rule 5. If you are fly casting and you feel as though you're working, you're not doing it correctly. The novice is always amazed when he watches a good fly fisherman pick up half a fly rod and effortlessly throw the entire line. It is the trademark, too, of a great fly caster—all of them seem to perform effortlessly. They appear not to be working—and they're not. Perhaps one of the greatest misconceptions about fly casting is the notion that the more power you apply the farther you can cast. Not true!

If you use the four rules already outlined, you can learn to cast a long distance without effort. It is not how *strong* you are, but how well you follow the rules.

The casting technique I consider the most efficient is one I developed entirely on my own, although I understand that others have developed the same technique independently. I got my first fly casting lessons from Tom McNally and Joe Brooks, and when they moved from my area after the first lesson, I was left on my own. Over the years, fishing three or more days a week when the weather permitted, I slowly developed a fishing-casting technique that I have been teaching to other anglers for twenty years. With this method you can cast all day at 60 to 90 feet with bass bugging tackle, and be no more tired than if you had used a spinning rod or plug casting outfit!

To me fly casting is simple physics, and the system that I taught myself through years of fishing is a "no-work" kind of casting. My favorite sport for many years was floating the limestone rivers of the mid-Atlantic area, fly rodding for bass. I realized very quickly that the more water I covered, the more bass I could catch.

The system I use begins *before* the fly is picked from the water and carries through to the final power application made to toss the fly to the fish.

My system begins with a detailed understanding of what is happening as line is picked from the water. Surface tension is what allows a metal sewing needle to float on water if it is carefully laid down. It also tries to keep a fly line from lifting from the water; so, you actually have to overcome surface tension, and *pull* the line loose from the water before you make any sort of backcast. Most anglers will begin their cast with the rod at about a 45-degree angle—or more—from the water. With a quick snap they rip the line loose from the water, jerking it, and most of the energy is absorbed in getting the line free from the surface. In order to do so they must give a powerful snap to the rod tip, causing shock waves, and the rod tip usually goes down too far behind, throwing a sagging belly in the line.

A highly efficient method of getting the most from your fly casting with the minimum of effort. The rod pointed is toward the fly, all slack removed from the line with the left hand.

The angler watches the leader and raises the entire rod in a swift but smooth motion in a horizontal plane.

As the rod hand reaches the head, the tip begins to sweep upward, lifting more line from the water. The point is that we are removing the line from the water and *have not yet made a backcast*. Removing the line from the water neutralizes surface tension, which holds the line on the surface of the water.

When the rod is in about this position, all of the fly line will have been lifted from the water—only the leader and fly are still wet. At this point a very brief power snap to the rear is made. You cannot make that snap too brief—the shorter the stroke, the tighter the loop will be.

As the line goes back, allow the rod to *drift* back with no power being applied to it.

Just before the line straightens out behind you, draw the rod forward, tilting slightly upward as shown.

Continue to bring the rod tip over, which will place a deep bend in the rod ("loading" the rod).

Note the high angle held in the cast; power begins at point "A" and ends at point "B." Also note the angle of the lower portion of the rod at the end of the cast. The shaded area represents the power stroke; the final power is applied to the line at a slightly climbing incline, rather than directing the line at the target. Again, the forward power stroke, shown as shaded, is incredibly brief. The shorter this stroke, the better and tighter the loop will be.

After the backcast has been made the angler usually stops his rod at 1 o'clock (or just past vertical), waiting for the line to straighten behind him; then he begins his forward motion. Remember—the fly won't move until the line is straightened, which takes up most of the forward stroke. By the time the line is straight and the rod is loaded, the tip is descending and the angler must give a sharp snap to propel the line forward. The snap again sets shock waves into the rod, and these are transmitted to the line. The whole cast is terribly inefficient, and becomes even more so as longer casts are attempted.

Let's use the system I prefer, and see how we can eliminate these problems—and cast with less effort. Lower the rod so that the tip points at the fly (*see photo 1*). At this point strip in all the slack line with your left hand. Lift the rod in a horizontal plane in a rather quick but smooth motion (*see photo 2*). As the rod hand reaches head level, the rod tip is rapidly elevated (*see photo 3*). At this stage of the cast you should be looking at the *leader*. As soon as all fly line has been removed from the surface (*see photo 4*), make as short a power stroke as you possibly can—*it can't be too brief.* It is this very brief, short stroke that forms the small, tight, efficient loop for the backcast; any longer stroke will begin forming a larger loop. *This short, brief stroke completes the power to be exerted during the backcast.*

As soon as the short power stroke has been completed, without any hesitation allow the rod to *drift* (with no power exerted) to the rear, as shown in *photo 5.* The line can be thrown at any height behind you, from very low to high above the surface, depending upon conditions. But the most efficient cast comes from a relatively low level behind you—which aligns it with the level of travel on the forward cast. A very high backcast has to be brought down and then thrown up again on the forward stroke. The most important point to be made here is that you should allow the rod to drift to the rear by its own inertia, adding no power to the line after the power snap. On a long forward cast allow the arm to drift back as far as possible; naturally, on a shorter cast, the rear drift will be less.

You may have read or heard that you should begin the forward cast when you feel the line tug against the rod behind you. That is absolutely wrong. It would be the same as shooting at a flying duck where it is, not where it is going to be when the shot charge arrives. The forward stroke should begin just *before* the line has straightened behind you.

The rod is shoved forward (*see photo 6*) until the hand passes slightly in front of the head. What happens, if this procedure is followed, is that all slack in the line is drawn from it by the forward shoving of the rod. The rod tip is tilted slightly upward, so that when the fly finally straightens behind you it can now *bend* the rod, loading it. The backcast should travel swiftly, so it can load the rod in the same way as a spincaster snaps his lure backward to load his rod. Then the rod tip comes over swiftly, continuing to store power as it loads the rod. This long turn-over, not possible in conventional casting techniques, permits a shock-free cast.

When the rod reaches the point shown in *photo 8*, it is under full load, and almost ready for the power stroke. In the last photo the incredibly brief power stroke begins at point **A** and ends at **B**. Note that at the end of the stroke the rod handle is pointing at a sharp upward angle. If the rod tip is dropped much lower the line loop will open, creating the typical big-loop, inefficient cast.

This is essentially the style of casting that is rapidly finding acceptance on salt water—but it is a type of casting that really applies to all fly fishing, from subtle dry-fly work to pushing a big streamer to a sailfish or amberjack. The only real adaptation in technique necessary is that the reach behind on the backcast should be much shorter when you're casting on a trout stream, where the distance is not needed. Not only does this system allow you to cast farther without as much effort, but it allows you to eliminate slack, simultaneously, with the long drop back and smooth push forward; and you can store immense power that will not shock the rod when applied.

For most shallow-water saltwater fly fishing, a cast must be made within five to seven seconds after the fish is sighted. A saltwater taper (a line with most of the weight concentrated at the forward end) is best, since most of the heavier portion can be held in the hands, ready for a cast, as shown here.

When the rod is snapped back, it is vital that the thumb and first finger of the left hand hold the fly tightly, forcing the fast traveling line to pull the fly from your fingers. If you toss the fly into the air, you will not be able to develop as much line speed.

After a quick backcast.

A forward cast is made, and ten to fifteen feet of line is cast to extend the fly.

As another rapid backcast is made, the angler sees that the fish is approaching the boat, so he drops to his knee, lowering his silhouette.

The line is not completely released by the left hand, as the running line flows through it. When the target is reached the left hand closes around the running line, causing the fly to drop to the fish. Before the fly actually hits the surface, the angler has moved the line in his left hand under his right finger and begun to strip retrieve. Using this technique he has the fly and line under control throughout the cast.

Another forward cast is made, and the fly is shot to the target.

Casting in a wind is a problem you will continually face in salt water; there is almost always an ocean breeze. The technique I've just described works beautifully when you're casting against a wind. The tight loop and the reduction of almost all shock waves from the line allow maximum casting efficiency. You should direct your cast lower when throwing a fly into the wind. It has nothing to do with making a longer cast, except that after the cast has ended and the leader has straightened out, the fly will blow back toward you if a high forward cast is made. So you increase accuracy by casting at a low angle to the water and the wind.

If you are throwing downwind—and you should always try to fish *with* the wind—throw the forward cast exceptionally high, at about a 60-degree angle toward the sky in the direction of the fish. The light line acts like a kite and will sail an astounding distance with the breeze. I have on many occasions made casts of over 130 feet with a standard floating line. What I did, of course, was simply make a good, long, high cast, which was kited by the wind.

If the wind blows from your right and you cast with your right hand, try this easy-to-learn technique: make a backcast slightly out to the right, as Bill Barnes is doing in the accompanying photograph. Note, in the second photo, that Bill has kept his rod hand in the same position as in a normal cast but has tilted the rod over to the left. This causes the fly to pass two or three feet to the left of Bill's shoulder. The forward stroke is straight toward the target, with the rod *tilted;* it is *not* a side cast to the front.

This is a typical good tight loop, required for competent fly rodding in salt water. Note the high angle of the rod at the end of the cast; the loop offers little resistance, and the forward portion of the fly line assumes a climbing attitude.

CAST
IN
THIS DIRECTION

BOAT DRIFTING IN
THIS
DIRECTION

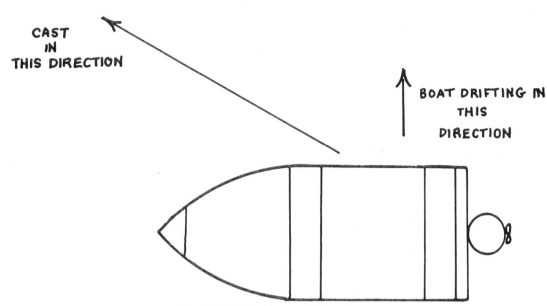

System for fishing from a boat on a windy day. If the angler casts downwind the boat will over-ride the fly and interfere with retrieve. Cast to the side and downwind, as shown in drawing; the fly can be thrown a long distance and boat does not ride over lure.

Bill Barnes shows how to make a cast when the wind is coming from his right side. A back cast is made slightly to the right.

The forward cast is made with the rod hand in the usual place, but the rod tip tilted to the right. This causes the fly line to pass several feet to Bill's left.

8 Angling Techniques

The mechanics of catching saltwater fish on a fly rod start with a thorough understanding of the role of the boat. It serves two purposes: it gets you within range of the quarry, and, once there, it becomes your casting platform.

Your boat should be considered fundamental, too, in your angling, and used as efficiently as your other equipment. Loose gear—including anchors and ropes—should be stored away from the range of your casts; windshields should be folded down to offer more area for casting; and you should obtain as much clearance in the cockpit as possible. Dropping loose coils of line on a floor that is filled with tackle boxes, gas tanks, loose rope, and other items could mean failure at a crucial moment. Saltwater game fish usually don't give you a second chance.

Since a crucial part of saltwater fly fishing is spotting the fish, communications between people in the same boat are important. When one angler spots a fish, he must be able to alert his companion as to the exact position of the moving target. Experienced Florida guides have worked out a system of communications that allows one angler to help his companion determine the direction of incoming fish instantly.

Imagine that you are standing in the center of a giant clock face—the boat. The front end of the boat, where the angler stands, is always considered to be 12 o'clock; the rear, where the guide stands, is always at 6 o'clock. To the immediate left of the angler who is facing the bow is 9 o'clock, and to his right is 3 o'clock. Look at the drawing to get a clearer explanation. No matter how the boat is turned, the bow always points at 12 o'clock and the motor end at 6 o'clock.

Let's see how this works in practice. You're motoring very slowly across a shallow bar and a striper swirls in the water, or the guide, standing on the stern poling you, spots a bonefish tipping its silvery tail into the air as it feeds. "Quick, ten o'clock, fifty feet away," the guide whispers urgently. You know immediately that 50 feet away to your left oblique is a fish; it's that simple. Without having to look at the guide, you can turn to 10 o'clock and make the cast, knowing full well that you will be able to see the fish very soon.

Much of the best saltwater fly fishing is done in shallow waters where actually spotting the fish becomes a primary task. The fisherman should wear polarizing glasses to help eliminate surface glare. However, banks of white clouds lying in the foreground often put a snowy

106

reflection on the surface that even polarizing glasses cannot penetrate. At such times the boat should be manipulated, if possible, so that the white clouds are to the side or rear.

The most important consideration in maneuvering the boat is that fly casters should always be in a position to cast downwind, if at all possible. A striped bass 50 feet away in a 20 mph upwind breeze is safe from nearly all fly casters, but an easy downwind target if the angler can get the line into the air with the breeze behind him. Your course is also important when you're chasing schools of feeding fish on the surface of the water. It's vital that the boat approach the school from an upwind position.

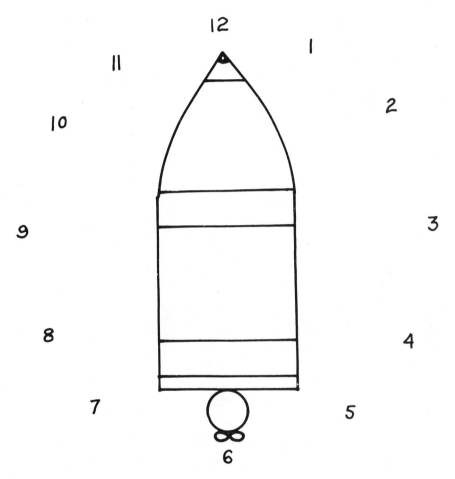

Fishing the clock system. The direction in which the boat is proceeding is considered noon, or 12 o'clock. The rear of the boat is considered to be 6 o'clock.

If your boat doesn't have a platform, you may have a problem handling the yards of running line that develop during the cast. Jim Green, a superb West Coast angler, told me of a technique that works better than anything else I've seen. Buy a piece of 7- or 8-foot square one-inch mesh netting from a marine hardware store or commercial fishing outlet (even some fishing tackle catalogs list netting). Attach half-ounce pinch-on sinkers along the sides and corners—usually a dozen is just right. Take the netting and drape it over the tackle boxes, spare rods and reels, gas tanks, and other gear that could catch a fly line. The sinkers will hold the net firmly in place, and because the netting is well ventilated, it won't blow away, as canvas or plastic often does. You can then strip your line so it falls into the netting. I carry the netting rolled into a small bundle, and it has saved the day for me many times when I was forced to fish from boats that would otherwise have proved frustrating.

A large garbage can placed beside the stripping hand can also be used to deposit the running line as it is retrieved. Be sure the line is dropped into the can. Placing 6 inches of water in the bottom will stabilize the container. A block of ice works even better: it soon conforms to the shape of the container, and the cold, slick ice stiffens and lubricates the running line so it performs better.

Use of netting on floor of untidy boat prevents line from fouling on the cast.

MAKING READY TO CAST

Once the angler has solved his boating problems, he can begin his actual fishing procedure. It starts with stripping the line from the reel and dropping it to the deck. Fly lines are made of a braided nylon core, over which a specially prepared softer plastic is coated to the desired thickness. The braided core, like all nylon line, has a quality chemists call "memory."

This refers to the fact that nylon tends to stay in the position it was last stored in—which was in tight little coils on your fly reel.

You can remove the memory by a steady, firm pull on the line—letting a companion help you speeds up the process. Or you can do it yourself by standing in the center of a loop of line and giving it one good pull, which usually eliminates the coils.

After the line has been stripped from the spool, and the coils removed, drop it to the deck. (When you first pulled the line from the reel, you dropped the forward portion of the line on the deck, and placed the rear part of the line on top of that; if you don't make a practice cast and reverse the order of the coils on the deck, you are almost certain to get a tangled mess when you cast to the fish. The fly must be cast one time and the line retrieved, and dropped to the deck in the correct position.

Be sure you are using the correct line for your particular fishing conditions. There are situations for which a floating line is most efficient, and others in which a slow-sinking or even a fast-sinking line is best. Many fishermen like to set up one rod to fish with, and prepare another rod, with a different type of line, in case a change in conditions occurs.

Author strips line from reel that falls to boat deck; the front portion of the line is on the bottom, while that last part pulled from the reel is lying on top of the pile of loose coils. This could result in a tangled cast.

Author makes a cast.

The line is stripped back in with rear of line on bottom: the cast
can now be made without tangling.

It's worth mentioning again here that before any cast is made, proper drag tension should
be set.

Prior to the first cast, double-check for casting hazards. Boat poles, being used as anchors,
stuck into the bottom and tied to the boat, should be set at a very low angle so they will not
interfere with the backcast. If there is a possibility that you may have to follow the fish after it
is hooked, rig a quick-release anchor. This is simply a float attached to a snap at the boat end
of the anchor rope. If you suddenly have to follow the fish, your companion simply opens the
snap and frees the anchor. Later you can return and pick up the anchor rope, which will be
buoyed by the float. A crab-pot trap-float works well.

If you are blindcasting, along the edge of a bar, for example, or outside the surf, and you
hook a big striper or blue, the anchor must be instantly available. Your partner may also get a
strike and not be able to operate the motor; tossing the anchor overboard will enable you both
to fight.

The purpose of the short belly section is to enable the angler to hold as much of this line
as possible outside the guides prior to the first cast. The more belly he holds outside, the faster
he can deliver the fly. There are a half-dozen ways to hold the line in the ready position, but
the simplest is to hold the rod in your right hand—if that is your favored hand—and to hold

the feathers of the fly clasped between the first finger and thumb of the same hand. The left hand holds the line coming back through the guides.

When a spot cast is to be made, rock the rod back sharply, allowing the 10 or 15 feet of line hanging outside the tip of the rod to pull the fly free from your fingers; two or three false casts and you can usually shoot the line to the fish. You *must* master this technique of spot-casting to fish on shallow water flats.

Line is held with most of the heavy weight-forward portion outside the guides. The leader and a portion of the head of the line are draped across the fingers of the left hand.

Close-up of how the angler should hold the fly and line for a speedy delivery to the fish.

The name of the game when you see a saltwater fish is speed and accuracy.

In shallow waters where the fish can be spotted, the angler and his companion search until they see a fish. At that moment a decision has to be made: one has to decide immediately how far in front of the fish to direct the cast. Several factors affect that decision: how fast the fish is moving; the closing rate; how deep the fish is; and from what direction the wind is blowing.

Most saltwater fly casters feel it's unethical to cast from a boat under power, or to troll a fly: the motor should be out of gear when the cast is made. The species of fish to which the angler is casting must also be considered in determining where the fly is to be dropped in front of the fish. Redfish (channel bass), for example, possess very poor eyesight; most of the time a fly that is slapped on the water near a redfish's eye will draw its attention. Amberjack and cobia often slash savagely at a loud, blurping popper; and jack crevalle love to hit a lure that falls with a plop beside them.

Other fish—permit, bonefish, mutton snapper, and often striper, if they are in calm water—demand a very silent entry of the fly into the water. In this case the fly should be cast rather far ahead of the fish, so as not to spook it. Few anglers would believe, until they witness it, that a 150-pound tarpon cruising over a white sand flat is spooked by a fly presented closer than 2 feet.

Know the habits of your quarry; but assume that a noisy entry will scare the fish, and that you should cast far enough ahead of the fish to prevent frightening it.

The angle at which the fish is approaching you is important. A fish coming toward the boat at a very slight angle is in the best position for a good presentation. The worst angle from which to present a fly is when the fish is going away from the boat, and the fly line must fall across a portion of the body of the fish; this almost always scares the fish.

SINK RATE

Closely linked to the problem of how far ahead of the fish to cast is the sink rate of the fly. You must know how fast your fly will sink in order to present it properly. Perhaps the

The saltwater fly rodder must get into action fast, and a method of carrying the fly that allows fast action is shown here. Bring the line down around the reel and back up along the rod.

The rod will then be rigged as shown. To get the fly ready, the angler slips it from the snake guide and flips the line off the reel base. At this point he already has 14 or 15 feet of line ready to cast. This same technique works just as well for freshwater fishing.

single most important thing to keep in mind in casting to a saltwater fish is that the fish and fly must arrive at the same spot on a collision course. Few fish will descend to snap at a fly, though they will often rise a foot or more to accept the lure. It is essential that you make your presentation far enough ahead of a moving fish that the fly can drop to the depth at which the fish is swimming.

The sink rate of the fly is obviously important in deep-water fishing, where the fly must get down to the fish's feeding level. Sea trout in basins and bays, for example, live on the grassy bottom, and the fly that rides just above that green carpet will appeal to them most.

It's just as important to consider the sink rate of the fly in shallow water—maybe even more so. Bonefish often feed in water so shallow that their backs partially protrude above the surface. A fast-sinking fly that dives into entangling grass is for all practical purposes useless. The fly must sink slowly, giving the angler time to manipulate it and allow the fish to notice it.

How do you control sink rate? There are several methods. The most basic way is to change the hook size; naturally, the same size fly dressed on a 3/0 hook will sink faster than one tied on a 1/0. Many times the fly's overall size can remain much the same, and a larger or smaller hook be substituted to control the sink rate.

Another way to increase the sink rate is to add a little lead wire to the fly body when it is made. You can also use the various types of sinking lines to pull a fly toward the bottom. And obviously you can also dress the fly with buoyant materials to make it resist sinking.

In summary, you must decide the type of fly pattern you need to control the sink rate, and then be able to determine how far in front of a moving fish to make the cast, in order to make a successful presentation.

LINE SELECTION

The various kinds of lines and their uses were covered in Chapter 4, but it bears repeating here that the angler must consider the type of line best suited for his specific fishing conditions. The right line is essential to success. For example, the angler wading along the edge of the shore casting to striped bass in 2 to 4 feet of water would be severely handicapped with a Wet Cel Hi-D line, which bombs toward the bottom when it enters the water. The line would constantly foul on the bottom. Here, the angler needs a floating line with a wet tip. If he cannot make long casts, he might do well to employ a shooting head, which would allow him to make longer casts and cover more water. An exception might be in early spring when the waters are still chilled and striped bass in the shallows are sluggish and lie on the bottom. Then a sinking line with a buoyant fly to keep it off the bottom would best present the fly to these fish. Such sluggish fish require a slow retrieve.

But if you're fishing from a boat and cast across a deep pocket or slough for stripers or bluefish, you certainly won't want to throw a floating line, unless the fish are surface feeding. The point, of course, is that you must select not only the proper fly for each specific fishing situation, but the correct line, too.

THE RETRIEVE

Since casting mechanics have already been covered, let's assume that you have made a correct cast, allowed the fly to sink to the proper depth, and are ready to begin the retrieve.

In a conventional retrieve in salt water under most fishing conditions, the rod should never be used to impart retrieve motion to the fly—yet that's exactly how it is used by most anglers.

They flip the rod tip in an upward motion, then strip in the accumulated slack. Then they repeat the process, often failing to hook the fish if it strikes on the retrieve. Here's why: when the rod tip is snapped upward, the line jumps forward and falls on the water in front of the rod in loose coils; should a fish strike before this slack is removed, the chances for setting the hook are poor, since there is no tension on the line.

Proper technique is actually simpler—almost foolproof, in fact—guaranteeing a slack-free line from fisherman to fish at all times. With the correct stripping retrieve the fish always strikes against a tight line, so if the hook is sharp the fish will usually impale itself on the fly. Proper procedure dictates that the rod tip be pointed toward the fly, with the butt at your belt buckle. The action is imparted to the fly by the manner in which you strip the line with your left hand (if you hold the rod with your right). You can vary the fly's movements by varying the strip. A series of short strips causes the fly to dart forward accordingly; long pulls will swim the fly forward in graceful strokes. When a fish hits the fly, the line is taut in the left hand and the angler can strike instantly.

When retrieving the fly, the angler can often see the fish and how it is reacting. If the fish is just following the fly, or showing little interest, change the retrieve manner—quick little strokes, or several long fast pulls—anything to get the fish into the mood to hit.

Since there are only a few cases when you should deviate from the retrieve described above, they are worth mentioning. King mackerel, barracuda, sailfish, and marlin often prefer a retrieve that is faster than most of us can perform with the left hand alone. If the fish can be seen, you can make a cast to it, then sweep the rod as far to the right as you possibly can—pulling in line with your left hand at the same time. This will cause the fly to streak through the water at eye-blurring speed for about 10 feet. These particularly swift fishes will often strike before they realize their mistake. Dr. Web Robinson developed this stripping technique to get a faster retrieve; and he was the first to take a billfish on a fly. Norman Duncan, one of south Florida's best fly fishermen, uses this same technique to take kingfish and has set records using that retrieve.

Dick Kreh carries a favorite tool for wading: a small block of Styrofoam with the necessary flies stuck into it hung around the neck.

When chumming fish to the boat, particularly in deep water, it's best to allow the fly to float dead in the water—just as the bits of chum are doing. This procedure works especially well if large chunks of chum or small baitfish are introduced to the feeding line.

Joe Brooks taught me another retrieve method that turns on some of the species that are notoriously difficult to coax into striking, like the wary barjack. Barjacks ride the warm seas, often feeding on the many small fish that gather and hide in floating weed lines that may string out for many miles in the current. I often cruised these weedlines looking for barjacks (yellow jack), but when I found them they frequently refused my fly. Then Joe told me his trick.

Drop the popping bug down on the water in front of the jack; pop it once, then lift it immediately. The jack will spin on his fins to see what happened. Then drop the bug back again, just in front of the fish's nose, and lift it again immediately. Repeat this several times and the jack will be frantic as it tries to locate this noisy, disappearing thing. Then set the bug down softly, make one or two slight popping sounds, and the fish will usually strike with abandon. I've worked this trick on cobia, cudas, dolphin, bluefish, amberjacks, and other wary fish.

Anglers often argue how far away you can cast and still strike successfully on the retrieve. I fish a full line for much of my fishing, and I have never had more than the normal problems common to hooking fish at any distance. If the hooks are sharp, and the retrieve is proper and the line taut, then most fish will hook themselves on the strike.

If you are teasing a certain fish with different types and speeds of retrieves without success, vary the size of the fly. If that fails, switch to a totally different type of fly. But first—*vary that retrieve.*

WHEN THE FISH TAKES THE FLY

When the retrieve is successful, the angler must learn what to do with various fishes. Tarpon, despite fabled stories to the contrary, strike so softly that many anglers are not aware that the fish has taken the fly. Tarpon give themselves away, however, in other ways. They will usually move up deliberately, slowly suck in the fly, then roll over to one side. When the fish rolls, or you see a silvery flash, strike! With small fish one hard, short backward thrust is generally enough—but on the larger tarpon (weighing more than 25 pounds) and other big fish, it's a good idea to make a series of short hard jabs, one right after the other, before the fish makes its move.

Bonefish often pick up the lure and swim off in such a manner that you are not aware the fish has taken the fly. Watch the line near the leader; if it starts to move through the water, lift the rod tip up quickly, but softly. That will set the hook in the rubbery mouth of the bonefish. There's no doubt about it when most fish strike: dolphin hit with blazing speed, as do barracudas, kingfish, and many swift fishes. Bluefish strike well and usually hook themselves. Cobia take a lure carefully, and since you can generally observe the fish when it strikes, you can react accordingly.

There are times when striped bass do not smash a streamer fly, but they will hit popping bugs with a splash. Many anglers use shooting lines for stripers, make a long cast, then start their retrieve. If you feel any resistance on the line, even while the fly is some distance away, strike. Striped bass will often hit almost as softly as tarpon.

Unlike freshwater fishes, a saltwater fish goes crazy when it feels the steel of the hook driven into its mouth. The line lying at your feet will come up through the rod guides like a striking snake, and unless you enter some controls at this point, you'll surely get tangles. When you strike a fast-running fish and you're sure the hook has been driven home, forget the fish for the moment. Your greatest problem now is to get all loose line under control. Your fish will undoubtedly make a blazing run, and you should curl the fingers of the left hand around the line so that the thumb touches the fingertip, forming a large ring guide. Looking at the line on the floor—and ignoring the fish—hold the rod high and use your fingers to get the line out from underfoot and off tackle boxes and all the other things fly lines have a habit of catching. Don't hold the rod lower than the hand. Control the line, for occasionally a loop of loose line will wrap around the butt of the rod and break the leader. Once the line on the floor is through the guides, and the reel is supplying the fish with line, you can play the fish just as you would on other types of tackle.

FIGHTING A FISH

Most freshwater fishermen who make the transition to salt water discover for the first time that many of the fish they hook cannot be brought to the boat at will. All of a sudden a new set of problems arises: there is a need for backing on reels, for some sort of mechanical drag, and for learning a technique of give-and-take battle tactics. In most freshwater situations, the angler plays his fish because it is fun—actually, he could have landed the fish most anytime he chose. In salt water it is often different. Of course small fishes can be boated quickly and easily, but others may take an hour—or *five* hours. Strain on the tackle and the angler often can be severe.

The most important rule in fighting any fish, freshwater or saltwater, is, *Never allow a sudden lurch or sharp jerk against the line.* As long as the pulling force exerted by the fish is a steady strain the line normally will hold.

To prove this, hold a piece of 6- to 10-pound monofilament line in front of you, each hand grasping an end. Snap your hands apart and you'll break the line easily. Now, holding the line in the same manner, snap your right hand to the right, and your left in the same path. Because your left hand follows the path of the force, no strain occurs on the line, so it doesn't break.

The same principle applies while you're fishing. When a fish makes a sudden surge away, the angler should thrust the rod *toward* the fish, to reduce the jolting impact on the line.

It is difficult to appreciate how much steady pressure can be applied to a line before it will break—as long as the pressure is even and steady. To test how much power you can get from, say, a 12-pound tippet, tie the line to a doorknob, then back off and begin to raise your fly rod, holding the line taut so no tension is released. The rod will take on a deep strain, your arms will begin to quiver, and you'll find it actually impossible with some rods, and tough with all rods, to break the 12-pound line with a steady pull. Remember—it's usually the sharp jolt that breaks the line.

Drag is essential for fighting many saltwater fish, so knowing how drag works, and how it can be used to advantage—or to your disadvantage—is vital. If the drag is set too light, the fish will strip the line from the reel; if it's too tight, the fish will break the line. Proper adjustment will allow the line to slip when needed, enabling you to keep control, so you can return line to the reel spool. Drag adjustment is really a complicated matter, but some simple rules will allow you to fish effectively—and experience will take over later.

How does drag work on a fly rod and line? You may think that if you run the line through the guides and adjust the mechanical drag so it slips when one pound of pull is placed against it, the drag will slip any time a fish exerts a pound of pull against it. Not true! After you make such a setting, raise the rod to about a 45-degree angle; then have someone attach a scale to the line and pull a deep bend in the rod. At 45 degrees you will discover that the drag doesn't allow itself to slip until more than 2 pounds of pull is exerted. Now, hold the rod so the butt points vertically. Repeat the process; as the rod forms a deeper bend the drag pressure will increase to more than 3 or 4 pounds—depending upon the rod's action—before the drag will slip.

If you watch the scale reading closely it will also be apparent that while the 45-degree angle allowed the drag to slip when 2 pounds' pressure was applied, it also took twice that much force to *get* the drag started. In other words, starting drag for most reels is about twice that of the force needed to keep it slipping. This is because the rod's action—the particular curvature of the rod under strain, and the type of guides—all affect the drag. While a fish pulls the heavy fly line through the guides, the drag will increase; then it drops off for awhile when the thin backing begins running through the guides.

However, as the diameter of the backing line on the spool gets smaller, the ratio of resistance increases radically. A Fin-Nor number 3 reel, set at a running drag that slips when 2 pounds is exerted on it, will, when only 100 yards remain on the spool, have a drag increased so much that nearly 7 pounds of pull is required on a straight pull just to get the drag to slip. Add the curvature of the rod, the guides, and any force exerted by the current, and you can lose a fish on a 12-pound-test tippet.

The problems seem immense. But by applying a simple technique, even an inexperienced angler can land fairly large fish with confidence.

When the fish has struck, the hook has been set, and the line is taut from its mouth to the reel, the actual battle begins. Most fish will make their fastest run the moment the hook is set. Saltwater fish roam freely in their domain, and they must experience a terrible panic when they first feel the steel of the hook and the tightness of the line. A saltwater fish will try to escape with every instinct and fiber of its being. During that first frantic run, try only to keep the fish from getting too far away from you. But do so with gentle pressure—your immediate purpose is to strain your fish as much as possible without putting too much strain on your tackle. And you must prevent any jolting pulls against the line!

Once the fish has settled down from its first run, you should do everything in your power to take command—either you or the fish should getting line. There should be few times when either the line is not coming toward you, or you are losing line to the fish. Many anglers put a deep bend in the rod, then merely hold it; the fish can often actually *rest* in such a condition, and this eventually prolongs the fight.

There is only one way to move a fish against its will toward the angler—by pumping. Pumping is simply raising the rod from a horizontal position to nearly vertical. This draws the fish several feet toward the angler. As the rod is lowered to the horizontal position, the angler winds in the accumulated slack. *The only time the angler should wind in line is when the rod is being lowered.* Pumping insures a *smooth* flow of power exerted against the fish, as the angler draws his quarry toward him.

Should the fish suddenly surge away from the angler, he drops the rod as quickly as possible toward the fish to reduce the shock. This will allow him to take big fish with *consistency.*

Jumping fish present special problems. A fish weighs several times more out of the water than it does under the surface. As a child you must have waded into a stream and lifted a large stone from the bottom with surprising ease, yet found when you got the rock into the air that you could hardly hold it. When a fish rises above the surface its weight increases several times. Let's take an example: a big fish takes the fly and dives for the bottom, shaking its head to rid itself of the fly. These jolts, while they are dangerous to the tackle, can usually be controlled. Suddenly, the fish leaps high above the surface, shaking its head. The fish can now throw several times as much weight against that leader, and what little purchase the hook has in the fish's flesh. (Experienced fishermen have noted that frequently a tarpon has been hooked and then rehooked several times during a fight.)

What do you do about it? When any fish jumps, bow toward the fish with your rod and shove it toward the leaping fighter. This creates controlled slack and the fish can only shake its head against a limp leader and the dangling fly. Of course, the instant the fish is back in the water, come tight with the line.

There is another danger in not bowing to leaping fish: should the fish leap and then *fall* on a taut leader or line, there's a good chance the line will part. But this is a secondary hazard.

So, the basic fighting strategy is this: allow the fish to make its first run against a lightly established drag. Then, begin to fight the fish as hard as you feel the tackle will bear. Be on the alert at all times to compensate for a sudden surge against the line, or if the fish leaps, shove the rod toward the fish to prevent line shock, and keep the boat to one side while fighting the fish.

If you begin the fight with a lightly established drag of about 1½ pounds, then you will have to apply additional pressure against the fish during the battle. As line diminishes on the spool (assuming you are holding the rod in the left hand) you can slip the fingers of your right hand inside the spool and apply pressure either against the line itself, or—as most experienced anglers prefer—push with the fingertips against the smooth inner side of the spool. The fingers allow you a delicate or a strong application of pressure. Naturally, anytime the fish needs to be given line, a quick release of the fingertips will put the fish against the lightly established mechanical drag.

Even more drag can be obtained by grasping the line against the rod with the fingertips of the left hand. It is surprising how much pressure can be applied this way. It can be especially handy when, the battle at an end, you raise the fish to the surface so it can be netted or gaffed (or released), and the fish bolts away. Simply lifting the fingertips from the line and the inner side of the reel spool will remove all but the small amount of adjusted mechanical drag. The better you become at fish-fighting, the less mechanical drag you'll use, and the more you'll rely on finger pressure alone.

Real familiarity with your rod—how it bends under stress and the particular curve it takes—is vital in fighting big fish. You can learn about your own rod's specific curves through a simple technique. Run the leader and line through the guides and attach the leader to a scale held by a companion. Then begin placing pressure against the scale by raising the rod. Have a friend call out the various scale readings as you increase lifting pressure. Study the rod to learn its curve characteristics. Later, place various amounts of strain on the rod and call out what you think the scale readings are; your friend can verify the guesses.

One other point: lifting a series of weights up to 7 pounds from the floor with the rod and leader will make you appreciate that it takes enormous pressure and a very strong rod to lift even 3 pounds. Few rods can lift more than that and still have any reserve power.

Let's take a typical fish-fighting example: We'll assume that you've hooked a jumping fish of respectable size. The column on the left lists the effects of drag and the reaction of the fish. The right column gives correct responses to the fish's actions and accumulated drag.

You're using 12-pound-test tippet. The aim of a topflight angler will be to apply 10 to 11 pounds of pressure *at all times* against the fish; this is the secret of light-tackle fishing (apply *maximum* pressure *all* the time). The angler must observe and judge the pressures that accumulate in the left column, and respond with proper pressures to build the resistance to 10 or 11 pounds—leaving just a few ounces as a safety margin. Naturally, inexperienced anglers would strive for about 7 or 8 pounds, leaving a larger safety factor. The following table describes top-efficiency fish-fighting:

ACCUMULATED RESISTANCE AT FISH'S END	ANGLER'S RESPONSES
Running drag is adjusted to slip with 1½ lbs. of straight pull; it takes twice that much pressure (3 lbs.) to get the drag moving. When fish strikes, rod bends and resistance is actually about 5 lbs.	At the strike, angler drives hook home with several sharp but very short jabs with rod. He allows fish to run, feeding the loose coils through his hand until line comes up on reel spool. He lets fish pull line as it speeds away. Drag safety margin is 7 lbs.
Fish has run off from boat 100 yards (30-yard fly line) and 70 yards of backing. (Many anglers clip 10 to 15 feet of fly line from rear end, to reduce water resistance against line and obtain more backing.) Drag resistance accumulated by pull of fish, water resistance against line, bend in rod, and mechanical drag is now 7 lbs.	Angler begins applying pressure as fish slows; 3 to 4 lbs. is a safe maximum.
Fish at 100 yards leaps—if line comes tight against fish with all drag resistances, coupled with the fish's weight, the leader will part.	Angler sees fish rising from water, realizes that total pull against his 12-lb.-test leader will exceed leader strength. Angler lowers rod and shoves it toward fish to create as much controlled slack line as possible.
Fish falls back into water.	As soon as fish descends from its jump and hits water, angler raises his rod and rapidly reels in all slack.
Fish swims slowly to one side, pulling line from reel. Resistance it creates against tackle is 8 lbs.	Angler applies 2 to 3 lbs. more pressure by holding his fingertips against the inside of the reel spool, or by using his fingertips against the line between the rod grip and butt guide. Angler attempts to pump fish and draw the fish toward him. He succeeds in bringing fish a little closer. He places line back on spool by reeling each time rod tip is dropped down toward fish.
Fish is brought slowly to boat against its will by pumping strokes. As fish is drawn closer, pressure at fish end due to rod bend, adjusted mechanical drag, line resistance, and swimming motions of fish is 4 lbs.	Angler now increases pressure trying at all times to keep 10 to 11 lbs. of force against fish. He applies 6 or 7 lbs. of pressure using fingertip controls, always bringing fish closer by pumping motions.

ACCUMULATED RESISTANCE AT FISH'S END	ANGLER'S RESPONSES
Fish refuses to come closer and begins to swim around boat, slowly beating its tail. Resistance is 9 lbs.	Angler keeps a good bend in rod and applies 1 to 2 pounds of pressure. At this time, angler is extremely alert in case fish bolts quickly, placing shock on leader.
Fish sees boat and swims under it.	Angler races to end where fish swam under boat, pushes several feet of the rod underwater and keeps it there, so line won't foul on boat (motor should be raised by companion if fish may catch line on sharp edges of propeller). Rod is manipulated so that the line under the boat is kept free and rod moved to side of boat where fish is, then rod can be brought back to fighting position.
Fish suddenly bolts away from boat.	Angler drops rod tip and shoves rod and reel toward fish to reduce shock on leader.
Fish continues to move away at a slower pace, creating 8 lbs. drag.	After initial surge by fish, angler should apply—with fingers to line and inside of reel spool—2 or 3 lbs. of pressure.
While fish is swimming away, the line picks up floating grass—increasing drag resistance to 10 lbs.	Angler should immediately shake grass from line or have companion move boat forward so angler can remove grass by hand. Light pressure should be kept against fish during this event. Angler should guide line away from floating grass when he can.
Fish swims slowly away creating 7 lbs. of resistance.	Angler applies 3 to 4 lbs. of force. It is very important that the boatman keep the craft to the side of the fish—*not* directly behind it—at all times. With the boat behind fish, the line falls across fish and leader or line could be cut by tail, or sharp portions of the fish.
Fish finally tires and nears boat. Resistance at fish end, from all factors, is about 3 lbs.	Angler now increases pressure to 7 or 8 lbs., always looking for a sudden surge by the fish.

ACCUMULATED RESISTANCE AT FISH'S END	ANGLER'S RESPONSES
Fish tires and angler can now move fish at will. Companion is ready with gaff or net.	Angler steps back in boat, while companion moves in front of him. This places the companion nearer the fish but angler should always have fish in sight. Boats with high freeboard can create visibility problems.
Fish is moved to boatside.	Companion is ready to gaff. Angler backs off on mechanical drag and alertly watches his companion.
Terrified, fish bolts away from the boat.	Companion strikes at fish with gaff, misses getting good hook-up and scares fish. Angler, with drag lightened and ready, drops rod tip toward fish. Then after initial burst of speed by fish, angler draws fish near again, and his companion gaffs fish and places it in boat.

During the battle, your fishing companion is part of a team that is trying to subdue the fish. Without his help you are severely handicapped—and a poor boatman can often cause a good angler to lose his prize.

Immediately after the fish has been struck the boatman must assay the situation. Is the fish going to strip all the line? Is the fish heading for an obstruction? Are sharks near?

If it appears that the fish will surely run all the line off the angler's reel, he must up-anchor, or get rid of the release anchor, start the motor, and head for the fish. During the entire fight the angler should try to keep to the side of the fish—*not* directly behind it. If the boat is directly behind it, the fish can exert the full pressure of its swimming ability against the tackle. The tail or rough back of some fishes can often slice through a leader, or even a fly line. A tarpon, in particular, often wears right through the fly line with its strong, beating tail. Sharks are even worse offenders; their skin is like sandpaper. Keeping to the side of the fish allows the angler to draw the fish to the boat much more easily, too. Remember, move the head of a fish and you move the fish.

The greatest mistake a boatman can make is overrunning the fish—that is, approaching it so fast that the angler cannot keep pace retrieving slack, and the hook falls free. The angler must constantly communicate with his companion; the boatman should watch the rod to make sure he is going slow enough to keep a bend in it. And he must keep a course to one side of the fish.

Should the fish be near an obstruction that could cut the fly line, the boatman can race ahead and place the boat between the fish and the obstruction, and sometimes putting the boat in neutral and racing the engine will frighten the fish into changing direction.

Angler makes a backcast holding onto the fly until the line pulls it from his fingertips.

Angler makes a forward cast to fish if they are close to him—if they are some distance away he may make a second backcast before shooting line.

Angler begins stripping line.

Second phase of line-stripping procedure. The length and speed of the pull determine how fly moves through water. Be sure to watch fish's actions and alter stripping manner to accommodate the fish.

Angler strikes as fish takes the lure.

The most important factor—clearing the line. As soon as angler has driven the hook home he holds the rod high and forgets the fish. Be sure to keep rod butt high, however, or line may catch on the lower portion of the rod and break the leader. The left hand forms an "o" ring around the line and the angler makes sure the line clears all obstructions.

Tarpon jumps.

126 •

Angler bows toward tarpon, creating as much slack as possible, so the fish cannot break leader.

Angler lets the fish run as he grabs the release anchor.

Anchor is freed from boat so companion can start motor and follow fish if necessary.

After initial run, the angler pumps the fish back toward him to put line back on the reel. Pumping motion is made by raising the rod to draw the fish toward him.

Angler forces fingertips against inside of reel spool to gain additional drag pressure. Should fish suddenly bolt away, angler can lift fingertips and drop rod toward the fish.

Angler lowers rod tip toward fish, reeling in accumulated slack line. This is really the only time the angler reels—when he drops the rod tip during a pumping motion, or slack occurs due to swimming actions of the fish.

Fish dives under boat and angler shoves rod underwater and works rod down to end of boat and around the other side.

Fish eventually tires and is brought near the boat. Note that the man using the gaff, Capt. Cal Cochran, is in front of angler, so he can be closer to the fish.

During the gaffing operation the angler has lightened his drag and when the gaff is struck the angler lowers his rod to create slack. This is insurance against the gaffer making a bad stroke and the fish suddenly bolting away from the boat.

The prize.

Many times, particularly near the end of the battle, the fish will suddenly turn and swim rapidly under the boat. Since most propellors are razor-sharp and will easily slice the line or leader, the boatman should shut off the motor, lift the lower unit from the water, and get everything out of the way that would prevent the fisherman from moving to the back of the boat.

Should the fish dart under the boat, the most effective thing you can do is to shove the rod tip deep underwater and allow the line to flow without striking the boat or motor. Then you can walk with the rod shoved down until you are at the far end of the boat, around the stern or bow to where you can safely raise the rod again to a fish-fighting position.

The angler should be warned before any sudden moves are made with the boat. The fisherman, intent on battling the fish, has his hands full; a sudden surge of power from the outboard could knock him off balance and break the line. WARN THE MAN FIGHTING THE FISH BEFORE YOU APPLY POWER TO THE MOTOR OR MAKE ANY SUDDEN MOVES WITH THE BOAT.

If, during a fight, the boat is moved over a long distance, or, often, if you are fishing an area carpeted with thick grass, a floating mass of vegetation will accumulate on the water. The line will catch this, and if too much collects on it, the increased drag will surely break the leader. Usually you can rid the line of grass by a series of sharp, short shakes of the rod. If not, step back and bring the grass near the boat where you or your companion can remove the grass. Note, however, that in many tournaments and for records, no one may touch the tackle but the angler himself.

GAFFING OR LANDING FISH

Most fish are lost either on the strike or at the boat. It has been my experience that more are lost near the end of the fight than at the beginning.

The landing net has to be larger than the fish you intend to land. That may sound obvious, but on a number of occasions I have been forced to land fish with nets entirely too small. In such cases all you can do is get the head of the fish in the net—and pray.

The landing net should have a mesh that has been dyed a neutral color. Bright nets, such as those made from white twine, scare fish. You can dye your net easily with household dye, but it's best to buy one with a dark color. Nets should have reasonably long handles.

Never chase a fish with a net. Hold the net motionless underwater at roughly at 45-degree angle and *lead* the fish toward the net. Once the head of the fish is near the mouth of the net bring it forward and upward in a swift motion. Never approach a fish from the rear with a landing net. If you touch the tail of most fish, unless the fish is exhausted it will surely bolt away. And—that sudden jerk may break the line.

Nets should be stored out of the way, yet where they can be reached quickly. Nylon or plastic nets are best, since they resist rotting.

Several nets on the market today have a mesh that resists snagging the hooks on the lure. Anyone who's netted a striped bass caught on a lure holding several treble hooks will quickly appreciate the benefits of such a netting.

Net all fish *headfirst*.

Gaffing a fish requires greater skill than netting. There are two basic types of gaffs: flying gaffs and hand gaffs. The flying gaff, outlawed by the Salt Water Fly Rodders of America and by many tournaments, is a gaff hook attached to a rope clipped to the handle; when the fish is struck, the handle comes free and the gaff hook, usually tied to the boat, allows you to fight the fish with the gaff. The larger game fish, like blue marlin (hardly a fly-rod fish), require a flying gaff, but for general fishing the hand gaff is more desirable.

Hand gaffs come in many shapes and sizes. Most boats carry at least two, and many good fishermen carry as many as five. The length of a gaff depends upon its purpose, the type of fish to be gaffed, and whether the boat has a high freeboard or is low to the surface. For general fishing, along both coasts, I'd recommend two gaffs: one with a handle 5 to 7 feet long for reaching out to get a fish, and a short hand gaff, approximately a foot in length, with a 3-inch bite. This gaff is perfect for reaching down beside the boat and lifting an exhausted fish; it is also a great gaff for assisting. The longer gaff, usually with a 3- or 4-inch bite, can be used to hook a fish several feet away from the boat. When the fish is struck, the gaffer often doesn't get the gaff just where he intended and so has an insecure hold. The angler can lay down his rod and use the smaller hand gaff, which is often referred to as a release gaff. With two gaffs in a fish, even a respectable-size trophy can be hauled aboard easily.

Tarpon is gaffed with an eight-inch gaff. Captain Cochran, as do many other guides, prefers to gaff a very large tarpon from underneath the fish and near the pectoral muscle. This allows the gaffer to upset the tarpon by turning it on its back and reducing the swimming efficiency of the fish.

Should the fish you catch be one you want to release, such as a tarpon, which is not good to eat, use the release gaff only, slipping it into the tarpon's mouth and pinning the gaff point against the side of the boat to immobilize the fish. It's a simple matter to remove the fly and release the fish. Barracudas are also released in this manner with no harm done to them.

Using a release gaff, the angler has pinned the fish against the side of the boat with the gaff point. This immobilizes the tarpon, and makes it easy to remove the lure.

Nearly all gaffs come with a round point, which is the worst type; it's nothing more than a puncturing tool. Experienced gaffers take a round-point gaff into a workshop and file it to make a far better point. They flatten the outside of the point, and then taper the sides toward the middle as you do when you triangulate a hook to sharpen it. This gives three cutting edges with a well-supported point that will shear through meat, bone, and gristle.

A piece of plastic or rubber tubing should be slipped over the gaff point when it is not in use. All gaffs should be stored where they cannot cause harm.

Barbed gaff hooks are even more dangerous, but flying gaffs should always be barbed.

If the gaff handle has a loop of cord on the rear of the handle through which the wrist can be slipped, remove it. Many fish will spin and twist violently when you stick them; sharks are especially prone to this; I have seen people suffer injuries from fish that twisted this cord so tight as to injure muscles and tendons that required weeks to heal. Unless you are a highly experience gaffer I recommend that you never use a gaff that has a rope.

Let's assume the proper gaff is at hand and the angler has tired the fish. The angler should always stand behind you, the gaffer, and draw the fish close to you. If you have the gaff and stand behind him you're rarely able to reach the fish. If the boat has a high freeboard, both the angler and the gaffer should stand so that they can *both* see the fish at all times.

The first, and most important, gaffing rule is always to place the gaff behind the leader and line. If you don't, and the fish bolts forward, the sharp point may strike the taut line and the battle will be over. Keep the gaff behind the leader at all times.

The second basic rule of good gaffing is that once you strike the fish you must keep coming until you have lifted the fish into the boat. Naturally, all tackle and loose gear should be removed from the boat deck before the fish is gaffed.

If the fish is heavy you can gaff it near the head. As you sink the gaff and lift the head, the fish will violently vibrate its tail, assisting the angler in bringing it aboard. If the fish is still "green"—not really tired—you may want to hit it near the tail. This allows you to lift the tail out of the water, which is where the fish gets its propelling power.

"Billing" a marlin: note that gloves are worn.

Thin fish are more difficult to gaff than wide fish, and those with hard scales, like tarpon, are tougher to sink the gaff into, than, for example, tuna. In a survey I once conducted among some top gaffers, all agreed that barracuda or king mackerel were among the toughest fish to gaff—simply because the thin body offered such a poor target.

The gaffer can place the gaff in the water with the hook up and wait for the fish to swim under it (never chase a fish with a gaff—you only make it more frantic) or poise above the fish with the gaff in the striking position. Most accomplished gaffers prefer to gaff by coming down and across the fish. The handle slides along the back of the fish as the point is rapidly brought into contact. As the point strikes home, the gaffer lifts the fish upward and swings it into the boat.

Don't strike until you are sure you can hit the fish correctly!

Charley Waterman once described an inept gaffer he knew as a fellow who looked like a monkey hoeing in a potato patch. I've seen people answering that description, and they usually lost the fish.

If you make a bad strike with the gaff, the fish becomes gaff-shy and will not come near the boat. And bleeding fish often attract sharks.

Fish react in all sorts of ways when gaffed. Cobia twist violently—stand clear! Bluefish will snap at anything they can get their teeth into, and some nasty wounds have been the result. Big tarpon can wreck gear; amberjack are like bulls, all muscle. If you have a large fish box, the gaffer can hit the fish, and, in one swift motion, deposit it in the box where it can beat its tail harmlessly.

A club, kept handy for the purpose, is essential for some strong fish. The fish is gaffed, brought aboard, and struck repeatedly with the billy club until it is subdued.

Remember, too, that the gaff point is very sharp and can cause you harm. Watch the gaff during the battle, and put it safely away as soon as it is not needed.

Billfish are neither gaffed nor netted. Sailfish and marlin are boated by a special technique: The billfish is brought alongside the boat. Most experienced charterboat skippers will not allow you to hand-gaff a billfish—they consider it too dangerous. The mate, wearing cotton gloves, will reach over the side and grasp the bill of a sailfish or small marlin and draw the head up to the boat. The fish is *always* brought up with the bill pointing to one side of the angler. Serious injuries can result if anyone grabs the fish with the bill pointed toward his stomach. One flip of the tail and he can be impaled on the sail's bill.

Once the head of the fish is brought over the boat transom, the mate grabs a billy club and knocks the fish out. Then it can be safely brought aboard.

The fly rodder who wades must beach or land his fish, and so has a different problem. The wader usually carries no landing net or gaff, although a short, folding gaff can be transported easily.

If the fish is beaten in a quiet water, the angler can slowly work his way backward, toward a beach. Often a pocket of water leads into the beach and the angler can slip the fish into this shallow water and then slide the fish up on shore. If the beach is sloping, the fisherman will slowly pull against the fish, using the rod, never grasping the leader, to manipulate the fish up on the beach.

If you're fishing where there's surf, you're in luck. After the fish is thoroughly beaten, back up slowly toward the beach, and watch the wave action as the surf rolls up on the sand. Wait for an incoming roller, and carefully lift the fish with the wave and run up on the beach while the wave carries your fish forward. As the wave recedes the fish will be deposited on the sand, but you must quickly grab it and carry it farther up on the shore to prevent the next incoming wave from lifting it seaward. Never, in an attempt to land a fish, kick it with your boot. The sharp spines can easily pierce boot and foot, causing serious injury.

Landing sharks requires particular attention. They are powerful and dangerous. They're unbelievably strong and have a hide like a coarse grinding wheel that can take skin from your hands with the same efficiency. Their teeth need no description.

Experienced fly rodders have a flat rule about sharks: *Never put a shark into a small boat.*

Too many times this is what happens: after serious punishment, a shark appears to be dead and is loaded into a boat. Suddenly, maybe an hour or more later, it comes to life. Bart Foth, one of the greatest bonefishermen, caught a lemon shark of more than 100 pounds on fly rod tackle a few years ago in the Florida Keys near Islamorada. It was hooked on the opening day of the giant Metropolitan Miami Fishing Tournament. The fish was subdued, and finally, after both Bart and his experienced guide, Captain Knowles, were convinced that the shark was dead, it was placed in the boat. More than a half hour later, the shark suddenly came to and thrashed and bit viciously. One bite took a hunk from a heavy-duty fishing chair; it resembled the first bite out of your morning piece of toast. The fish was again beaten, thrown overboard, and finally dragged to the dock. It was hung there and weighed, and more than an hour later, while I was taking pictures, it came to life again! Fortunately, no one was hurt.

Several precautions can be taken. The very best tool with which to kill a shark is the bang stick, which is a handle about 5 or 6 feet long, to which is attached a cylinder that holds either a shotgun shell or a high-powered rifle shell. When the fish is brought alongside the boat, the mate or companion forcefully brings the loaded end of the bang stick down on the head of the shark. The explosion almost always kills the shark instantly.

Billy clubs are ineffectual against sharks. But one hand weapon that does do a pretty good job of immobilizing the shark is a heavy ball-peen hammer. Several blows on the top of the skull will usually quiet the beast, but a stunned shark still should not be brought aboard a small boat.

My favorite method is to get a rope on the tail of the shark, and drag the fish backward to the landing, if I am going to weigh it. Dragging seems to drown the fish, and is probably the safest way to handle sharks when you're in a small boat.

Sharks have no bones. Their body structure is cartilage, and they can twist and turn easily. I've seen many pictures of anglers holding up small sharks; those sharks, if they decided to, could curl up like a yo-yo and bite the angler's hand. *Don't hold a shark!*

HANDLING FISH THAT HAVE BEEN CAPTURED

Nearly all freshwater fishes can be handled safely. The catfish has spines that can give you trouble, and pike and pickerel have pointed teeth, but, in the main, freshwater fish are relatively safe to pick up. Saltwater fishes are a different matter; almost all species can be hazardous to handle.

The bluefish has sharp teeth. As with barracuda, mackerel, and others, not only are its teeth sharp at the ends, but both *sides* of the teeth are honed to razor edges. If you see teeth in the mouth of a saltwater fish, know that those teeth will probably be dangerous.

Nearly ever saltwater fish has coarser and stronger gill rakers than freshwater varieties. You should not put your hands inside the gill flaps of *any* saltwater fish unless you know exactly what you are doing. The channel bass has extremely rough rakers, and many other species can inflict deep cuts, especially if the fish flops around while your fingers are inside those gill covers.

Most saltwater fishes, except those with extremely sharp teeth, crush their food. But any fish that has rubbery or rather smooth lips must do something to the prey before it can swallow it; such fish usually have strong crushers in the rear of the throat. The fish grabs its victim, flips it back to the crushers, which come swiftly together with the force of a steel vise, and crush the prey to a pulp. I have seen permit pick up a crab, crush it, swallow the soft parts, and spit out the shell as easily as you could do it to a peanut. Any angler who sticks his hands inside the mouth of a fish with smooth, leatherlike lips is taking a good chance of losing those extremities.

A jack crevalle lies motionless in your hand when the rear of the gill covers is pinched together, as Jim Green is doing here.

Snook should be handled as shown.

Some fish present hazards that are not really apparent to the angler with little saltwater experience. The jack family, which has many subspecies, usually have soft rays in the dorsal fin. However, some jacks carry a small pair of stiff spines on the belly near the anus that can stab painfully. You can paralyze any member of the jack family by gripping the fish across the back of the head and clamping with the fingers at the junction of the gill covers. For some reason the fish is immobilized by this grip.

This small cutter, shown lying on top of the thumbnail, is sharp as a razor blade and can injure an angler not familiar with the snook.

The snook is another fish that can easily injure you. In the middle of the outer area of the gill cover on a snook is a transparent cutter blade that is as sharp as any knife. About the size of a nickel, it can slice your fingers if you carelessly grab the fish. In fact, most snook fishermen use a heavy monofilament leader when fishing for the species, since thin line is often sliced into by this weapon. Most guides place their thumb inside the mouth, and curl their first finger inside the gills at the point where the cover meets the throat.

Barracuda, mackerel, king mackerel, and other thin, hard-to-hold fishes are best grasped with a towel or with a pair of cotton gloves.

Billfish, next to sharks, are perhaps the most dangerous fish to land. Long, extremely strong, and very active, billfish must be properly subdued before they're brought inside the boat. The generally accepted procedure is to wear a pair of cotton work gloves. Grab the bill,

Snappers and other fish that have short, stubby but very sharp spines on the back should be handled across the belly, as Capt. Gene Montgomery is doing.

not the fragile leader, and hold onto the fish until it quiets. There are a correct and an incorrect way of grabbing the bill. The right hand should grab the bill so the thumb points toward the fish's head. The left hand should grasp the bill so the left thumb also points toward the head. Held in this manner, and always to the side of the angler, the fish can cause no harm. If the fish lunges forward, the person holding it can easily force it away from him, if he has the recommended grip.

Before any billfish is brought aboard it should be stunned with a billy club, kept handy for that purpose. A billfish thrashing about in a cockpit is a dangerous fish indeed.

GUIDE TO DANGERS OF HANDLING FISH

SPECIES	SPECIFIC DANGERS	SPECIAL PROBLEMS	HOW TO HOLD AND REMOVE FLY
Barracuda (Great and Pacific)	Very sharp teeth, leap a great deal.	Be aware of leaping fish near the boat.	Hold fish firmly and use pliers or similar tool to remove fly.
Channel Bass or Redfish	Has strong crushers in mouth and gill rakers are very sharp.	Never put fingers inside mouth or gill covers.	Grasp fish behind head and pinch gill covers together. Large fish should be placed on deck or ground, and held firmly.
Striped Bass	Gill rakers can cut.	Keep fingers outside gill covers.	Hold fish firmly with a rag; smaller fish can be grasped by lower lip.
Bluefish	Extremely sharp teeth.	Use special tool for removing fly.	Hold fish with a rag to keep it from slipping, and use metal tool to remove fly.
Bonefish	No dangers, but fish is considered inedible and should be released unharmed.	"Crushers" deep inside throat can mangle fingers.	Gently.
Cobia	Extremely strong and muscular.	Fish should be tired before attempting to land.	Don't try removing fly from fish until it is tired; place fish in fish box until it calms.
Dolphin	Thrashes about violently and bleeds profusely.	Same as cobia.	Same as cobia.

SPECIES	SPECIFIC DANGERS	SPECIAL PROBLEMS	HOW TO HOLD AND REMOVE FLY
Black Drum	Same as redfish.	Same as redfish.	Same as redfish.
Jack Crevalle	Small cutting projection next to anus; very strong fish.		You can paralyze fish by holding behind head and pinching behind head.
Mackerel (all kinds)	Extremely sharp teeth.	Fish thin, a little slippery and hard to hold.	If possible, hold with a rag or towel.
Marlin (Blue, White, Striped) and Sailfish	Bill can inflict serious wounds.	Fish are powerful and the leader cannot be grasped to control fish.	Fish should be completely exhausted, then handled first by lifting by the bill. Gaffing not recommended on larger fish.
Permit	Crushers in throat.		Can be lifted by tail, netted, or gaffed.
Pollock	Crushers in throat.		Should be netted or gaffed; fly can be removed by hand.
Roosterfish	Extremely strong and could inflict damage by thrashing.		Hold with a rag.
Shark	Terrible teeth, very strong, can thrash or chop the angler.	Fish is often alive and dangerous when it appears dead. Has no bones, can curl around and bite person holding it.	Don't hold. Cut leader and let in fish.
Snapper	Have caninelike teeth which can snap closed like a steel trap. Spines on back are sharp and can cut.		Hold fish across belly to avoid spines. Keep hands away from mouth; use a tool to remove fly.
Grouper	Crushers in throat, stout spines on back, gills raspy.		Fish should be tired before fly is removed, and should be held firmly.
Snook	Cutter blade on side of gill covers.		Grasp fish with thumb over lip and first finger through lower opening of gill cover.
Tarpon	Big ones are powerful, and can thrash and hurt angler.	When being gaffed, giant tarpon can pull angler into water, so fish should be exhausted before being gaffed.	Small fish to 35 pounds can be held by lower lip. Larger fish: leave fly in until fish is very tired.

SPECIES	SPECIFIC DANGERS	SPECIAL PROBLEMS	HOW TO HOLD AND REMOVE FLY
Tuna (all kinds)	No specific dangers, except that fish are extremely strong.		Fish should be tired before fly is removed.
Wahoo	Very sharp teeth.		Use tool to remove fly; teeth are very sharp.
Weakfish (Sea Trout)	Some sharp caninelike teeth.		Teeth are not dangerous, but can hurt.
Yellowtail	Same as tuna.	Same as tuna.	Same as tuna.

RELEASING FISH

Many fly-caught fish are inedible, and if not kept for a trophy mount, should be returned to the sea. Some fishes are so exhausted when captured that they require special handling if they are to survive. Bonefish fight so valiantly that they arrive at the boat in a state of total collapse; if released they will usually sink to the bottom and die. Tarpon often meet the same fate, as do many other species.

Fish you are not going to eat or have mounted should be released. The author is shown reviving a big tarpon by working the fish back and forth vigorously so that water can be pumped through the gills. This technique works well with many species of fish.

The general technique for reviving distressed fish is to hold the fish in the water in its normal swimming position, then swish it back and forth rapidly. This motion pumps water through the gills, reviving the fish. There is no need to wonder when you should release the fish; when it returns to normal, it will easily slip from your hands.

Any fish that can be lip-gaffed or netted should be captured that way if it is to be released. The number of fish in the sea may *seem* unlimited, but it is not, and conservation of our great game fish is something every fly rodder should consider paramount. The excitement and pleasure derived from capturing a truly great fish should be reward enough.

Paul Crum returns a snook to Everglades waters.

Handle fish carefully when you capture them if you do not plan to kill them. Capt. Bill Curtis is gently lifting the bonefish by the belly, without squeezing the fish. Many fish can be handled in this manner.

PART THREE

INSHORE AND DEEP-WATER

Species and Strategies

9 Inshore Fishing

Most saltwater fly fishing is done in relatively shallow waters, or very close to the shoreline. Defining inshore fishing is difficult. It includes wading a northern beach for stripers, and poling across a flat seeking bonefish. But it is more than that. Roosterfish are caught within 100 yards of rocky points in the tropics, but, since the shoreline plunges almost straight down, the water may be 300 feet deep. Striped bass are often sought several miles from shore in large boats by men trolling atrocious rigs; but for our purposes, let's consider the striped bass an inshore fish. Bluefish are caught far out at sea, and right under the docks—so we'll call it an inshore fish too.

The list of inshore fishes would include the following: barracuda (great), channel bass, rockfish (West Coast types), striped bass, bluefish, bonefish, bonito, cobia, corbina, flounder, halibut, jack crevalle, jewfish, ladyfish, mackerel, permit, pollack, pompano, roosterfish, shark, snapper, snook, tarpon, and weakfish (sea trout).

That's a lot of fish, and they live, breed, and eat under a variety of conditions. Some, like the sea trout, or weakfish, prefer areas with a grassy bottom, for that protective cover holds much of their food. Roosterfish like surf piling against the rocky projections of a shoreline, where they can voraciously slash into baitfish. Tarpon like to live under the mangroves in the quiet shade when they are young, then move into channels adjoining the flats when they grow larger. Striped bass move around so much that they confuse even biologists. So, it's a good idea to specialize, if you really want to become a successful saltwater fisherman.

Blind casting—casting into what you assume are fruitful waters and retrieving your fly with the hope that a fish will see and strike it—is one type of inshore fishing. Striped bass, sea trout, flounder, bluefish, and other species that either lie deep on the bottom, or swim well beneath the surface, are often caught by blind casting. If you locate a school of such fish, or you know your area well enough to predict your catch, this kind of fishing can be very exciting and rewarding.

But *sight*-fishing just has to be the most exciting kind of fishing. You can either anchor a boat in shallow clear water and wait for fish to approach, or wade or boat across these shallows, looking for the fish. In any case the fish is usually sighted long before it is time to cast. This is a combination of hunting and fishing, and for many who have practiced it, no other kind of fishing can quite compare. Bonefishing is the best-known kind of sight-fishing, but many other species can also be taken by this method. Cobia, tarpon, striped bass, permit, snapper, shark, jewfish, channel bass, and snook—all can be successfully sight-fished.

A basic law of shallow water fishing is that the angler lower his silhouette if the fish follows the fly to the boat. Notice that the man poling the boat has also dropped to the deck.

A third kind of saltwater fishing, not widely practiced but highly successful for some species, is called chumming. The angler picks out a choice location, anchors, then puts out the sort of food that will attract the species he is interested in catching. This technique works well with bonefish, permit, bluefish, striped bass, mackerel, bonito, and shark.

Chumming is not really a haphazard technique; it requires knowledge of the traffic patterns of the fish (chumming in an area where the fish do not pass would be futile), and the selection of the type of chum most likely to attract these species.

The well-equipped angler will have at least two tackle outfits to fish the shallows. One will be a floating line and, depending upon the species sought, he will have the reel loaded with either a saltwater taper or a weight-forward taper, and this will be the line that he'll probably use most of the time. Many West Coast fishermen would use a floating shooting taper instead of a full-length line; that is simply a matter of choice—both will accomplish the same purpose. This floating line (ranging from size 8 through 12, again depending upon the size of the flies) will be the workhorse line that will catch most of the fish.

The angler will also have with him either a spare shooting taper, or another reel loaded with a sinking line—in most cases an extra-fast-sinking line, which will enable him to position the fly deeper, or on the bottom when necessary.

Other lines may be called for by specific conditions. For example, an intermediate sinking line is very helpful in fishing for giant tarpon. A sink-tip line may be a wonderful tool for fishing permit, when you'll want the fly to bomb to the bottom, but prefer the remainder of the line to float. But first, equip yourself with a floating and a fast-sinking line. As you gain experience, you'll probably find plenty of reasons for using other types of line too.

An inshore reel should be just as good as the one selected for offshore. If you fish for many species of inshore fish a reel with a small line capacity and little or no drag will do, but it may not suit for that trophy you are always seeking. Certainly, if you fight bonefish or permit—both long-running, fast-moving fishes—you will need some sort of drag device, whether it's a hand or a mechanical one. If you pursue giant tarpon, big cobia, or rough roosterfish, you'll need a stout reel with plenty of backing and a good drag. For flounder, channel bass on the flats, weakfish, striped bass, bluefish, jack crevalle, snapper, and other fish that will slug it out over a short distance, an inexpensive reel that can resist the ravages of salt water will usually suffice.

HOW TO LOOK FOR INSHORE FISH

Learning to spot inshore fishes is an acquired skill. The ability to see what others do *not* often means the difference between success and failure. It really is like stalking; there are many "signs" that will help you determine where the fish are.

Almost any fisherman knows that hovering birds indicate fish beneath. Circling gulls, they think, mean fish are below. But often such is not the case. Many times gulls are just circling a pod of baitfish, waiting for stripers, bluefish, or other predators to begin the carnage. The *action* of the gulls will tell you if larger fish are disturbing the bait: when the bait is lying near the surface, unconcerned about predators, the gulls will often wheel in slow spirals, watching and waiting, but when the gulls drop down in quick tight circles, or dart to the water and obviously pick up something as they tower upward—that's the time to head full bore for the birds. Field glasses are often a help; some of the newer ones are made from glass fiber and are completely waterproof, even if dropped overboard.

If you can see baitfish showering above the surface, that's the best time of all. A cast into that spray of fish will draw an immediate strike.

Sometimes, while running and looking, especially for striped bass, you'll come across a huge flock of gulls sitting on the surface. Unless you have an urgent destination, hang around for a few minutes; break out a sandwich and wait. The gulls are there because, from aloft, they have located a large school of baitfish and they are simply resting until a school of larger fish find the food.

You'll scatter a feeding school of fish by racing your boat through it. When you see a school of surface fish tearing into baitfish, work the boat from the outside edges—never run it through the school. The fly rodder is aided immeasurably if the captain manning the boat will also approach the school from the *upwind* side, allowing him to toss his fly with the wind into the feeding fish. If you are the only boat, and stay on the edges of the school, you can often catch a number of fish before the school moves on or is frightened and sounds.

Another bird that aids in spotting fish is the man-o'-war bird, or frigate bird, easily identified by the peculiar **W** shape of the wings and its seven-foot wingspan. Seen only in the warmer seas, the frigate bird usually follows a single large fish, rather than a school of fish. It will drop to the surface, grab a tidbit from the water, and lift again into the sky in a display of incredible flying skill. The huge bird, which has the lightest wing bones for its size of any bird, will often put to sea and stay aloft for a week. Lacking the oily coating on the feathers that many sea birds have, a frigate bird that falls to the water will probably drown as soon as its feathers become saturated. I have frequently seen fish chasing a school of larger baitfish, making the bait leap frantically from the water; the frigate bird, hovering above, would swiftly dart seaward and catch the hapless baitfish in midair.

This bird flies in wide spiraling circles when hunting. When it sees a fish that may produce a meal, it will begin hovering over the large predator. If the bird makes swift passes toward the water—head for the spot; chances are the large fish is now actively feeding.

Discolored water, usually brownish or greenish, often indicates fish. That's why good charter boat skippers prefer to handle the boat from topside, rather than from the comfortable cabin below. They can see water discolorations or moving fish from above. Many captains can actually tell you what kind of fish cause a specific discoloration. In Key West in the wintertime huge schools of jack crevalle roam the Gulf side, feasting on tiny sardines. These schools of jacks often cover more than an acre, with individual fish ranging in size from 8 to 20 pounds. They show under the water as a yellow-amber color.

School fish moving along in relatively shallow waters will often give off a series of ripples unlike any natural wave pattern. Whenever you see waves that do not appear normal, it will pay to check them out.

Fishermen for striped bass and bluefish spend much of their time cruising and looking over the surface for feeding fish, or birds. But not many know that on days when there's a chop on the surface, splashes from feeding fish can best be spotted from a downwind angle. Unless the splashes are so pronounced as to disturb the top of the waves, they are often hidden under the waves' curl. With the wind in your face, looking toward the breeze you will see the telltale white splashes on the downwind side of the curlers.

High rolling waves will often reveal hordes of baitfish, frightened right up to the shore by larger fish lying just seaward. Maneuver your boat close to the shore and cast right into the surf. Fishing this way along the North Carolina coast in November and December produces some fantastic catches.

Barracuda and king mackerel often give away their presence by spectacular thirty-foot leaps. One of these mighty fish skyrocketing out of the water in a curving arc is a sight to remember. When fish are skyrocketing they are actively feeding, and a well-placed fly will often draw strikes. Mackerel, while much smaller, also skyrocket, although their leaps usually carry them only a foot or two above the surface.

When fishing from rocky jetties or an offshore bar, you will often see fish chasing bait right against the obstructions. Cast to any boils or swirls you think may be fish. In some areas, pilings produce great fishing. In San Francisco Bay, striped bass often show themselves by surface movement as they feed near pilings.

At night in warmer seas the angler often can locate feeding fish, especially snook and tarpon, around bridges. They almost always lie on the up-tide side of a bridge, but inside the shadow line cast by the lights on the bridge. However, their dark shapes, lying near the surface awaiting drifting shrimp, crabs, and other food, give them away.

Birds dipping among the frightened baitfish that are leaping from predatory fish below make a fisherman's soul leap with joy. A fly quickly tossed into such action will produce an instant strike.

Sharks often betray themselves as they bask near the surface with their dorsal fins protruding. A careful approach must be made to basking fish, for they're easily alarmed and will dive at the slightest noise.

Big blacktip sharks, and sometimes lemon sharks, cruise the shallow flats looking for food. Often the whole upper third of a shark's body sticks above the surface. In shallow bays along the East Coast, sharks feed for crabs right up along the sod banks. It's hard to intercept them, but they do betray their presence occasionally as the dorsal fin protrudes above the surface. Usually, for such specific fishing it is best to locate the sharks by their movements, then set up chum lines in anticipation of the fish reappearing in the area.

Tarpon are able to breathe air from the atmosphere and are frequently seen as they roll to the surface, exhale and inhale, then slowly submerge. In calm water you can spot a rolling tarpon at several hundred yards—a standard method of locating this fish. In backcountry of the Ten Thousand Islands you can often determine whether tarpon are in the area by watching for bubbles floating on the calm surface. Where there is little current the air bubbles exhaled by tarpon will linger for several minutes.

Early morning in calm, protected areas tarpon can often be found asleep near the surface, their dorsal fins clearly showing in the air. One of my son Larry's favorite fishing places is a quiet lagoon in the lower Florida Keys; if we can arrive there right after dawn we often see both permit and tarpon sleeping contentedly side by side in the dim light, their sharp-pointed fins protruding above the surface like a poorly installed picket fence. These fish are extremely difficult to approach; silence is essential if you want to score.

The depth of water also determines how you must look for fish. If you are searching for fish on the flats in water less than a foot deep, do *not* look at the bottom: it's the surface that will give you clues. The fins or tail will often stand out of the water as the fish swims, or tips up on its head to root out a morsel. Clearly defined **V** wakes indicate moving fish, and remember that the fish will be a foot or more in front of the wake it creates.

There is another phenomenon, called "nervous water," which is simply tiny ripples that form no real pattern on the surface, which tell that fish are swimming directly below. It's important to keep in mind that in extremely shallow water, if you look at the bottom instead of the surface, you'll miss many of these fish-indicators.

However, when bonefish, redfish (channel bass), and similar species are swimming in 1 to 3 feet of clear water, it's vital to search the bottom. You may miss a fish ghosting over a changing bottom if you're looking at the surface. And it pays to know your fish, of course. Bonefish, permit, and snapper move constantly; when you see a 2-foot green object lying motionless on a Florida flat, you can bet that it will be a barracuda (although on one occasion I stopped Leon Martuch from casting to a huge bonefish that I mistook for a cuda. I don't think he'll ever let me forget it).

You should know the depth of water that the fish you seek prefers. Permit, for example, like at least 18 inches of water on a flat, while bonefish will feed in water just deep enough to allow them to maneuver. Mackerel will be in 6 or more feet of water, and bonito like even more. Striped bass seem to go wherever they can find food—an outside sandbar boiling with heavy water, or the quiet shallow mud flats of San Francisco Bay.

Polarizing glasses are the single most valuable aid to spotting fish. There are a number of different tints, ranging from a bright tan to yellow, through green, blue, and gray. Brown is the most popular with experienced anglers; smoke-colored glass seems to be the second choice. Yellow or tan is preferable on overcast days. Regardless of color, these glasses are designed to polarize the light waves usually encountered in fishing; and you may find that under certain light conditions, by tilting your head a little to one side or the other, you'll be able to remove even more glare.

Even the type of hat you wear can help you spot fish. The brim should be long enough to shade your eyes. The "Florida style" hat has become very popular of late; it shields the eyes and protects the neck and ears from sunburn. The underside of the brim of any hat you wear should be a dark color. Test this theory for yourself: put on a hat whose brim is light colored on the underside and look at a distant object in the bright sun. Then exchange the hat for one that has a dark underside. Baseball players who range the outfield have been darkening the areas around their eyes for years to obtain this same effect.

Captain Bill Curtis, perhaps the best bonefish guide in the world today, anchors his boat by "staking out." The sharp end of the boat pole is inserted into the flat. Care is taken that the pole is slanted low to the water so the backcast won't foul on the pole.

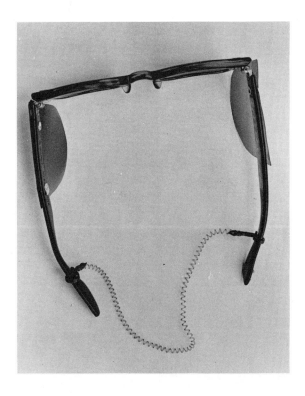

Polarizing glasses are a must in sight fishing, and side shields (made from old sunglasses) will prevent much glare from entering the backside of the lenses. The coiled monofilament line on the back is a product called Snuggers, which keeps the glasses from falling off.

When fishing shallows, always approach the fish with the sun over your shoulder. Even polarizing glasses are of little help when you approach *into* the sunlight and into a water surface filled with glare.

The background sky affects your spotting fish. Large banks of white clouds lying on the horizon act in much the same way as the sun, reflecting light off the water into your eyes. It's obviously much easier to see fish in flat, calm water than in water that's wind-rippled, and water in the shadow of cliffs or shore vegetation appears to be transparent.

Wading is another great way of fishing inshore waters with a fly rod. But one immediate word of caution: *Never wade potentially dangerous water alone.* It may make the difference if help is only a few yards away.

Wading at night, a specialty of many northern striped bass fishermen, can be especially dangerous if you're not familiar with the terrain. You should be aware of every drop-off, local tidal rip, boulder-studded area, or other local hazard. If you're trying out a new area, be sure to explore it carefully before wading after dark.

Rock jetties can be extremely dangerous, since there's usually treacherous water at their base. Many anglers wear shoes with golf cleats imbedded in them when fishing from jetties; certainly, you should avoid rubber-soled sneakers for such work. Even felt-soled wading shoes are inadequate.

Do all wading on jetties with great caution.

Your wading pace must be slow. Carefully place one foot forward and ascertain your footing before moving on. If you're ever caught in a stiff tide, turn sideways so your body presents less resistance against the water; this will also brace your feet better for a return to shore.

If you wade in colder climates, protect yourself with chest-high waders; a belt around the top will prevent you from shipping water on a fall. Your waders should have rubber soles; felt simply wears out too quickly on raspy sand and gravel beaches. You can glue outdoor carpeting to the boot soles with contact cement, giving them a tough, nonslip surface. When the carpeting wears out it can be removed and another section installed.

If you're fishing where surf may at times flood over you, a raincoat with a hood is good insurance. Specially designed short-waisted rain jackets (no zippers or snaps; the waist ties down with a cord), made just for waders, are a blessing.

In tropical areas, cold and high surf are not usually problems. But stingrays and sea urchins are. Proper wading techniques will allow you to fish free of concern.

A sea urchin looks like a tennis ball that's turned into a porcupine. The sharp, brittle spines that stick out from the ball at every angle will penetrate the foot. They break off, and usually have to be removed by surgery. The best protection is to wade with a conventional wading shoe, a basketball-style sneaker that covers the foot to several inches above the ankle. The instep has wire strainers built in, to filter all bothersome gravel and dirt, and the bottom is felt-coated. This heavy canvas shoe, with a stout rubber bumper on the front, will prevent even urchins from penetrating. High-topped sneakers work about as well, but they allow grit and gravel to drop into the shoe, making your wading uncomfortable.

A stingray that you can see, and that sees you, will present no problem, for, like most snakes, all it wants to do is get away. But stingrays have a habit of hiding from their natural enemies by settling their bodies into the soft mud. They flap their wings a number of times and the descending mud completely covers the ray, camouflaging it perfectly. The stingray has a protective device in the form of a sharp, rough stinger on the tail. Should you step on a hidden

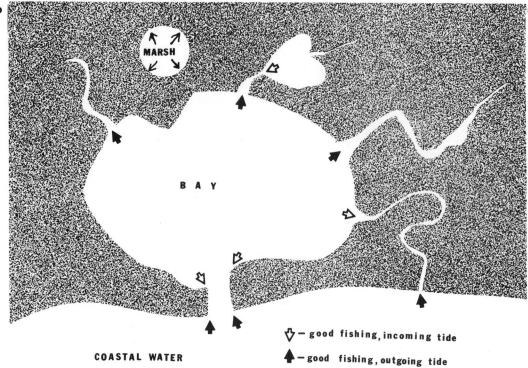

MARSH

B A Y

COASTAL WATER

▽ — good fishing, incoming tide

▲ — good fishing, outgoing tide

A typical inshore fishing situation: a bay fills on incoming tide and drains on falling tide. A fundamental concept of inshore fishing is to fish at the base of a "funnel," which is the outlet portion of flow. The funnel on outgoing tide is marked by all dark arrows—note that this includes the mouths of creeks. On incoming tide, the funnel reverses itself and is on the other end of the flow; see the outlined arrows. This principle holds for almost any type of inshore fishing.

A typical beach fishing situation. The arrows mark current flow and the "X"s mark where the fish will hold and feed. Note the funnel effect and that fish also feed in eddies, where food collects.

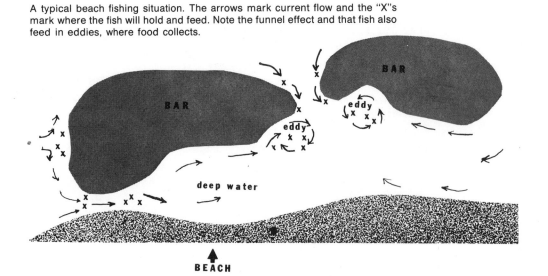

BAR

BAR

eddy

eddy

deep water

BEACH

stingray, in self-defense the ray will try to drive the stinger into you. This is extremely painful, and people have been hospitalized for treatment from stingray attacks. However, it's important to realize that the ray doesn't *want* to get into a fight, and will willingly leave if only you warn it of your presence. This you can do easily. Instead of picking your foot up in a normal walking manner as you wade a flat, allowing the foot to descend on the ray, slide your foot along the bottom to your next position. If your sliding foot hits the ray it will flee in panic and leave you unharmed.

I have not heard of a single attack on a wader from a shark or a barracuda. Obviously, if a large shark is acting aggressively, the proper thing is to retreat, although my experience has been that the larger the fish in shallow water, the more easily frightened. Apparently the fish feels out of its element, and the slightest unusual sound or movement will generally cause it to run. The same can be said of barracudas. In fact, the unusually large fish are often the most difficult to catch, simply because they're so difficult to approach. It's my belief that you can safely ignore sharks and barracudas on clear-water flats. If a flat is murky, and a shark cannot see you clearly, then it may strike. I've often fished the lower west coast of Florida in Everglades Park at Cape Sable; on a number of occasions I've battled a snook, jack, or tarpon right to the beach, and just before I landed the fish in the murky waters, a large shark has inhaled the prey. Wading in such a place would indeed be a dangerous stunt. But where waters are clear, in my opinion sharks and barracudas offer no threat to a wader.

A makeshift stripping basket can be constructed from an old dishpan. Here Lou Tabory, one of New England's finest fly fishermen, had one tied to his waist with a rope (a wide belt works better) when he and the author fished for bluefish and stripers near Shelter Island.

Unlike his companion in a boat, the wading fisherman is severely restricted in his movements. He can only search as much water as he can cast a fly over. The fisherman who wades a great deal should seriously consider using a shooting basket and a shooting-taper line. A basket can be simply made from a plastic dishpan through which your belt is strapped, or you can purchase a commercial type. Some people like to carry the basket in a position in front of them, others like it on their side. The shooting basket keeps running line out of the drifting tide and away from entangling feet. And the angler can reach at least fifty percent more water because he can cast so much farther. The one drawback to using a shooting taper while wading is that correcting a faulty cast is harder. If you've cast to a cruising fish, and the fish turns in a direction not on course with the fly, you must quickly make another cast. A shooting head requires that you strip in all the running line, then pick up the head, and *then* shoot it. Sometimes this procedure takes so long that the fish escapes. But it is perhaps the shooting head's only liability for the wader.

Since angling for the different species of inshore fishes varies in so many details it may be best to treat each major species separately, even though basic technique for many will overlap.

STRIPED BASS—WEST COAST

No other fish is as popular with fly fishermen throughout the country as the striped bass. While other fish may be stronger, jump higher, run faster, fight longer—even be better to eat—the striped bass is where the people are. And for that reason alone, it is the most prized and sought after. The major concentrations of people in this country—along the coast from North Carolina to New England, and along the California coast to the Oregon shores—duplicate exactly the concentrations of the striped bass.

Striped bass are not native to the West Coast. They were transplanted there in 1879 from East Coast stocks, but they have fared well, and at this reading all the records kept by the Salt Water Fly Rodders of America for striped bass taken on a fly were made on the West Coast.

The heaviest concentration of striper fishing on the West Coast is in San Francisco Bay and adjoining inland waters. Fishing in the Bay begins sometime in June when the big fish return from their spawning grounds on the upper Sacramento and San Joaquin rivers. The peak period is generally agreed to be from June through November, and by mid-December most of the good fishing is over. The four weeks that produce the most big fish are the last two weeks of August and the first two weeks of September.

San Francisco Bay is huge, with much of it covered by mud flats separated by channels. The mud is too soft for wading, so shallow draft skiffs are used to get around on the flats. The prime foods for the Bay stripers are jack smelt, herring, and anchovies. As tides rise on the flats the anchovies and other baitfish will move with it, and the striped bass sometimes work in water barely deep enough for them to swim in, in an effort to get at this tasty food. Anglers who fish these flats in shallow draft boats do so in a manner much like that used for bonefish or tarpon. Much of it is sight fishing: the angler moves up on the flat as soon as the rising waters permit, and looks for nervous water, wakes, or other indications of fish.

Occasionally, the bass will herd anchovies and other fish into a school, then several fish will blow the water apart in an effort to get at the baitfish. If the fly caster can arrive on the scene quickly, while the big bass are still aroused, he stands a good chance of a hook-up.

There is an enormous amount of unfertile water on these vast flats. Therefore, if you can arrange to go with someone who knows the area and has successfully fished it, you have an advantage. Good feeding flats for stripers one year will probably be good ones the next, so patterns can be established and followed.

Casting in open water is rarely successful, but blind casting in known hot spots is practiced among the more successful fishermen, like Dan Blanton, Bob Edgely, and Lawrence Summers, who have also developed a technique for fishing the many hundreds of pilings driven into the Bay bottom.

In water from 4 to 15 feet deep, these men use shooting taper lines. A 30-foot head of lead-core line and a floating shooting line is the standard outfit. This rig allows a long cast with heavy flies, even on windy days.

They'll locate a piling and anchor within casting distance. The best anchorage is on an up-tide side from the pilings, so you can keep the fly from sweeping into the piling, as well as swimming it fast or slow on the retrieve. The fly is dropped very close to the piling, allowed to sink, then retrieved in rapid 2-foot pulls toward the boat. Another method is to anchor off to one side of the piling, within casting distance, and cast across-tide, letting the fly sink deep and be swept in near the piling, then retrieved away from it.

Several fly patterns repeatedly take fish: the Givens Barred-N-Black, the Whistler series developed by Dan Blanton, and the Lefty's Deceiver. Most flies are weighted, so that they can be cast close to a piling in a moving tide and still get deep before they are swept into the piling. Bead chain eyes are popular on many of the West Coast patterns. Some anglers, like Dan Blanton, claim that the bead chain eye imparts a "jigging" motion, causing the fly to rise on the strip and fall at the end of the strip retrieve.

Most flies are dressed on hooks from 2/0 through 5/0. The Mustad #34007 and Eagle Claw 318 models are standard selections, although stainless hooks in other patterns work very well and sharpen better.

The very best time to fish pilings is the first hour before sunrise.

During this golden period just before dawn, fish will feed on any tide, but during the daylight hours, when striped bass are more reluctant to strike, a moving tidal current seems to produce better.

Neap tides, rather than spring tides, are the best tides to fish. This is especially true on the flats, for extremely low-falling water brings the flats above the surface, driving all fish from them.

Other obstructions in the Bay harbor striped bass; for example, duck blinds, wrecks, and rocky shorelines. Some good fishing occurs at times at the outflow of warm water from a local power plant.

A big problem when you're fishing around barnacled-covered pilings is that when a large striped bass takes the fly, it will frequently get on the other side of the piling, and the sharp barnacles will slice through the line. Keep a spare line in the box, and apply as much pressure as possible to prevent a fish from reaching the pilings once it is hooked.

Bass in the San Francisco Bay area average 10 pounds, with a few reaching as much as 40-plus pounds.

Bass also concentrate at night in lighted areas in the Bay, but remember that night fishing from bridges is forbidden by California law. Hal Jansen and Myron Gregory have taken many huge striped bass on a fly when fishing at night. Gregory is a real pioneer in West Coast fly fishing and had much to do with the national acceptance of the lead-core shooting taper.

The size of the fly is extremely important. Striped bass are among the most selective of fishes when it comes to lures. The fly caster getting refusals should alter fly size rather than pattern as a first step; often a relatively small change in length will make a great difference.

Other areas nearby also produce good fishing. Jansen and Gregory fish the Richmond, San Rafael Bridge area, and both feel that predawn fishing (under the lights) at the west end of the bridge is the best, and that incoming tide seems to produce the most fish. Small bait inhabit the area, and so small flies usually take the fish best.

The Brother and Sister Islands, located in the narrows between San Francisco and San Pablo Bay, often give good striped bass fishing, particularly in the tidal rips.

The Golden Gate Bridge area is relatively unexplored by fly fishermen. The water is deep and holds swift currents, so you'll need lead heads and a big boat. This water can get nasty.

Pacific Ocean stripers range up and down the coast in the summer months. The heaviest concentration is in the area from Golden Gate Bridge to Half Moon Bay. These fish follow the schools of bait, sometimes right up into the breakers. This is tough fly fishing, since much of it is in the curling waves that break on the beach, but the fish are there.

Boat-launching areas are few in this area. Small boaters can rent a skiff at Pedro Point in Pacifica, but launching a skiff there is not for the faint-hearted. You're sent down a pole ramp into the surf, where you must row beyond the breakers before starting your motor. Pick your day *carefully* for getting out of Pedro Point.

Half Moon Bay has a good launching area at Princeton. This is a protected harbor, fine for small boats, and it can produce big stripers. It was here that Dan Blanton and Bob Edgely, one day near dark, saw a surface movement, and Bob made a cast into it with a Lefty's Deceiver. When the battle was over he had landed a new world-record striper of 32½ pounds.

Stripers are taken by fly casters at the mouths of several rivers in Monterey Bay, including the San Lorenzo, the Salinas, the Pajarro, and the Moss Landing Slew. At Moss Landing Slew a power plant sometimes sucks bait into the turbines, kills it, then spews it into the outflow, where stripers rush in to feed. It can be terrific fishing, if you time it right.

Tomales Bay, north of San Francisco, produces a lot of stripers, but they seem to be smaller on the average; and because the Bay faces northwest, which is the direction of the prevailing winds, the water is often very choppy.

Coos Bay, Oregon, is about the northern limit of striped bass fishing on the West Coast. The many miles of estuaries offered by the Umpqua and Smith rivers are perfect for stripers, although winds frequently plague fly fishermen. Blind-casting the channels that drain these flats is one method of taking fish on a fly. Chumming, while generally not practiced here, could be effective.

Dick Wadsworth is a former East Coast striper nut who now fishes the Umpqua River in the Reedsport, Oregon, area. He also likes the Smith River, which is nearby. Dick fished these two rivers every day in 1971 from June until August 1. "My diary tells me that I landed two fish of 23 and 26 pounds the day I arrived, and ran into fish every day thereafter," he says. "The month of June was the best month for numbers of fish. There were lots of school fish that averaged 4 pounds, and enough large fish that I was landing one to three fish a day that exceeded 20 pounds."

Dick goes on: "About the middle of June school bass became scarce, but the big ones began appearing near the surface where we could see them. These were bright, unspawned fish, fresh from the ocean. Where we were casting blind for them, we were now able to stalk individual fish. On July 9, a huge school of large fish appeared daily. They would lay off the mouth of the slough we were fishing and stay in one spot on slack high tide. These big fish would lay about three or four feet under the surface and appeared as if a cloud was casting a shadow on the water. We hooked fish from this school daily until July 30, when they all disappeared. I left for home on August 4 and my friends at Reedsport told me the big fish did not appear on the surface again until the following year . . . all fly fishing was over after July 30.''

Dick caught the current world-record striper, a giant 40¼ pounder, on 12-pound-test tippet. He says his favorite fly imitates the pogy, a small saltwater smelt that migrates up the river as the stripers come in to spawn. Size seems to be critical: a 3-inch fly produces small fish, but a 4-incher will interest the larger bass. His tie is simple and colorful: tail the same as a Mickey Finn fly, yellow then red then yellow. Variegated Mylar chenille body, and a wing of white bucktail with yellow above it and a little green, topped with blue. Hook size is a number 3XL 3/0.

Dick felt that flies were more effective than plugs. He fishes from a 12-foot skiff, which he admits can be dangerous, but he thinks that the silent approach to these skittish fish is a great advantage.

Not too much is known about the striped bass fishing in this area. Dick and several others are experimenting with fish earlier in the year, and using other tactics. I've never fished the area, but I do know that huge stripers are caught on deep running lures in the spring. It might be the best place of all for fly rodders to take a truly giant striped bass.

The author with several typical striped bass taken while wading in the upper Chesapeake Bay.

Bob Edgely, one of the West Coast's leading saltwater fly fishermen, with a world record striped bass, 32½ pounds.

EAST COAST STRIPED BASS

There are many gaps in our knowledge of the East Coast striped bass fishery, despite the fact that so many people have fished—commercially and for sport—for these fish since the country was settled in the late 1600s.

It is generally agreed that from Maryland north along the coast striped bass move into deep inland waters during the winter months and lie nearly dormant. The main population centers during this time are in the Chesapeake Bay and the Delaware and Hudson rivers. Farther south, in North Carolina, is a separate fishery on a slightly different time schedule.

Striped bass, so the biologists say, do little feeding or swimming when water temperatures are lower than 40 degrees. When the water warms into the high 40s the fish become a little active, and begin to move from deep-water havens into the headwaters of the estuaries to spawn. Immediately after spawning the famished fish head toward the concentrations of bait, which are then usually in the shallows, the first waters to warm in the spring. After feeding well, they begin to fan out. The frigid waters along the coast have kept them hemmed into the deep-water sanctuaries until now. The bass swarm along the coast from North Carolina into Canada, the main bulk of them staying close to shore from Virginia through New England.

Reaching good feeding grounds during the summer, the fish stay in a specific locality for several months, then move southward toward their winter sanctuaries to repeat the whole performance again in the spring.

The striped bass is an anadromous species—it lives most of its life cycle in the salt, but returns to freshwater estuaries to spawn. This is a vital reason why sport fishermen must protect the marshlands and the estuaries from pollution and encroachment by developers. Ruin of these waters means the demise of the striped bass.

North Carolina has a resident population of striped bass, concentrated mostly in the northeastern corner of the state, with some in the Cape Fear delta area. The best inshore fishing occurs in the Roanoke, Croatan, and Albemarle sounds and the rivers draining into them.

During late March and early April stripers begin ascending the rivers of North Carolina to spawn. The major waterways are the Roanoke, Pasquotank, Perquimans, and Little. One of the most popular fishing sites for light-tackle buffs is on the Roanoke River near Weldon, almost 100 miles upriver from the coast. Fishing is good around the mouths of these rivers when the fish move up them to spawn, and when they return in late April and early May.

The fish seem to scatter throughout the sounds, where anglers still can catch them until early June, when fishing tapers off. It begins picking up again in September.

North Carolina has never been thoroughly explored by fly fishermen seeking striped bass. There are plenty of stripers in its waters; and in my opinion it offers one of the great, still unexploited areas for striped bass fly fishing.

The greatest nursery ground in this country for striped bass is the Chesapeake Bay. Chesapeake is roughly 120 miles long, extending from Hampton Roads, Virginia, to the northern border of Maryland. It is a haven for striped bass. The fish are not, on the average, as large here as they are in other waters to the north, but nowhere else can the angler find such vast numbers.

Many freshwater rivers rise in the Appalachian Mountains to the west, sweep through the fertile farmlands of Maryland, and pour into the upper reaches of the Bay. This mingling of fresh and salt water produces the brackish water that furnishes the vital spawning grounds of the striper. Biologists say that much of the stock of fish produced in this bay moves out in the spring, up the coast, scattering into the thousands of bays and rivers all the way to New England. So, the northeastern coastal striper fisherman is really dependent for much of his fishing on what the big bay to the south produces, even granted the significance of the Hudson River system spawning.

Most Chesapeake Bay stripers average from 1 to 5 pounds—and 8-pounder on a fly is regarded as a really fine fish. Above the Bay Bridge, near Baltimore, the fish average even smaller than that. I lived much of my life in Maryland, and I have caught more than a thousand stripers on a fly rod. The biggest I took from the Bay was a 13-pounder on the lower Eastern Shore, near Crisfield. But under good conditions, it is not unusual for an accomplished fly rodder to catch fifty striped bass in a day of hard fishing.

Old-timers in the Bay area swear the best fishing occurs four days before the full moon, and four days afterward. Fly rodders can expect to take fish with some consistency as soon as Bay waters get into the 50s, which is usually in May. Fishing remains pretty good all summer; in August and early September the fishing is almost always most productive early in the morning and late in the afternoon.

October is the favorite month of Bay fly rodders. During this month, and sometimes the first two weeks of November, the number of schools of striped bass feeding on the surface will astound a striper addict from New England. I have seen schools of these 1-to-4-pound fish that range more than four or five acres across, tearing into bait, the tiny white splashes indicating a feeding orgy was on. Many boaters carry field glasses. The Bay is full of gulls, which know, or seem to know, exactly where the stripers will push bait to the surface. We ride constantly on the alert, looking for birds, and when gulls begin diving quickly to the surface, with other gulls from the surrounding area converging on the spot, it's time to move—and fast!

The approach to feeding schools is important. Running into a school of feeding fish will only put them down; you must stay on the outside edge of them. More important for the fly rodder, bring the boat in so you are upwind; it's hell to try to cast a streamer or popper into the stiff breeze. If you gain one thing from this chapter, let it be the following tip; this technique has allowed me to take fish with a fly before a companion could open his spinning reel bail and make a cast.

As you approach the fish, assuming you are right-handed, get in the right rear side of the boat (starboard) and pull off some running line, letting it fall on the boat deck. Hold the running line in your left hand as you cling to the jumping boat. Allow the weight-forward portion of your line to slide through your right hand and the rod guides, until the entire head, leader, and fly are streaming on the surface behind you as you skim across the water toward the fish. Make sure that you approach the fish from the *upwind* side; the best approach is so that the wind is blowing from directly behind (or at least a little behind) and from your left. The instant your companion kills the motor, you can come forward with a strong sweep of the rod hand, coupled with a double haul, and shoot the entire line right into the school. You can do this while he is turning off the switch and reaching for his own rod. It takes a little practice, but if you learn this technique you'll increase your chances of catching a striped bass from a feeding school immeasurably. (Surprisingly, the fly line or the fly rarely tangles when the line streams behind the boat.) This technique works equally well on bluefish, mackerel, tuna, and other surface-feeding fish for which a quick approach and immediate cast are required.

The larger the fish, the larger the fly size must be. The smaller fish, to 10 pounds, feed mainly on smaller baitfish. For general fishing, from 1½ to 3½ inches is the best length of a fly

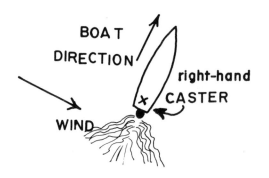

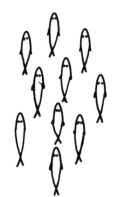

Properly approaching the school of fish, the boatman has the right-hand fly caster in the right stern portion of the boat, allowing the angler to keep his back and forward cast over the water. The boat is placed in front of the fish so the angler can throw the fly far enough ahead of the school that every fish will swim by it.

APPROACHING A SCHOOL OF FISH

for stripers throughout the East Coast fishery. Since stripers are highly selective as to fly length, it pays to carry a number of the same patterns in different lengths.

Popping bugs will take stripers, and standard-size largemouth bass popping bugs are about right for most striper fishing. Hooks from 1/0 to 3/0 on extra-long shanks make the best poppers for conventional fishing for up-to-10-pound bass. Color of bugs does not seem important, but the bug should be easy to lift from the water for the backcast, and it should be capable of creating a good splash when retrieved. Widely used bug materials are balsa wood and cork. Both are good, but both can fall apart if a number of stripers are taken on a single lure—so carry extras. Because the bug works on the surface amid pops, gurgles, and splashes of water, the striper does not get a good look at it, and its length is never as critical as that of the streamers.

My favorite section of the Bay lies near Crisfield, which is near two of the deepest bodies of water in the Bay, Tangier and Pocomoke sounds. Separating these deep waters is a network of channels, sod banks, bars, and islands; as the tide flows from one sound to the other, baitfish are swept along with the current. Often floating grass presents a problem here, which Keel hook flies can solve. Popping bugs work well in this area, too. Crisfield, on the lower Eastern Shore, and other nearby areas have a number of launching ramps for the fast small boats vital to this kind of fishing. Try the Broad Creek area connecting Crisfield with Pocomoke Sound. The Tangier Sound side of Fox Island is where I took my 13-pounder; the Kedges Straits near Smith Island are also fruitful water.

Good feeding areas are around old underwater stumps, along the shores where the banks drop off steeply, and the tidal rips. Throughout Chesapeake Bay, the best fish action seems to come on the change of the tide—with some local exceptions.

A sea robin, a fish frequently taken by fly rodders in the New England area when they fish striped bass with a sinking fly line.

The best striper fishing in the upper Bay occurs along the Eastern Shore from the mouth of the Choptank River north to the Bay Bridge, near Baltimore. Popular Island, not too far from the mouth of the Choptank, can furnish great sport for fly fishermen. During the fall, especially in October, the river mouths on both sides of the bay see a lot of surface action as the school fish plague the baitfish that ride near the surface. By late November the striper fishing falls off radically in the Chesapeake Bay area for fly rodders, who usually turn to duck hunting, for which the Bay is also famous.

There are many public launching sites in the upper Bay on both shores; a list of these can be obtained from the Department of Natural Resources, Tawes State Office Building, Annapolis, Maryland.

The Eastern Shore of Maryland has been famous for its hospitality and good food for two hundred years. It has many fine private homes, motels, and lodges that furnish excellent accommodations for the fly rodder.

May is a great month for striped bass in the shallow estuaries of New Jersey and New York. These waters are the first to be warmed by the sun, and the fish move there for comfort. The fish average from 5 to 10 pounds; a 15-pounder won't raise too many eyebrows. Occasionally some bass will overwinter in Great Bay, Barnegat Bay, and Long Island Sound.

These fish will appear a little ahead of the normal schedule of fish arriving from distant sanctuaries. It takes persistence and patience to catch these early stripers. No well-defined feeding habits have been determined, and anglers have not yet tuned in to exactly where the fish are at a given moment.

Properly rigged boats move swiftly over the waters of the inland bays and creeks, searching for stripers. The helmsman usually stands, to have a better view. He will look for breaking schools of fish, but in the spring these are unlikely, so he will keep a sharp eye turned toward the bottom. If he happens to run over a school of resting stripers, indicated by the silver flashes of the scattered fish, he shuts down immediately, allows things to calm a bit, then begins casting. If he is in an area that he feels is potentially good he will drift with the breeze, blind-casting in hopes of locating the fish.

There are a wrong and a right way to drift and cast for any inshore fish. Most anglers shut down, drift, then cast straight downwind, which allows the longest cast—and usually the shortest retrieve. Remember that the boat is moving downwind, the same direction in which you made the cast. Your boat will drift rapidly toward your fly as you strip. Unless you strip very quickly, you may get little or no action for your fly as the boat overtakes it.

The most efficient method of fly casting from a drifting boat is to cast in a downwind quartering direction. The wind will carry the fly as far as you can cast, but you will be bringing the fly back at an angle to the boat, which prevents the boat from overtaking the fly, and extends your effective retrieve distance.

By June the striped bass have swarmed out of the rivers and are all over the bays, furnishing the angler with even more exciting fishing. The bass will remain until late October.

From Southport all the way up the northern shore of Long Island Sound to Shelter Island you can find good bass fishing starting in very late May and lasting through October. The Penfield Reef Rocks, off the mouth of Ash Creek, and the area near the mouth of the Housatonic River, both the south point near Stratford Light and the entire cove to the northwest of the river mouth, are excellent places to fish throughout the summer for bass.

Night fishing is practiced by experts throughout the entire Jersey-New England area. They wade the shoreline and use a shooting taper or floating line to take many stripers (shooting tapers allow you to search more water, and you know in the dark when your head is just outside the rod tip). Where small streams enter the bays you will often catch both stripers and weakfish. My best luck wading these areas has come with streamers, and while most Yankee anglers use white flies, I prefer all black or dark-colored flies. I have had such poor luck with popping bugs at night that I have given them up entirely, even though stripers take these bugs well in the same areas during the daylight hours.

The many jetties along the shorelines of New Jersey-New York-New England produce excellent fishing—but remember, jetty fishing can be dangerous.

Most people who know how to fish jetties agree that the lee side of the jetties will produce the most fish. Bait and fish congregate in the eddies formed on the lee side. Cast downwind when you can; this allows you to bring the fly back at whatever speed you desire. Frequently, if you allow the fly to hold against the current it will produce a strike. Streamers work better than poppers, although on occasion the surface lures do better.

Don't forget to cast alongside the jetty, for this is natural cover for baitfish. Large boulders often tumble from the jetty into nearby waters; if you see one standing above the surface, cast around it, or to any water that indicates boulders lying on the bottom. Any rip formed by the jetty is always a place to investigate.

Your first fishing trip on a jetty will try your patience, for the running line will catch on rocks as you make your cast. Jim Green, West Coast rod builder and a superb fly caster and fisherman, developed an idea for casting for bonito from California jetties that solves the jetty fly rodder's problem. Jim takes a 7-foot square piece of regular fish netting. I like the 3/8-inch size, but anything up to 3/4-inch works fine. I pinch a sinker on the netting at each corner, add one in the middle of each of the four sides, making a total of 8 sinkers. Carry the net out on the jetty where you intend to cast (it takes up only a little room) and throw it across the rocks where your running line will fall. The breeze will blow through it, so it doesn't act like a kite, and the sinkers will hold the netting over the rocks. The fly line will lie on the netting and come out of it as if it were lying on a lawn. This same netting will also save you when you're fishing in a boat loaded with line-grabbing gear.

Striped bass come well to chum and it's one good way for the fly rodder to catch this fish. This same technique works well on bluefish, too.

The best chum, which is hard to obtain in many areas because of pollution of the estuaries, is grass shrimp. These tiny crustaceans used to be found in almost all bays and sloughs along the East Coast.

Ground clams, when you can get them, are great for chum, but any ground sea fish will make good chum. Anchor 100 feet up current from where you think stripers might be. The up-tide side of a bridge abutment, a rip, or a bar is a prime place; so is the mouth of a canal on outgoing tide. Some of these places are hard to fish with normal methods, but chumming can bring the fish right to boatside.

Striped bass do not require a large quantity of chum, but it must be fed to them steadily. Sometimes the chum is not what attracts the stripers, but it will pull in the tiny baitfish, which in turn attract the stripers. Don't expect to put chum overboard and minutes later have fish appear in the slick behind the boat—though sometimes that does happen. Give a position at least one half hour before you decide to move. Be reluctant to move once you have established a chum slick. If you see baitfish working in the slick, be even more reluctant to relocate.

Other kinds of chum will work. Several companies manufacture a canned bunker chum that works especially well. The half-gallon cans can be carried aboard for months before being used, and when you need one you can punch a few holes in it and hang it overboard.

In an emergency you can use an onion sack or a burlap bag. Put a few rocks in it, and place a few dead fish inside. Pound the fish to a pulp, and anchor the bag near the boat. Occasionally raising the bag and flopping it back against the bottom will stir the chum and pull fish.

You can make your own chum from the fish you catch. Take the insides, heads, and skins and grind them; then freeze them in half-gallon packer cartons. Wrapped in newspapers, this chum can be carried aboard a small boat for several hours before it will start to thaw. It takes about ninety minutes for a 10-pound bag of chum to thaw in the water during the summer season. You can buy commercial chum bags, but an onion sack or a piece of netting will serve as well. I wash the chum bag by letting it hang outside the boat, inverted, on the return trip home—the bag is scoured clean by the time I get to the dock.

One basic fly-fishing outfit will serve for your striped bass fishing, from the Carolinas to New England. Almost ever-present breezes require that you use a line from size 8 to size 10. The rods matched to these lines are a little stout for landing smaller fish, but they're necessary to deliver the fly into the wind. The wader might want a 9 or 9½ foot fly rod, since this will aid in keeping his backcast from striking the water; the boatman might prefer one of 8½ to 9 feet.

Striped bass are not known for long runs, so you don't need the large-capacity, expensive reels associated with tarpon or sailfish. The Pflueger Medalist 1495½ or 1498, Scientific Anglers' System 9 or 10 reel, or the Valentine Model 375 are all excellent striped bass reels. Twenty-pound Dacron or Micron makes perfect backing.

Leaders can be tapered, and the tippet need not be heavier than 10- or 12-pound test.

Flies for striper fishing along the coast, for fish under 10 pounds, need not be longer than 3½ inches. The most popular patterns are dressed on 1/0 to 3/0 hooks. In addition to a few strands of Mylar, the fly generally has a two-color wing, with the lighter color on the bottom, and dark green, blue, or brown on top, to resemble one of the many small baitfish stripers feed on.

There are other areas on the East Coast and the Gulf of Mexico that hold striped bass, the best known being the St. John River drainage in Florida, but here stripers are much fewer or have much less importance than the stocks from North Carolina through New England, where the striped bass reigns as the king of fishes.

BLUEFISH

Bluefish are found throughout much of the world, and in this country from the Gulf of Mexico to Cape Cod. During the winter months some bluefish are taken in the Gulf and along the extreme southern end of Florida's east coast. The fish migrate up the coast past Georgia and the Carolinas in March and April; the Chesapeake Bay begins receiving fish in late April or early May. When the warmer weather comes the fish move past New Jersey, and usually by early June a few are being taken by fly fishermen in New England. All the way up the coast groups of bluefish will break away from the main migrating schools and remain in a relatively local area throughout the summer.

During this period they may be located anywhere from the small bays and mouths of tidal creeks to many, many miles offshore. The farther you get from shore the larger the fish seem to be. Jeff Dane caught a world record on a fly miles at sea off Norfolk, Virginia—the fish weighed 17 pounds 7 ounces. Fish caught near shore and in the estuaries are usually small, a 5-pounder being considered a good one.

By late October the bluefish begin pouring down the coast toward warmer waters. Bluefish can be enormously abundant one season and almost nonexistent the next; what causes this cyclic pattern is still to be determined.

No fish feeds more voraciously than the bluefish. There are many tales of bluefish eating until they can consume no more, then disgorging everything, only to start killing and eating again. Their teeth are especially dangerous; not only the point but both sides of the tooth are like a razor blade.

Fishing for bluefish with a fly rod is done in the same manner as fishing for striped bass. The same flies, outfits, and techniques are used, except for the shock leader. You'll get more strikes if you use a shock leader of 50- or 60-pound test monofilament in front of the fly, although you stand the chance of losing an occasional fish. If you do use wire, a short section, no more than 4 inches, will catch more fish than a longer length of wire. Number 2 or 3 solid trolling wire is better than nylon-coated braided wire, for bluefish tend to strip much of the nylon from the braided wire so that it hangs in tatters, resulting in refusals by the fish.

If you find bluefish splashing into bait on the surface you'll note that they seem to be more densely packed in the school than stripers, and the baitfish seem to be even more frantic in

Dick Lohr is very careful not to get near the sharp teeth of the bluefish he has just taken on a fly.

their effort to escape these voracious fishes. If you move quickly up to schools of breaking blue-fish and make quick casts, floating lines are best suited for the work. But if you are actually searching for bluefish, or working in a chum line, a sinking line will produce more bluefish. And bluefish can be chummed as well as any inshore species. Menhaden or the canned bunker chum mentioned earlier are highly effective.

Paul Kukonen knows a bay in Rhode Island that fills up with bluefish in September. He made a 16-mm film of 4- to 7-pound blues herding menhaden against the shoreline, then slashing into them. All of this is going on in water only a few feet deep. Paul's film vividly shows the schools of fish eagerly taking flies; it's certainly one of the most exciting films of inshore saltwater fly fishing I've ever seen.

SHAD

Winter is a long, dreary period for the angler, made livable only by reading good books, tying flies in anticipation, and talking about the sport with cronies. Then, along both coasts, the first flowers of spring herald the arrival of the shad. The shad is not the biggest, toughest, or wisest fish that swims—but the shad will take a fly, and the hickory shad performs like a tiny tarpon when hooked. If for no other reason than that it means the beginning of another fishing season, the shad is a welcome visitor to anglers on both coasts.

Shad are anadromous; they live most of their life in the sea, moving into the freshwater rivers to spawn during the early spring. Their normal diet includes small baitfish, but biologists claim that during the spawning period shad do not eat. Yet they will take flies; perhaps they are reminded of the small baitfish they have eaten so often.

The American shad is the larger of the two species that fly fishermen concern themselves with. (A number of other kinds of shad are unimportant to the fly rodder.) The average size of an American shad will run from 1½ to 8 pounds; the record is over 12 pounds. On the East Coast the heaviest concentrations occur from the lower Chesapeake Bay up the coast through New England. The American shad (often called the white shad) was introduced to the West Coast by Seth Green in 1871. Fish from the Hudson River drainage were placed in the Sacramento River. Within a decade the fish had spread as far north as the Frazier River in British Columbia. On the West Coast today, the major American shad centers are the watersheds of the San Francisco Bay and San Joaquin and Sacramento rivers. They are also abundant in the American, Russian, and Feather rivers.

American shad prefer to spawn in the larger river systems. They concentrate at the head and tail of large pools. Sometimes they're so thick that the water seems solid with their silver bodies. Most of the time they stay close to the bottom.

Boyd Pfeiffer with a stringer of hickory shad, taken from Octoraro Creek, in Maryland.

The other important species of shad for fly fishermen is the hickory shad, a smaller version of the American. The hickory, called a jumping jack in the mid-Atlantic area, comes out of the water the instant a hook is impaled in its mouth. It fights well for its size, and reminds many fishermen of a tiny tarpon, to which it is related. A large hickory is 3 pounds, and a very few reach 5 pounds. Hickories are caught all along the East Coast, but are less abundant than the American shad north of the Chesapeake Bay area.

Both species of shad take flies readily, and because you'll frequently fish for them in fast water (especially the American shad) you'll need flies that sink well. When fishing for hickories in smaller tributaries, where they prefer to spawn, you'll find a sinking fly less helpful.

It's important to remember that the shad has a "papery" mouth of clear, fragile tissue, and so you must play it gently. Many shad have been lost because the angler "horsed" the fish along, or tried to lift it from the water by grasping the leader.

The most desirable water temperatures for shad are from 55 to 63 degrees; this is when they prefer to spawn. When temperatures rise above 66 or 67, shad will leave.

Because there are so many exotic and more publicized species of fish in Florida waters, few fishermen realize that there is a major shad fishery in the St. Johns River drainage. Almost any portion of the St. Johns River from Lake Monroe and Puzzle Lake south to Lake Poinsett holds shad in February and March, when the fish come up this huge river drainage to spawn. The major spawning occurs from Sanford to Lake Poinsett. The fish average 2 to 5 pounds, occasionally more. The shad like to collect in the deep-water bends on the river.

Shad fishing peaks in late February, but continues until late March, when the shad leave the system for the open ocean.

Standard shad flies, to be described later, are all effective. However, the river is so large in many areas that many fly fishermen will troll with small spoons on spinning rigs to locate the shad. Once the school is discovered the boat is anchored and the angler uses fast-sinking fly lines to present his tiny streamers to the fish. The closer the fly is worked to the bottom—almost a universal rule for shad fly fishing—the more strikes are forthcoming.

In North Carolina the hickory shad run precedes the American shad by a week or two. The hickories begin running up the Neuse, Tar, and Cape Fear river systems in early March, followed shortly after that by the large American shad. While there are many shad in these river systems, fly fishing for them has not yet caught on. The record shad taken in North Carolina is 5½ pounds.

Maryland has good fishing for both species, although the major number of fly fishermen concentrate on the hickory. They move up the Susquehanna River until they are blocked by the Conowingo Dam, then into Deer and Octoraro creeks. Good fishing also is had farther down the bay at Red Bridges. Octoraro Creek is a paradise during the week for the fly fisherman. Very narrow, and rather shallow, the small creek jams full of hickories about the time the dogwood blooms, which is about April 15. Standing belly-deep in the cold water, you can drift your small fly down to the fish, usually lying at the tail of the pool. Frequently an angler will take 20 or 30 fish in a day with a System 6 or 7 trout outfit. Leaders can be light—4 to 6 pounds in test.

Irv Swope, one of the regulars who fish this stream, has designed a nonfouling fly that really takes these shad. He relies heavily on fluorescent colors in his materials, and the shad seem to approve. The fly he uses is shown among those in Chapter 6.

Joe Zimmer, another avid shad fisherman, has developed the other most popular style of fly used by those who fish the creek frequently. Joe uses the same hook as Irv (3XL8) but he prefers to make a chenille body (the color doesn't seem important), and he makes a single wing of calf tail that is as long as the hook. Both patterns take fish with regularity, and I've found them successful also on other small streams.

However, these small flies are not as effective for the American shad, which prefers to stay in the larger rivers, where the water is deep and swift. In Maryland, for example, I have taken the larger American shad in the large pool on the west side of the Susquehanna River immediately below the dam, with a sinking fly line and a bright silver-body, white-wing fly, dressed on a number 2 hook. The smaller flies that are so good in the little tributaries will not get down well enough to reach the larger Americans lying near the bottom.

The Delaware River in New York has some excellent shad fishing and during Colonial days shad was a major source of food there. It was caught and eaten fresh, or sliced in half and cured in salt, which allowed the pioneers to store it indefinitely. Pollution and damming have reduced the shad fishery on the Delaware, but it's still viable for the fly rodder.

In New England about the time the lilac blooms, late May and most of June, the Connecticut River has to rank as one of the finest of all shad fishing streams. Any local fly-fishing shop can give you the latest specific information on where to fish in the area.

In California the water warms in early April and the shad swarm into the Russian, Sacramento, Klamath, American, Feather, Yuba, Trinity, and San Joaquin rivers by the thousands. Just outside and upstream from the city limits of Sacramento, on the American River, is a fly rodders' hot spot in early and mid-June.

Oregon shad fishing is also excellent; the Coos Bay area can be great. Upriver from the public landing on the North Fork is a favorite fishing area; slack tide generally brings the first strikes. In the Roseburg area the shad will take flies from mid-May through mid-June; the Umpqua River, just below Roseburg, is especially good. The giant Columbia River, separating Washington and Oregon, probably holds more shad than any other western river. It's so big, however, that you need a local guide to help you locate the proper places to fish.

Mackerel, a good inshore fish that prefers a fast stripping retrieve, and bright flashy flies from two a half to four inches in length. Use 40- to 60-pound monofilament or light wire for a shock leader.

Shad fishing is done with the same basic technique everywhere. In the smaller streams the flies like those Zimmer and Swope use work exceptionally well. In larger rivers, especially when trying for the American shad, you'll need patterns that are bright, sink well, and are dressed on number 4, 2, or even 1 hooks. Sometimes anglers wrap fuse wire or copper wire around the hook to make it sink quicker. Lead-core shooting heads work especially well in heavy water, although they seem to have caught on with anglers only along the West Coast.

Mylar added to the fly gives off reflective flashes that help you keep track of your fly, as well as induce the shad to strike. Fluorescent materials, both for bodies and wings, have become increasingly popular.

The migrating fish seem to follow current lines, and are frequently taken on the outside of bends. But once they have settled into a pool they seem to prefer the head and tail, with the lower portion the most heavily populated.

A dead drift with a sinking line is my favorite method of presenting the fly. Seldom does an erratic or rapid retrieve bring strikes. Few anglers do it, but adding a dropper fly often produces additional strikes, especially if you're blind fishing.

Shad seem to move the most on an incoming tide, but to strike more readily during slack tide periods.

BONITO

One of the fastest fish that swims is the bonito. There are three species of this fish: Atlantic, Pacific, and striped. The Atlantic bonito occurs only along our Atlantic coast, and the Pacific only from Baja north to British Columbia.

Bonito roam the green waters close to land but a little offshore. In Florida they are most frequently found a mile or two from the beach. They feed on small baitfish, and once you have seen a bonito splash as it feeds on the surface, you'll always be able to detect it.

On the East Coast when a school is sighted and the angler rushes to the area, much as he would for striped bass or bluefish, he casts ahead of the fish, not where they are actively feeding. Small flies, from 2½ to 4 inches, are best; bonito rarely take a fly larger than 4 inches. Polar-bear wing with Mylar strips in it, and a bare hook or body of white chenille, is the favorite pattern.

On the West Coast bonito are fished for a little differently, although free-roaming schools near the beaches can be as successfully fished for as on the East Coast. In Monterey Bay during September, when the Japanese Current swings close to shore, a large run of bonito can be expected. Surface-feeding schools are easily seen. Bonito can be in a local area for days, and then suddenly disappear. It's usually a waste of time to blind-fish for them. Surface activity is, most frequently, just after daybreak.

But the real bonito fun for West Coast fly rodders is at Redondo Beach in the vicinity of King's Harbor, in southern California. The bonitos will average 3 to 6 pounds; some will top even that weight by a pound or two. The best fishing occurs when other fishing is nearly dead—in February—although bonito are in the harbor all winter.

The fishing is done in the harbor, which is surrounded by solid-rock jetty walls. The warm-water discharge from the electrical generating plant seems to attract the fish, but probably just as important is that anchovies are constantly escaping from the live-bait receivers located in the center of the harbor. For that reason, many anglers try to cast as close to the receivers as possible. The mouth of the hot-water exit is another choice location.

Chumming with live anchovies is very effective, and you can rent a bait sled right in the harbor. White bucktail, polar bear, and white marabou seem to be the preferred wing materials. Mylar is recommended on any pattern you use, and the flies should not be much longer than 3½ inches; smaller is even better.

When the fish are on the surface a floating line will work. But most of the time a sinking line, even a lead-core shooting taper, is recommended. The harbor is 50 feet deep, and fish are taken all the way to the bottom.

The proper retrieve for bonitos is a matter of controversy. Many anglers feel that the fastest retrieve possible is the best; some will make a cast, position the rod and reel between their lower legs, and, bending over, retrieve as fast as possible by bringing the fly line in hand over hand. When a strike occurs they sometimes break the leader, but this method really makes a fly zip through the waters. I've found that sometimes no retrieve at all, or a very slow one, is most effective; so it pays to experiment on bonito.

Bonito are strong, and a run of 100 yards can be expected. Use a light drag with a reel loaded with plenty of line and you'll have a sensational time fishing these very strong, fast fish.

SPOTTED SEA TROUT AND WEAKFISH

The spotted sea trout, according to a state survey, is the most popular fish among Florida fishermen. It is abundant on the grass flats along the east coast and all the way up the Gulf of Mexico side to Texas; New York marks its northern boundary.

Often confused with the sea trout is the weakfish, which looks somewhat like it. The largest populations of weakfish are located from the Chesapeake to Peconic Bay, Long Island.

The spotted sea trout, which are larger on the average than weakfish, live almost entirely on grass flats of inshore waters. Here they feed on shrimp, pinfish, small mullet, menhaden, and other little fishes.

The weakfish have a more varied diet, eating almost anything small enough to ingest. Included in a long list are sand launce, crabs, mollusks, shrimp, and sea worms. Weakfish will live over almost any type of bottom, from mud flats to sandbars.

Both species have a delicate mouth; in fact, the weakfish gets its name because its mouth is so fragile. The angler must set the hook lightly on these two species, and play the fish gently. Both species splash about on the surface but fight poorly.

Spotted trout remain in their local waters almost all year, depending upon water temperatures. Real trophy spotted sea trout are taken in the Cocoa–Cape Canaveral area of the east coast of Florida, from the Banana and Indian rivers. For years anglers in this area have dominated the *Field & Stream* contest with their catches, which are called "gator trout." In most areas 5-pound spotted sea trout will draw sighs of admiration, but here it takes a 9-pounder to bring cameras out of the regulars' bags.

Spotted sea trout fishing is excellent in the thousands of shallow, grass-covered bays from the tip of Florida into Texas. The best technique for the fly fisherman is to use a popping cork and spinning rig with bait to locate the fish. The popping cork sits on the water; dangling several feet below it is a piece of shrimp impaled on a 1/0 hook. A yank on the rod brings a gulping sound from the suddenly immersed popper. Any trout in the area come rushing over to see what all the racket is about and inhale the shrimp. Once the school of fish is located—and they almost always travel in schools—the fly rodder can break out his tackle and begin casting. It's a good idea to carry a plastic bottle with a cap on it, to which are attached a long string and a

Doug Swisher, of freshwater trout fishing fame, shows how to catch a nice spotted sea trout. Fly used was a red and yellow Lefty's Deceiver.

weight. When you have caught several fish from a drifting boat, drop the bottle overboard: this will act as a buoy, marking the whereabouts of the school. Fish around the bottle until no more strikes are forthcoming, then retrieve your bottle and continue your drift.

Weakfish are perhaps most abundant in Chesapeake Bay, but they rarely move in numbers above the mouth of the Choptank River. The fish arrive in the Bay in late May and stay until cold weather runs them out.

Another species of trout important in the North Carolina waters, and fished in the same manner as the spotted sea trout and weakfish, is the gray trout; it runs much smaller, on the average, than the other two species.

The three varieties of fish are sought with the same basic fly-rod technique. All three prefer shallow bays near the coast, and rarely leave these areas unless cold weather drives them to deep water.

I have not heard of a spotted sea trout's being caught on a fly at night. But weakfish will readily strike a streamer after dark. All three species react well to ground-fish chum. Anchor in an area you feel will be fruitful, and set up a chum line; weakfish and trout are not alarmed by a boat and will come up the chum line to within a few yards of the boat.

The "papery" mouth of the trout and weakfish requires a gentle strike and fight, and the use of a landing net.

Streamer flies are the most effective, for all three species. All-yellow, or red and yellow, is the universal selection of top fly rodders. All-white and red and white are second choices. All the flies include Mylar strips in the wing. Hook sizes range from 2 to 1/0.

One of my favorite methods of fishing for spotted sea trout is to locate a shallow bay with a grassy bottom, and drift across it. I cast a fly dressed on a Keel hook on a fast-sinking line, allowing the fly to bomb to the bottom. I retrieve the fly very slowly as the boat drifts. Because the Keel fly rarely tangles, I like to crawl the fly right in among the grass stems. If I catch a trout I'll anchor and cast in a circle around the boat, making sure the fly gets all the way to the bottom each time.

Keel flies are very effective for weakfish, too, and a godsend in fishing over any rough bottom, where conventional hooks would constantly foul.

Spotted sea trout will readily take a popping bug—a great thrill to see—but a streamer is far more effective.

Sometimes barracudas grow large inshore, like this one held by the author. A 6-pound barjack had taken the fly, when suddenly this giant cuda took both fly and barjack. Although the fish was landed on 10-pound test leader, because the barracuda actually took the barjack instead of an artificial fly, it was not eligible for a record.

CHANNEL BASS (RED DRUM OR REDFISH)

The channel bass is one of the most popular game fishes among coastal fishermen. It's caught from New Jersey down the eastern coast and around Florida, all the way up the Gulf of Mexico into Texas. In Florida and the Gulf states a channel bass will average from 2 to 10 pounds, with an occasional 12- or 14-pounder caught. The all-time fly record for the Metropolitan Miami Fishing Tournament is a 25½-pounder caught by J. T. Littleton, but that size fish wouldn't raise an eyebrow among the bait- and plug-casting fraternity along the coast of Virginia and North Carolina.

North Carolina has the most consistently good channel bass fishing of any state. Anglers fish both from the beaches and from boats working the nearby offshore waters. A 90-pounder is the current record for the state.

Most channel bass in North Carolina are caught just off the beaches in water a little too deep for fly rodding. Normal procedure is for the angler to cast a large hunk of dead bait as far as he can, and allow it to soak on the bottom until a hungry channel bass locates it. Further complicating the fly caster's problem, channel bass feed much better at night.

The best technique for the fly caster who wants to take a large channel bass is sight-hunting, as practiced by Florida charter skippers. Sighting from a tower on the boat, or working from a flying bridge, the skippers slowly cruise the waters to locate schools of channel bass, frequently numbering 500—or even 1000—fish of 40 or more pounds. The school will appear as a bronze-colored mass, moving very slowly just under the surface. They move through in late April and May and again in October and November.

You need a precise combination of conditions to fish in this manner. The water, usually a little murky, must be rather clear if you are to see the fish. Calm seas are a must, and bright sunlight should prevail.

The schools are difficult to approach, especially if other anglers have been harassing them lately. The art, as practiced now, is to use a 9- or 10-foot surf stick and a lure that can be thrown 100 yards. The boat is quietly brought that close to the fish and the long cast is made. If skippers knew the fly casters' limitations, they could possibly put them into position to get a cast into the fish—and it would almost certainly be a world record for the angler who landed one of these huge channel bass.

Another type of sight-hunting is being perfected by some pioneer anglers in North Carolina. In the Hatteras and Ocracoke areas some pilots, flying very slow-moving aircraft, hover aloft to locate large schools, then direct fishermen to the fish. This has been a practice for several years over the normally murky summer waters of Pamlico Sound, where these fish spend much of their time.

In Virginia, Maryland, and New Jersey coastal waters the big channel bass feed in the turbulent, murky surf, which offers the fly fisherman little chance at them. I'm certain that all the world records for channel bass will come from North Carolina waters as soon as fly rodders perfect techniques for taking this grand fish.

Channel bass are commonly called redfish in Florida, where they are found, in limited numbers, along the northern coast. But Florida Bay, especially the northeastern half, offers the finest channel bass fishing of all to the fly rodder. The very clear waters average less than 3 feet in depth, and the muddy bottom, carpeted with a dense growth of grass, is unbelievably rich in aquatic foods. This area is generally regarded as the main nursery grounds for most of the channel bass caught along the Atlantic Coast.

The water here is rich in shrimp, crabs, small pinfish, and other foods that redfish appreciate. Most of upper Florida Bay is shallow; the flats have less than 18 inches of water on them at high tide, and are dry at spring low tides. The strategy here is sight-fishing. Shallow draft boats, either light aluminum or fiber-glass, are poled across the flats, while the anglers look for swimming fish. The channel bass are easy to see. Their copper-red bodies with the black spot on the tail show well against the dark green or brown grassy bottom. Even easier to see are the tails of the fish when they stand on their heads and try to worry a crab or shrimp from the grass below. The cherry-red tails wave back and forth—on a calm day you can see a tailing channel bass more than 100 yards away.

Larry Kreh hefts a nice fly-caught channel bass. Note the black spot on the tail.

Channel bass have extremely poor eyesight, and the fly rodder must position his fly close enough for them to see it, but not so close that it will alarm the fish. This is best accomplished by throwing a fly 6 to 10 feet ahead of the fish, then retrieving it so that the path of the fly and the fish will intersect. Channel bass will take almost any color fly, but a combination of orange and red, or red and white, seems best. Both of these patterns are also easy for the angler to see, so he too can easily keep track of the fly's course as it approaches the fish.

In Florida Bay you can see channel bass swimming right in the grass. At low tide they will often be swimming in just 6 inches of water. Conventional flies, however, work poorly, because they are constantly entangled in the grassy bottom. Two underwater patterns have been developed that work exceptionally well. The Keel hook is used for one tie, with usually just a large amount of fluffy marabou, red, white, yellow, or orange, tied to the hook, and a few strips of Mylar added for flash. It's a simple fly, but you can drag it through the grass with only a rare hang-up or two.

The other fly is called a hackle streamer. This fly is tied on a conventional hook, usually 3 XL in length. Attached to the tail are 6 to 8 saddle hackles; then the full length of the hook shank is wound with as many saddle hackles as can be tied on it. The whole thing resembles a multilegged caterpillar with a supple saddle-hackle tail.

It works something like a dry fly, in that the palmer-wound hackles along the hook shank support the fly so well that it simply does not sink far below the surface. In fact, if several false casts are made, the angler frequently has to jerk the fly to get it to drop below the surface. Once underwater the fly sits almost suspended, with the hackles on the shank flexing back and forth and the saddle feathers at the rear working in a manner that excites any channel bass that sees it. The fly, because of its buoyancy, can be manipulated along in inches of water, and the palmer-wound hackles usually brush the fly away from most grass, making it relatively weed-proof.

A popping bug works wonders at times, and scares hell out of the fish on other occasions. It should be tested each day to see what the fish's reaction will be. Channel bass on the flats will pounce on a popper most of the time; color seems unimportant. The trick is to cast 4 to 6 feet away from the fish, then make soft popping sounds instead of loud splashings, to attract the fish.

The redfish is not known for its fighting ability. The fish will make short determined runs, then stand on its head and try to rub the fly out against the bottom. Shock leaders of 15- to 30-pound test are frequently used because of this grubbing trick, but most of the time the channel bass can be taken on a straight leader tippet.

Florida Bay channel bass fishing is hot from late April through October, and many redfish remain on the flats all year. They depart when a cold spell hits, and the water drops into the 50s, but return again as soon as waters warm.

Farther up the coast and along the shore of Louisiana there are many shallow oyster bars and flats that hold large numbers of channel bass. When waters are clear and the winds abate, the fly rodder can have excellent fishing. The Texas coast has miles of shallow flats, somewhat similar to those of upper Florida Bay. Here anglers skim over the water in shallow draft boats, and fish much the way they do in Florida. The flats are grass-covered, and the fish, which average a little larger than they do in Florida, can be seen both swimming and tailing. One good spot is the flats in the Laguna Madre area of south Texas. The fish are there all summer, but April and May are the choice months.

A lot of light-tackle spinning specialists in Texas have been fishing these channel bass for years, but fly rodders have not scrambled yet to some of the finest fishing in Texas. Certainly, as word spreads, more will be seeking this husky fish with a fly rod.

Redfish, or channel bass, can be handled easily like this. But the gill rakers inside the covers are raspy and cut deeply. Stay away from them.

BONEFISH

Most bonefish must die from ulcers. They feed and swim in a constant state of alarm. Bonefish do *not* have lockjaw, super-sensitive noses, or any sort of radar that can pick up an enemy angler a half mile away, although all of these possibilities may seem reasonable to a bonefisherman at some time during his career.

Bonefish are scattered throughout much of the world, but as far as fly fishermen are concerned, they're found only in Central America, the Caribbean, and the Florida Keys. In all other areas bonefish feed in deep water, inaccessible to fly fishermen.

I've fished most of the places where bonefish can be caught, and nowhere have I seen them so abundant as in the water around the Turneffe Islands, off the coast of Belize (formerly British Honduras).

A bonefish looking for food. Note the turtle grass, and how large the eye is on a bonefish.

I remember my first trip there with Bob Stearns. Bob and I had left the comfortable lodge at Keller's Caribbean Sports in Belize and spent a lazy four hours on a 44-foot houseboat cruising from the mainland to the Turneffe Islands. We towed two 18-foot skiffs behind the boat. On arriving we got into the skiffs and Phillip Andrewin, our guide, poled us to what looked to be the richest bottom growth I've ever seen on a bonefish flat. Suddenly Phillip yelled, "Bonefish! Quick, get out and wade to them!"

Bob and I could certainly be considered experienced bonefishermen, and yet at first we didn't see the fish that Phillip was so desperately trying to show us. Then, "My God, Bob, there must be a thousand of them," I yelled as we both jumped over the side, dragging fly line behind us.

The fish were pushing a 6-inch wake in front of them as they advanced. Second estimates placed the school at maybe 200—a lot of fish any way you think about it.

Bob and I each took a fish on a Keel hook fly as they surged forward. The fish were small by stateside standards, weighing maybe 4 pounds. During our five-day stay we saw more than 2,000 bonefish a day; I once caught four and hooked another while standing in one spot. These fish average 4 pounds, but Vic Dunaway took a 9-pounder there, and a 12-pounder has been caught. Even though larger fish are rare, because there are so many fish here, Turneffe is probably the best place in the world for the fly rodder to learn how to catch bonefish.

Yucatan Peninsula is almost as good, and three spots in the Bahamas hold tremendous numbers of bonefish: Ambergris Cay, the south end of Exuma, and the middle bight area of Andros Cay.

These are the stout crushers on the inside of the bonefish's mouth. The bonefish can smash a crab to pulp with one snap.

In the Florida Keys the best bonefishing occurs in Biscayne Bay, Key Largo, and the Islamorada area. Good bonefishing continues down the Keys through Marathon, past which it slowly tapers off. It's peculiar that the flats in the Key West area, which would appear to be excellent bonefish territory, have very few bones, but teem with the wily permit.

Three locations in the world consistently produce the largest fly-caught bonefish. In late January huge bonefish, full of milt and roe, move onto the flats on the east side of Bimini in the Bahamas. These fish will remain there until sometime in late March or early April. The current world-record bonefish (caught on spinning tackle) was taken there by Jerry Lavenstein, on February 25, 1972; it weighed a whopping 16 pounds. Shell Key, on the Florida Bay side of Islamorada, is another hot spot for trophy bonefish. Bart Foth, one of the world's most successful fly-rod bonefishermen, annually wins the coveted bonefish trophy in the giant Metropolitan Miami Fishing Tournament. He holds the 39-year all-time record for the tournament with a bonefish he took on a fly that weighed 13 pounds and 3 ounces. Perhaps 90 percent of Foth's trophy bonefish came off the small flats around Shell Key. Nearby Aresnicker Keys are also excellent places to look for giant bonefish.

In April and May giant spawning bonefish invade the flats of Biscayne Bay. Captain Bill Curtis, who has perhaps the finest record of all the bonefish guides who take on fly rodders, works the flats of Biscayne Bay, within sight of the skyscrapers of downtown Miami. It's not unusual for one of his clients to catch six or more bonefish with a fly in a single day, and they constantly catch bonefish from 8 to 12 pounds.

Fish caught in Biscayne Bay will range in weight from 7 to 9 pounds, trophy size in other areas. If I could not get to Bimini, and I was interested in catching a world record, or at least a trophy, on a fly, I'd fish in Biscayne Bay. It has produced more record and outsized fish than any other body of water in the world. No one seems sure why this is so. The fish have had to accommodate water-skiers, fast-traveling pleasure boats, and other invaders, but they have adjusted admirably well.

The front end of a bonefish; note the large eye and small mouth—two reasons for approaching the fish cautiously and presenting a small fly.

As with other kinds of angling, knowing the strong and weak points of the bonefish, and using this knowledge to advantage, is the road to success. The bonefish is a tough quarry; it's hard to deceive, and gives a good account of itself once it is hooked.

There's no substitute for learning how to bonefish with a guide or angler experienced at the art. Watch him, listen to everything he says, question him constantly about his techniques, and learn all you can about the habits of the bonefish. Just one day with a guide or good bone-fisherman is worth a year of study on your own.

Bonefish are very sensitive to water temperatures; you'll see none on a flat if waters are cooler than 68 degrees. At 70 degrees a few fish will be around, but they'll be reluctant to strike, even at a tasty shrimp. Once the temperature rises above 73, however, the fish become very active.

In Florida during July, August, and September bonefish feed at dawn for an hour or two, and very late in the evening—few fish are caught during the heat of the day. Yet in Mexico, Cuba, and the Central American waters the fish feed throughout the day, regardless of the time of year.

Bonefish travel in schools, in singles, and often in a group of two or three fish; the extra-large fish are almost always loners. Even if there are several on a flat, they seem to prefer being alone. Single bonefish are much more difficult to approach, and less likely to strike a fly. School fish are apparently more competitive in their feeding habits, and accept a fly more readily.

Many people have caught bonefish on bare, white sand, but in these cases the fish are usually crossing the sandy area either to get to a food source or to return to their sanctuary in deeper waters. When over light sand the fish are almost always more easily frightened, so the fly must be cast much farther ahead than normal. Dark flies seem to work better on sand than do light-colored patterns.

Bonefish are bottom feeders; their mouth is located on the lower portion of the head, so they can easily suck up food. One scientist wrote a description of a bonefish that, while accurate, was certainly unflattering: "The bonefish has an elongated, torpedo-shaped body with a slender head and a small inferior mouth."

Bonefish feed on crabs, shrimp, small worms, and small minnows found on the flats. Few good bonefish flats are devoid of turtle grass. This plant resembles lawn grass, except that the stems are about 3/8 inch wide, from a foot to 18 inches long, and dark green. Turtle grass is breeding ground for small sea life, vital in the food chain. I can't think of a single good bonefish flat that does not have at least sprinklings of turtle grass.

Some flats are "hard"—that is, firm enough to wade; others have a mushy bottom. Bonefish feed on both types, but if you prefer to wade it's a good idea to select a hard flat.

It's easier to spot a bonefish on flats that are light in color. Some of the best bonefish flats, however, are completely carpeted in turtle grass, and the dark bottom makes it very difficult for all but the most expert to see the fish. Bonefish apparently can adjust their coloration somewhat to suit the bottom they feed upon. Bones that feed regularly over dark turtle grass will be dark in color, those that live over light sand or a bright bottom have few vertical markings and are almost pure in color. In fact, Al Pflueger, a marine taxidermist, always ascertains where a trophy bonefish was caught, and then colors it accordingly.

Polarizing glasses are a must when looking for bonefish. The tint preferred by Florida Keys guides and anglers is brown, which offers a functional compromise between bright and dark days. Bright yellow glasses are wonderful on dark days, for they build contrast and so actually appear to brighten the scene. However, these same glasses can cause headaches if the day is very bright. Smoke-colored glasses work well on hazy days. The inexpensive polarizing glasses found on most drugstore counters will work for a limited amount of time, but the soft lenses scratch easily and you must take extreme care to keep them in good condition. Most old-timers have purchased glasses that have a polarizing section sandwiched between two pieces of hard-to-scratch optical glass, and such glasses will last a lifetime; I have one pair that has gone through two pairs of frames and is still usable.

If the angler is being poled across the flats, the boatman should be careful about placing the foot of the pole on the bottom. Many bonefish have flushed when the boatman clanked the pole against the hard coral.

Even the type of clothing you wear when bonefishing is important. Bright white or yellow reflects light that will frequently alarm the fish. If the bonefish follows the fly toward the boat you should crouch low, to avoid casting a high silhouette that will warn the fish. Should bonefish suddenly appear close to the boat, and not have detected you, make all your casting motions at a slow pace. A quick drop to the deck or a fast rod movement will surely flush the fish.

The water depth determines a great deal about how you should look for a fish. If the water is very shallow, less than a foot deep, look at the *surface*, not at the bottom. In such shallow water the bonefish's progress can be detected by the dorsal or tail fin above the surface, or by the distinct wake it makes as it moves across the flat. Bonefish will often stand on their head and jet a stream of water at the bottom to dislodge a crab or other morsel. The whole tail will protrude above the surface, one of the most exciting sights in light-tackle fishing. If you miss the tail exposed above the surface, you'll see a telltale puff of mud made by the bonefish's water-jet.

If the water on the flat is more than a foot deep you should be looking at the *bottom*, not at the surface. Underwater, bonefish resemble a light gray shadow. Their course is never steady; they'll move a few yards in one direction, then suddenly dart off to the side. One of the greatest problems in presenting a fly to a bonefish is that often, about the time you have decided where the fish is going and made a cast, the fish will bolt off in another direction, and a hasty backcast and another shot must be made.

A school of bonefish traveling in a foot or more of water will cause ripples (called nervous water) that are at variance with the surrounding surface. This condition is difficult to describe, but once you have seen it, you'll recognize and be alerted for it in the future. Bonefish moving in a school also produce distinct wakes, even in water three feet deep. Look for ripples moving *against* the wind and wave pattern, a sure tip-off that fish are below.

Watch for stingrays working on the flats. Often permit and bonefish will track alongside the slower moving ray, which is scouring the bottom, flushing food in its path. If a crab or shrimp darts away from the ray the swifter bonefish simply slip in and grab it before the ray has a chance.

Joe Brooks taught me another trick in looking for bonefish. We were fishing with Captain Jack Brothers near Key Largo. Jack cut the motor well away from the flat and poled us up in the clear, shallow water. Joe offered me the casting platform, but I refused and insisted that he take the first try at a fish. Joe stepped up, stripped line, made a false cast, and stripped the line back onto the deck. He held the fly in his left hand and looked over the flat. Nothing was said for perhaps ten minutes; only the water dripping from Jack's pole interrupted the silence. Joe suddenly turned and smiled at us. "We should see some fish here," he said. "There are lots

This cobia was taken from a marker along the Gulf coast of Florida by the author. During the spring and summer months many cobia are caught around offshore rigs, near buoys, and around channel markers. Best tide to fish is slack, but with a noise-maker lure, like a chugger, you can often pull a cobia to the surface, and toss a fly to the aroused fish.

of sharks around. I've noticed that when sharks are missing from a flat, or no stingrays are working, few bonefish are around."

Since that day, I have verified his observation many times. In fact, if I begin poling a flat and it is devoid of fish life, I give it five minutes to produce; if nothing happens, I move on.

There is no single best tide for bonefishing, despite the many articles maintaining that bonefish are best taken on a rising tide. It really has to do with the terrain. Usually flats located directly against deep water are most productive as the tide begins to rise and fish in the deep-water sanctuaries come out to feed. Portions of the same flat located several hundred yards from the deep water may not be productive until the tide has risen almost to its peak, simply because the fish cannot swim that area on lower stages of the tide. Flats on the bay side of an ocean are usually best late on the tide. In many areas bonefish will feed on one flat as the tide rises, move to another flat during high tide, then cross over that flat and move to another on the falling tide. Bones feed only on a certain portion of some flats, always ignoring the other parts of it. Why this is true is not really understood. But it clearly illustrates that you need the services of a guide or a skilled bonefisherman if you are new to a specific bonefishing area.

In the Bahamas, Cuba, and portions of the Central American bonefish waters, you'll find huge muds. They're usually depressions in the flat that hold some water at low tides, maybe a short blind channel, a pothole, or a similar feature. Bonefish that have been feeding on the flats collect in these holes as the tide lowers, and continue to feed. Their thrashing about creates a thick yellowish mud. The angler who sneaks up to such a mud—often several hundred square yards in size—and casts his fly around its edges can get several bonefish before they are alerted.

Bonefish seem to be in a constant state of alert, ready to flee at the slightest alarm. They move constantly. Should you see a greenish fish, resembling a bonefish in color, but lying perfectly motionless on the flats, it will almost surely be a barracuda. If a cuda starts tracking your fly, slow it down, let the fish look at it, and it will move away. Speed up the retrieve, however, and the cuda will move in, make one snap of its jaws, and collect your fly.

On any flat the bonefish seem to prefer moving against the tide or the wind, whichever is stronger. Frequently you can follow the path of a bonefish by the silvery showers of minnows that flush in front of it. Many flats have little runs or depressions in them, maybe a few inches deeper than the rest of the water. Bonefish prefer to move in such troughs.

The type of tackle for bonefishing varies but slightly. You should have a reel that holds a minimum of 150 yards of backing. The backing should be Micron or Dacron; 18- or 20-pound-test is perfect for bonefish. If you're fishing on wind-free days, or for smaller fish, you might like to try a System 5, 6, or 7 rod and line. Since bonefish flies are relatively tiny, trout tackle will do. A 7-pound bonefish taken on a little trout rod is a revelation.

The leader should be long. In calm, clear water, where the fish are especially spooky, I prefer a 16-foot tapered leader. I make my leaders in a special way showed to me by Bob Stearns. I put a butt section of approximately 4 feet of 30-pound on the fly line, followed by 3 feet of 25-pound-test monofilament. On the fly end of the 25-pound monofilament I make a loop. Then I loop a 2-foot section of 20-pound-test, followed by 18 inches of 15-pound, 18 inches of 12-pound, and 4 feet of 10-pound-test, for a 16-foot leader. Sometimes I substitute 8- or 6-pound-test for the final tippet section. If the wind comes up, such a leader can be tough to cast; so I remove the looped third piece of leader (the 2-foot section of 20-pound test) and loop on a foot-long section of 20-pound, another foot of 15-pound, and a 2-foot section of tippet. It may sound cumbersome, but it works well and is really easy to do.

The diet of a bonefish is so varied that almost any fly, if small enough, will take bonefish at one time or another. But some established patterns have emerged, and it's foolish not to use them.

Bonefish have a small mouth. They simply cannot ingest a 6-inch minnow or dollar-size crab. So you must present them with a fly they think they can eat. The maximum length of a bonefish fly would probably be 3 inches, but few are more than 2½ inches long. The more skilled the bonefisherman becomes, the smaller the hooks he uses. Bart Foth, who's probably caught as many large bonefish as anyone on earth, ties almost all his flies on number 4 and 6 hooks—and sticks mainly to a single fly pattern.

Since bonefish feed on bottom life, the fly should generally be worked there. Most of the patterns worked out by those who fish regularly for bones are designed to be either completely or relatively weedproof. The inverted tie, discussed earlier, achieves this—so does the Keel hook.

Bonefish have a soft but leathery mouth, so no shock tippets are required on the leader. But the mouth is so tough that sharp hooks are a must.

Almost all beginning bonefishermen work their flies improperly at first. Bonefish are startled by a fly darting through the water in rapid 1-to-2-foot jerks. More fish have been scared by this retrieve than have been caught. The retrieve should be in short (1- to 6-inch strips) motions, and if the current allows, the fly should often be held motionless for a moment. If you have properly calculated the path of the bonefish, you can let the fly fall to the bottom.

As the fish approaches the fly, move it by dragging it in little jerks along the bottom.

The rod tip should be low, even actually immersed in the water. If you're casting from a boat and you strip, holding the rod 3 or 4 feet from the surface, you'll ruin your retrieve. As the fly is stripped toward you and you pause, the line will sag between the rod tip and the water, causing the fly to continue to move. Keep the rod tip either in the water or within a few inches of it to guarantee that when you stop stripping, the fly will stop moving.

The presentation of the fly to the fish is important. Bonefish have super-sharp eyesight, and a bright-colored fly line unrolling toward it will often reflect light and frighten the fish. Lines neutral in color (I prefer a medium shade of gray) are recommended.

If the fish is tailing, the fly has to be presented within a foot of it, and dragged right under its nose before the fish will see it. But when a bonefish is swimming along in a foot of clear, calm water, the cast should be at least 8 feet in front of the fish. But be ready—if the fish changes direction, as it is most likely to do, you must quickly pick up the line from the water and make another cast. The fly should be directed at least a foot or two above the surface of the target area; driving the fly into the water will create too much disturbance. It pays to be "down sun" from the fish when you cast too, to prevent throwing a line shadow over the fish. Should the fish swim into or under the leader or line, keep perfectly still. If the fish strikes a moving leader or line, you've had it! Once it has passed under the line, you can quickly pick up and make another presentation.

The full strip of the line to move the fly when bonefishing should usually be no more than the distance shown here.

After you spot a bonefish, you have a maximum of about 6 seconds—often less—to make a cast. Remember that you are standing in the boat, holding the fly and leader, with much of the fly line lying on the deck at your feet. The procedure for making a quick cast is outlined in Chapter 8; study it well. Before you make your first trip for tarpon, bonefish, or permit (all three are flats dwellers) you should practice at home until you can make that delivery in 6 seconds or less. And don't forget that casting speed is not all; you must get the line into the air, all the while calculating the speed and direction of the bonefish, then make the presentation of the fly at the right spot, at the correct moment.

Shooting taper lines are not recommended for bonefishing. First, since most fish will be caught within 60 feet of the boat, distance will not be a problem. More important, you lose the ability to correct a bad presentation quickly. With a conventional saltwater taper, if the fish makes a change in direction after the cast has been delivered, a good fly caster can pick up all or most of the line, make a hasty cast, and get in another presentation. Shooting tapers require that the running line be retrieved all the way back to the head before a cast can be made, and this almost always eliminates the chances for a second cast.

When the fish does take your fly, you need only lift the rod and tighten your line; the sharp hook will easily penetrate the bonefish's mouth. But it is exactly at this point that many fishermen lose the battle.

Lying on the deck are yards of line, which will soon disappear through the guides. Your immediate concern, once the fish has been hooked, is to clear that line—which will be *smoking* through the guides in an instant. Hold the rod high, then form an **O** ring with the first finger and thumb of your other hand around the line. As the running line begins tearing up off the deck, keep your eye on *it* (disregard, for a moment, the escaping fish), and with the **O** feed the line from under your feet, off the gear on the deck, and allow it to flow smoothly through the guides. Remember to keep the rod hand higher than the hand feeding the line. If the rod is lower, the line can tangle around the reel or the rod butt.

Once the fish has pulled all loose line from the deck, fight it from the reel. The drag pressure should be set at about a pound. It's vital that you do nothing to restrain a bonefish during its first long run—which will be from 50 to 150 yards, perhaps farther. As soon as the fish has ended its run, immediately begin to pump the rod and recover line. Generally the fish will fight sluggishly back to the boat. But when it sees you, it will make a second run that is almost never quite so long or fast as the first. The fish may repeat this several times before it tires.

Bonefish fight until they are totally exhausted, so you must revive the fish when you release it. If you simply unhook it and drop it back, it will sink to the bottom and die. To revive it, grasp the fish around the tail and hold your other hand under its belly. Swish it rapidly back and forth underwater. Don't worry about how to tell when the fish has recovered: when a bonefish is ready to leave, you won't be able to stop it.

The most popular kind of bonefishing is done from a boat poled across the flats. A guide moves the boat with a long pole, to which a shoe of some sort is attached, to prevent the pole from sticking in the bottom. The angler stands on the front casting platform, line carefully coiled in readiness on the deck while the fly is held in his hand. When a fish is sighted, the guide manipulates the boat so that the angler gets a clear shot at the bonefish.

Wading is the second important method. Here, a boat is often used to get to the flats, and then the boat is generally moved until fish are actually sighted. Then the angler steps out and carefully wades to within casting distance. Wading is for some a pleasant preference—at other times it's a necessity because the boat cannot approach the bonefish if the water is too shallow.

A third method of taking bonefish is by staking out, or anchoring in a choice spot that bonefish frequent. You can stand alert and wait for expectant bonefish to arrive, or you can chum them into your area. Some guides position the boat by sticking the pole into the bottom and tying a short rope to it. If your guide does this, make sure he has inserted the pole into the flat at a very low angle. If he doesn't, the fly line will surely catch on the pole on the backcast.

Chumming is an effective method of bringing bonefish to the boat. But it does require some knowledge of the area. You can't chum bonefish if there are none around. Once you've determined that a flat is a good spot for chumming, cut up a half dozen live shrimp and throw them into the area you want the bonefish to come to. It's a good idea to chum a bright spot, so that you can more easily see the fish when they arrive.

Be sure to anchor the boat on the upwind side of the area chummed, and, if possible, on the up-tide side, too. Captain Bill Curtis does this, and has great success. He has his anglers cast a Blue Tail Fly to the feeding bonefish, place their rod tip underwater, and then strip the fly in, only an inch or two at a time. The bright Mylar sparkles in the water. Anchored up-tide of the chummed spot, the current will hold the fly in the water; bonefish find it irresistible.

I have read articles claiming that catching this fish is a snap. The writers obviously hadn't done much bonefishing with a fly rod. Joe Brooks rightly called this fish "the grey ghost of the flats." Bonefishing with a fly rod is one of the most intricate challenges in the sport of angling. It can also be one of the most satisfying.

Captain Bill Curtis, right, stands with a client and peers into the light-colored sand hole (see arrows). Curtis has thrown a handful of cut-up shrimp into the area for chum.

PERMIT

The permit is the supreme challenge to fly fishermen in the salt. This fish is more wary than a bonefish and nearly as fast, it has incredible eyesight, swims even more erractically, is infinitely stronger, grows bigger—*and rarely takes a fly.*

No one has yet figured out exactly how to take permit on a fly. This fish has defied the innovations of fly tyers for as long as we have fished for it. Someone will catch a permit on a specially designed fly, and others will show it to a number of permit, and get refusals; another pattern succeeds once, and then fails. And so it goes.

The permit, the fly rodder's supreme trophy.

I caught my first permit on a fly almost by accident—after casting fruitlessly to thousands of them. Mark Sosin and I were fishing near Key West, trying to catch a permit on a crab so Mark could get some pictures for a story he was writing. A school of small permit, perhaps 6-pounders, came rushing toward us over a clear sand bottom. Mark had a spinning rod ready and made a quick cast, and the whole school rushed the crab. One grabbed the bait and Mark soon had the husky little fish at boatside. I began to pole the boat toward the shoreline where we could set up our pictures. Mark started yelling to me that the school was coming back. I ignored him, complaining that we should get the pictures, then go back to fishing. Mark picked up the fly rod and threw it to me. I dropped the pole in the boat, grabbed the rod, and began to strip line. It lay in a tangled mess in the boat bottom. Seeing the disaster, Mark just picked up the line and threw it overboard. I knew it wouldn't work, but desperately stripped more line until it came untangled and the fly fell in front of the fish.

One surged forward and took the little pink fly. A few minutes later I boated the permit. It could not have weighed more than 5 pounds, but I was so overjoyed at finally catching a permit that its size did not diminish my happiness. I picked the permit out of the water and kissed it, ignoring the clicking of Mark's camera shutter.

Why permit will hit a fly one day, and then for a *year* refuse everything, is not clear. Several facts that we do know, however, will aid the angler seeking permit. Permit are even more sensitive to cold water than are bonefish. It has been my observation, and that of two superb permit guides of long experience, that once the water drops below 72 degrees the permit disappear. Also, permit are most often seen on the flats in water deeper than that preferred by bonefish. The best water height is from 30 inches to 4 feet, although I have several times seen permit swim on their side in a foot of water to get at an escaping crab.

In the Florida Keys permit are seen more in summer than in winter. May is perhaps the best month. During June most of the permit seem to disappear from the shallows, and we find them concentrated around deep-water wrecks. We think they're spawning, because the fish are filled with milt or eggs. By August the permit are back on the flats and remain there until cold weather drives them off. You can find some permit on the flats anytime the water warms during the winter, but it will be late April before they appear in appreciable numbers.

Some unexplainable things happen in permit fishing. Jim Lopez, who holds many world fly records, was fishing with Sid Coogler in July 1971 on a wreck far out in the Gulf of Mexico from Key West. They established a chum line. Using a sinking fly line and flies dressed on 3/0 hooks, Lopez caught an incredible fifteen permit in four consecutive days of fishing. Sid caught four. The largest fish Lopez took was 17¼ pounds, and Coogler's top fish went 21¼.

It was an incredible feat, and had Lopez and Coogler not been so well known for their honesty, the story would probably never have been believed. They used a short strip retrieve, allowing the fly first to drop deep into the chum line; they tried three different flies. With such success under their belt they felt as they went home that they had finally found the answer to catching permit on a fly. Returning to the same wreck the following week they observed the large number of permit, set up their chum line, began to cast their sinking lines and special flies—nothing. They never caught another permit—neither on that trip nor on any subsequent trips.

"We must have hit a certain weather condition, and the fish were hungry," Lopez explains, baffled by it all.

Permit fishing is still an unsolved angling technique. Enough have been caught on the flats—more than fifty in all of fly-fishing history—to encourage fly fishermen to keep trying; but not enough have been caught to establish workable techniques or effective patterns. This is a pity. For, once hooked, they are explosive fish.

SNOOK

Florida Sportsman once polled its readers, asking, among numerous questions, which fish was their favorite target. The snook led by a wide margin.

The snook is also the favorite fish of thousands of northern light-tackle anglers, and for a good reason. Northern anglers have been fishing smallmouth and largemouth bass most of their lives. They understand the type of cover, feeding locations, and lure manipulations it takes to catch a bass. Apart from the fact that bass take plastic worms, the snook and the bass are very similar. The snook grows much larger, and being a saltwater species will fight longer and harder, but the bass fisherman can feel at home fishing for snook. Others, like Art Flick, compare snook to the brown trout.

Joe Brooks and Rocky Weinstein—two fly-rod pioneers. This picture was taken many years ago of a snook that Joe and Rocky took from the Tamiami Trail canal, where Rocky was a pioneer guide.

Perhaps the finest fly rodding for snook is in the area along the west coast of Florida from Naples east to U.S. 1. What can be said about fishing this area also applies to fishing the mangrove shorelines and creeks in Central America, where there is some fantastic fishing in still relatively unexplored water.

The lower west coast below Naples sees a huge run of spawning snook in late spring, but these fish move along the outside shoreline through the deep passes. They don't offer the fly rodder a consistent target, although it's sensational when you hit the right spot at the right time.

But on the inside—the vast complex of bays, creeks, mangrove islands, and bars—is an area called the Ten Thousand Islands. On your first trip you may be amazed as the guide moves at top speed over the water, through narrow, treelined passes into a small creek, through another pass—and in no time you may feel completely lost. Yet once you have fished the area a while you'll begin to notice subtle signposts—a peculiar twisted dead tree, an odd-shaped oyster bar, an osprey nest; such indicators will tell you where you are.

Though some snook live inside all year long, it's in the winter that tourists insist on coming there to fish. Fortunately, the fish that have been living and dining outside along the coast will either move away into deep water, or swim inside, where there is more comfort. It's on the inside that fly rodders fall in love with snook fishing.

On the inside, the normal procedure during falling tide is to manipulate the boat along the mangrove shoreline at a comfortable casting distance; the angler tosses his flies into the small pockets and creek mouths, and under the overhanging branches.

A mangrove tree resembles a spider turned into a bush. The multileg plant stands in the water like a giant spider, ready to pounce on a fly that comes too close. The snook lie under the mangrove bushes, waiting to ambush any unwary baitfish that swim by. They'll mistake an all-yellow, red and yellow, or red and white streamer for a baitfish, too.

The best line for such fishing is number 9 through 11. These heavier lines allow you to develop considerable speed, so you can throw a tight loop, a requirement if you want to present a fly under an overhanging bush. Floating lines are best for most snook fishing, since the water will range from a foot to 6 feet in most places. You may find, on occasion, a fish in a deep hole or pass so that a fast-sinking line would be preferable. Leaders need not be longer than 7 feet, but you must have a shock tippet attached to the fly that will test from 30 to 40 pounds. It should not exceed a foot in length. The shock tippet is necessary because the snook carries a small razor-blade-like cutter on the rear portion of the gill flap. It will go through a light tippet like butter. And obviously you should use care when handling a snook, to avoid cutting yourself.

If you're new to the Ten Thousand Islands area, it will help to have a guide, for much of the water is not good for fishing. If you insist on renting a boat (and they can be rented at Flamingo, in Everglades National Park, and at Chokoloskee Island) then you should know a little about assessing a shoreline for snook. You can spot a poor shoreline quickly. Obviously no fish is going to lie under a mangrove bush in only a few inches of water. It takes 18 or more inches of water to make a snook feel secure. So if the roots are in deeper water it can be a good spot.

Creeks 10 to 50 feet wide that have birds feeding around them are excellent spots to try. The wading birds feed on small baitfish, and their presence indicates that the snook's food is available. Tree stumps, bushes, and other debris are swept to the mouth of a creek at times of high water. The water from a creek is usually running off a marsh behind it that is at a higher elevation, so the swift current will have eddies where snook can lie and wait for bait being swept to them.

Northern bass fishermen have the perfect rig for fishing the mangrove shorelines. Their bass boats will work over shallow water, and their electric motors allow them to control the boat silently and keep it within range of the snook without alarming the fish. Guides can get to snook water from Chokoloskee by running inside creeks and so you need not fear running open salt water with your boat.

During winter cold spells the snook on the inside will gang up in deep holes. I have on several occasions taken as many as ten snook (Florida law limits daily possession to four) in a single day by fishing these deep holes with a lead-core shooting head and a bucktail fly, or an extra-fast-sinking fly line. I like to use a heavily tied Joe Brooks Blonde fly (all-yellow) with the bucktail tied much thicker than normal. Bucktail floats, and I use the heavily dressed flies for a good reason. I allow the lead-core or extra-fast-sinking line to drop to the bottom of the hole. Then I crawl the line across the bottom. The bucktail fly tries to float, so it moves across the floor of the hole just inches off the bottom, right in front of a snook's nose.

When the sun comes out after a cold snap, the first waters to warm are the shallow, mud-bottom bays on the inside. You can motor quietly across a bay to check for snook. The fish will be lying still in three to four feet of water. As the boat approaches they flee with a powerful sweep of the tail, which sets up a yard-wide boil of yellow mud. If you see this, start drifting and casting; other snook are likely to be around.

Flies for snook fishing need not be dressed on large hooks. I like number 1 or 3/0 hooks, with extra-long shanks. My favorite two patterns are the Lefty's Deceiver and the Joe Brooks Blonde; I prefer all-yellow or red and yellow. A slider, which is a popping but that doesn't pop and looks like a bullet-shaped lure, can be very effective on snook. It makes a nearly silent retrieve but darts erratically over the surface when retrieved, a motion snook find appealing. A typical slider bug is shown in Chapter 6.

Joe Brooks holds up a 16¼ pound mutton snapper taken on the flats near Key West. Many knowledgeable anglers regard the mutton snapper, which feeds on the flats like a bonefish, as more difficult to take than a permit. Only when a mutton snapper is following a sting ray in search of food does the fish strike readily. At other times the mutton snapper is very easily alarmed.

There is some good fishing, especially in the spring, along the outside shoreline from Naples to Flamingo, where you can blind cast either streamers or popping bugs. Located along these shorelines are thousands of old oyster bars. The best tide to fish here is often the high falling. The snook will lie on the Gulf side of the bars waiting for bait to be swept across the bar. When the tide has completely fallen, snook will often concentrate in a deep hole between the bars, where an extra-fast-sinking line is best.

Between Flamingo and Islamorada you can catch snook on a fly in two ways. Poling the flats and casting to yellow-colored pockets up on the flats can produce some good snook. Almost always, a streamer fly is best for this work. The trick is to approach the pothole quietly, and to cast the fly beyond the hole and then bring it through the pocket. Snook will set up a feeding station in such a pothole and wait for moving bait to swim over the hideout.

The other and more exciting snook fishing in this area is sight-hunting for these fish. A guide or fellow angler poles the boat over the shallow flats to nearby keys. Poling silently around the key, both men look intently for snook that will be lying up under the mangrove roots. The angler, spotting a snook, makes a long cast with a streamer fly. These fish are tough to take, but they are best caught on a fly rather than on other fishing gear.

Snook take on the color of the waters in which they live. A snook on the inside, living among the dark mangrove-stained waters, where the bottom is red-black, will have an almost jet-black back. A snook that lies in a light-colored pothole will be almost yellow in appearance.

Though snook are generally written about as a fish of the mangroves, they are distributed throughout both coasts of Florida, and occur in heavy concentrations on the lower half of both the Atlantic and Gulf of Mexico shores. Some of the highest concentrations of huge snook (much bigger than those found in the Ten Thousand Islands area) hide, eat, and die within the harbors of the major cities of Florida.

Their favorite hangout is a bridge or causeway. Since these structures are lighted at night, the snook will lie, usually on the up-tide side, within the shadow line created by the lights of a bridge. Here they wait for drifting shrimp and bait. These fish can be seen as dark shadows, just under the surface, almost unmoving for minutes at a time. Suddenly they dart forth, snatch an unsuspecting baitfish, and return to their feeding stations.

You can blind-fish for such snook by anchoring up-tide from a bridge and casting white flies at least 5 inches long into the shadow areas. You should dress the fly heavily; I like a Lefty's Deceiver on a 3/0 hook, but carrying at least 15 to 18 saddle hackles. The fly should have Mylar in it; it will sparkle with the reflections from the bridge lights. Experience has proven that a very rapid retrieve is best. Cast the fly 6 or 8 feet into the shadows under the bridge, then strip it out as fast as you can. Once the fly has emerged 10 or more feet from the shadows, it can be picked up and recast.

A more exciting method of fishing these snook is to anchor the boat at the base of a bridge pier, then crawl up on the base and walk to the up-tide side. You can stand there with only a few yards of fly line outside the guides and peer into the dark waters. You'll easily see any fish. The fly is cast 3 feet beyond the fish and zipped right past its nose. In many cases it strikes from instinct. If you show the fly to the snook several times and it refuses, move on and locate another fish. You can take tarpon in the same manner with the same flies.

Snook find waters cooler than 60 degrees intolerable, so in cold weather a thermometer is a great aid to the snook fisherman.

TARPON

I was a striped bass addict for most of my life—until I caught a tarpon. I have boated nearly every species that will accept a fly, and none compare, for me, to the tarpon. I suppose there are many reasons, and if you have fished tarpon I really need not justify my statement.

Tarpon come in many sizes. You can fish a canal ditch with a System 4 fly rod and line for tarpon as small as freshwater trout, and they strike the same flies. Or you can stake out on a tarpon flat in the lower Keys in the spring, and toss a streamer to a 150-pound giant. Nothing makes me feel more inadequate, or thrilled, than to stand on the casting platform of a skiff, armed with only a fly rod, and see a log of a tarpon coasting across the flats. The big ones, more than 100 pounds, make you feel inept and foolish as you stand there, poised with a 3-inch streamer fly in your hand, wondering how in the hell you are going to win over this 6 feet of scale-encased muscle—so big that you can describe the fish by its *width!*

Legs become rubber, arms inoperable; your eyes misjudge. If the fish actually takes the fly, you'll probably strike too hard. The tarpon catapults from the water like a giant jack-in-the-box, throwing water all over you.

Tarpon are found along the coast of the United States and all through the tropics, on the Atlantic side. But it is from lower Florida through Mexico and the Central American countries that tarpon are considered the king of fish for fly fishermen.

Tarpon are sensitive to cold, and in the winter periods only a few fish will be found even in the Florida Keys. As waters warm in late March the giant tarpon, on their annual migration, move up onto the flats. There is probably no place in the world where such large fish can be so easily fished for with a fly, as in the middle and lower Keys. By late April, the Florida Bay side of the Keys teems with schools of giant tarpon, many in excess of 140 pounds. By June the fish have moved to the Atlantic side of the Keys and remain there for several weeks before disappearing.

During the summer months tarpon in the 5- to 40-pound class frequent many of the shallow basins, channels, and pockets among the many keys.

During late May a migration of large tarpon appears off the lower southwest coast of Florida, beginning in the sloughs and estuaries around the Shark River, where fly rodders can take these fish by blind fishing with a sinking fly line and bright-hued streamer fly. The fish move on up the coast off Punta Gorda in June, then on to Grand Isle, Louisiana, in mid-July. A few weeks later they arrive off Port Aransas, Texas. But north of Shark River the tarpon are usually in deep water, where dead baits, crabs, and live mullet are the best bait. Then the silver king shows up along the coast of the Yucatan Peninsula in the fall, and by winter is working its way through the waters of Belize, Panama, and Colombia. While it is not certain, it is suspected that the tarpon at that point cut across the Gulf of Mexico to start the cycle all over again in the lower Florida Keys.

The peak months for a fly rodder seeking a real trophy tarpon are May and June. The best locations are the Islamorada area and near Marathon. Excellent skiff guides, who thoroughly understand the fly fisherman's problems, are available. The boats are tailored for fly fishing, having large, open casting platforms, and no line-entangling gadgets aboard.

Some large and small tarpon remain around the Florida Keys and other fishing hangouts all through the tropics throughout the year. The power plant in the harbor at Key West has a permanent population of small tarpon that may go to 60 pounds. I went there once with Jim Green, and in the harbor filled with shrimp boats we watched schools of 25- to 50-pound fish swim five feet below the boat. Jim tried every fly and trick he knew, but in two hours of casting didn't get a single strike. Yet I have pulled into the harbor on a few occasions when the fish cooperated by eagerly grabbing our flies.

That's typical of the tarpon.

Soon after I first moved to Florida, I told Vic Dunaway I had finally figured out a bunch of tarpon I had been fishing for several weeks. He smiled, and with a condescending air said, "Lefty, about the only thing you can be sure about a tarpon is that it is a tarpon." The next week I again fished the tarpon I had "figured out," and never got a strike. No fish is more unpredictable.

The outfit for big tarpon is a specialty tool. The single most important piece of equipment is a stout reel with a superb drag. The drag must be whisper-smooth, for it is not uncommon for a big tarpon to run 200 yards at full bore. Any lurch in the drag could mean a broken leader.

The reel should carry a minimum of 250 yards of Dacron or Micron backing. I like 20-pound-test, but many anglers of rich experience swear by 30-pound. To obtain a little more room for backing, most anglers will cut 10 to 15 feet of running line from the rear portion of the fly line.

The leader should be at least 6 feet long. Most of us now use the quick-change leader. This is a 3-to-4-foot section of 30- to 40-pound butt leader that has a loop in the forward end. The 12-pound-test tippet section is looped to it, and that is attached to a 12-inch section of 80- or 100-pound monofilament butt section.

The rod has to be stout. Bamboo is out. When that fish is lying five or six feet below the boat, exhausted, the only way you can claim your trophy is to lift it to the gaffer, and this takes a rod with enormous power. Bamboo will not stand this strain. Every year I hear reports of bamboo rods that failed the test.

Jim Green casts to rolling tarpon in Key West Harbor; arrows point to backs of fish rolling in front of Jim.

An angler who has never fished giant tarpon may pick up a rod designed for such heavy work, heft it, and shake his head in disbelief. He'll feel no one could ever cast such a rod all day long. He's right. But no one does. You cast to a giant tarpon only after you have seen the fish; on a good day of fishing these giants, you may have made only a dozen casts. The rod is primarily a fighting tool, and as long as it can deliver the fly to the fish, that's all that's required. Good tarpon fly rods have large snake guides, bigger than anything used in freshwater fishing. Two reasons: the fish exerts tremendous pressure on the guides as it fights and is lifted from the water, so the guides have to be large and held securely on the rod; and an escaping tarpon will frequently bolt away after the strike, and the line coming off the deck will go through the guides in a clump. If the guides are tiny, the line catches and the fish breaks off.

The reel seat on a tarpon rod should be stout, either chrome on brass, high-grade anodized aluminum, or tough plastic. It should carry double-locking rings to insure that the reel doesn't fall off in the middle of the fight. Another trick is to run a little tape over the reel-locking rings to make doubly sure that the seat will not loosen.

No fish takes a fly better than a tarpon. It still amazes most of us that a giant tarpon will move ten feet out of its way to suck in a 4-inch streamer fly. Along the west coast of Florida the fish seem to go for a relatively large fly, perhaps 6 or 7 inches long. But in most places I have fished in Florida and the tropics the big fish prefer a streamer from 3½ to 4 inches in length.

Two patterns reign supreme among tarpon fishermen, although many experts have their own favorites, and other patterns certainly do take fish. The Stu Apte tarpon fly is made with two to four orange saddle hackles tied at the rear of the hook shank. Two or three yellow saddle hackles are placed on either side of the orange ones. Several turns are made, palmer style,

Norman Duncan frantically reaches with the net for a leaping tarpon he took on a fly at night.

around the hook shank where the hackles are attached with an orange and a yellow hackle. It's a simple tie, but one tarpon fall for. Some people say it reminds the tarpon of a particular worm the fish are fond of feeding on, others say it looks like a shrimp, another choice food. However it does it, it certainly takes tarpon.

The other fly, which Norman Duncan designed and John Emery made popular, is the Cockroach. This simple fly has 6 grizzly hackles tied at the rear of the hook, with either a collar of bucktail tied around the hook shank, or a few turns of red hackle. It's a drab fly, but very effective. Neither fly exceeds 4 inches in length, and for smaller tarpon the flies are further scaled down. This fly is often used, too, with the shank painted a fluorescent bright orange.

For giant tarpon, hooks from 3/0 to 5/0 are used. Since such hooks are difficult to set into the concretelike mouth of a tarpon, the points must be well sharpened. The triangulation method of sharpening the hook, which makes three supporting edges, is preferred by many. I like to sharpen the hook on the outside bend into a **V** shape.

Three types of line are used for tarpon fishing. The most popular is a heavy, saltwater taper floating line; it is used by perhaps 90 percent of all tarpon fly fishermen. Since most giant tarpon are caught in five to eight feet of water, the angler can usually cast his fly far enough ahead of the fish to make a good presentation. However, when floating grass clutters the surface, these lines funnel the vegetation right to the hook on a retrieve.

The Intermediate line sinks very slowly, unless dressed with buoyant material. This line gets the fly down quicker to tarpon in deeper water, and it tends to settle through floating

The mangrove snapper is a good fly rod fish of the shallows. They hide beneath the roots of mangrove trees and will bolt from hiding to strike a noisy popping bug, as this one did.

The roosterfish, one of the toughest fish that swim, is one that few fly rodders have taken. This Pacific fish roams far at sea, but also lives right up in the surf. Only a few have been taken on a fly, and it has to be regarded among the six top trophies a saltwater angler seeks.

grass. There is one disadvantage to using an Intermediate line, however. If you make a cast and the tarpon suddenly veers off course, you must get the fly back quickly and make another presentation. The Intermediate line has often sunk so deep that a hasty backcast is impossible.

The third line, used rarely on the flats but often in deeper water, is the extra-fast-sinking. This line will bomb a fly to the bottom of a hole or channel and crawl the lure before the tarpon. It must, however, be brought back close to the boat and a roll cast made to lift the fly from the water before another presentation can be made.

You fish for giant tarpon in two ways. A guide can pole you along the banks and over the flats. Jack's Bank in Marathon and Buchanan Bank near Islamorada, as well as the vast Nine Mile Bank offshore from the Everglades, are areas where guides practice this art. Tarpon frequently breathe air from the atmosphere, as we do. They rise to the surface, exhale, inhale, and roll under. In calm waters, an experienced angler can see a rolling tarpon for a half a mile.

The fish moving along just under the surface will create a wake or nervous water. Most of the time the fish lie rather motionless in the water, or move very slowly, either in singles, pairs, or large schools. If you see a school of moving fish you should cast in front of all the fish, so that should you get a refusal from the leading fish, the remainder of the school still have a chance to examine the fly. Also, casting into a school of fish can alarm them. A fly line, delicate as it is, dropping over a tarpon will usually cause it to panic. If it is a single fish the fly should be cast far enough ahead to allow it to sink to a depth that will enable the fly to meet the fish on a collision course.

Most beginners work the fly too fast. The tarpon likes a fly that swims along, undulating slowly up and down. However, if a big tarpon starts stalking the fly, but won't take it, a sudden increase in the speed of the fly will often get a strike. The tarpon must feel that the fly is escaping.

How should one strike a tarpon? The fish will either approach the fly from the side, rolling away as it strikes, or come from directly behind and inhale it. If the fish comes from the side, you're lucky. As it moves away it will drag the hook against its mouth. But if the fish is stalking the fly, you must follow a definite pattern. The fly is moving at a certain speed, which the tarpon has already determined; as it moves in, it expects the fly to continue on at that speed, so it times its strike accordingly. Watch the tarpon; as it moves in to swallow the fly, cease stripping. If you do, the fly will go deeper into the tarpon's mouth and guarantee you a better hook-up.

When the tarpon turns away with the fly, strike. But don't pull back in a long sweeping arc with the rod. The tarpon may decide to go in the opposite direction at the same moment and a broken leader will be the result. Instead, make your strike by a repetitive series of short, hard jabs.

Then if the tarpon comes out of the water, as it surely will, you have a chance to recover. When a tarpon or any large fish jumps, you must bow to it. This bowing technique has to be

The ladyfish, rarely more than 3½ pounds, is a tiger when hooked. A first cousin of the tarpon, this small, sleek fish is found in all subtropical waters and takes streamers well. Since it's not good eating, ladyfish should be released unharmed.

mastered or you will lose most of the fish you hook. The bowing technique prevents the fish from falling back on a taut leader, possibly breaking it—but that is not its major effect. The tarpon weighs much less in the water than it does in the air. Anyone who has tried to lift a rock from a river bottom in his youth knows that getting the rock up to the surface was easy, but often it was too heavy to carry once it was in the air. A leaping tarpon throws its full weight against the line as it rises into the air, and by bowing you shove the rod toward the fish and create as much slack as possible. The only thing that weight can do then is shake the fly. Most of the time it will hold.

It is at this point that the knots you tied get their test. Only the best of knots will do for such work. If you plan to fish for bigger tarpon, then you should master the knots suggested in Chapter 5. Guides spend as much time and care building their leaders and knots as they do on anything. It pays, too, to keep a number of extra leaders made up, ready for use. Should you break a fish off, it will take only moments to re-rig.

If you fish from an anchored boat rather than one that is poled across the flats, you should have a release anchor attached to the line. This is simply a quick-release snap tied to the anchor line. To the snap is attached a buoy of some type. If the tarpon is hooked and begins tearing away, your companion can unsnap the anchor line and begin chase. Later, he can return to the buoy, retrieve the anchor, and reposition the boat.

The cast to a tarpon, bonefish, permit, or any other fish moving on the flat must be very accurate—and it must be made immediately.

There are, of course, other kinds of tarpon fishing aside from fishing for the giants. One of the most interesting is night fishing for tarpon, especially in the Florida Keys. All during the warmer months of late spring, summer, and early fall, tarpon roll and feed under most of the bridges in the middle Keys. Tom's Harbor and Long Key are two of the best, but many of the bridges hold tarpon. Usually a silent two-minute wait will tell you if tarpon are around. In the quiet darkness you can hear them rolling and crashing on bait. It's best to fish when the high slack tide begins to move from the Gulf toward the Atlantic; you can catch fish throughout the fall of water. That is not to say that you can't hook fish on an incoming tide.

The procedure outlined for snook fishing generally applies, although you cannot get on any abutment bases of bridges. Blind casting, since there are often large numbers of the fish, is fruitful. Be sure to fish the up-tide side of the bridge. Most of us prefer a moonlit night.

In the Gulf of Mexico along the Yucatan Peninsula coast the flats hold thousands of smaller tarpon, in the 20- or 40-pound class. The fish can easily be seen swimming in the four feet of water, and take flies well. A System 8 or 9 fly rod is preferable. It's possible in some of these areas to hook and jump forty or more tarpon a day.

In the Turneffe Islands of Belize, large schools of tarpon live in channels from February until May. They feed in the deeper channels that cut through the island, and fast-sinking lines do the best work.

One of my favorite methods of tarpon fishing is with a medium freshwater trout outfit, throwing a number 7 line. Using scaled-down tarpon flies 2¼ inches long, I like to pole on high spring tides around the little mangrove islands of the Florida Keys and other tropical areas, looking for the 5- to 30-pounders that lie back under the mangrove roots. It's tricky fly casting, and the best of sport when one of these 20-pounders hits on that fragile rod. Many of them make several jumps through the bushes and are gone. Enough leap toward open water to encourage you to try again.

The current world record tarpon taken on fly tackle is this 154-pounder caught by Stu Apte.

SHARKS

One of the most difficult fish to take on a fly rod is a large shark. Not because of its power and ferocity—it's more complicated than that.

Sharks in very deep water are almost beyond the realm of the fly rodder. You can successfully boat medium-to-small sharks in blue water, but the truly large ones—over 100 pounds—will simply strip your line and be gone. It's on the flats and in the shallow bays that sharks offer you a chance.

Throughout the tropics and extreme southern Florida, sharks get up on the flats and cruise, seeking food. Occasionally, they get in water so shallow that their huge dorsal fins stick above the surface, reminding me of black sailboats cruising the flats. They may not seem to be moving fast, but you'll soon find that it is very difficult to keep up with them when you're poling a boat, and to make things tougher, they rarely swim in a predictable course.

Sharks have poor eyesight, and this really causes problems for the fly fisherman. The angler must cast the fly so it lands near the eye and alongside the head, *not* in front of the fish. Then during the retrieve the fly must be kept there as long as possible, to give the shark ample time to see it. If the fly is positioned in front of the shark, it will never know it's there.

Since the amount of time the fly remains near the shark's eye is crucial, the boat's and the angler's position prior to the cast is important. If you cast to a shark that is going away from the fisherman, the fly, no matter how well placed, will zip by so quickly that the shark will either not see the lure, or miss it on the strike. You need to approach the shark at such an angle that it swims toward you. Then you can make a cast and maintain the fly near the eye. As the shark moves close to the boat you should kneel, for though its vision is poor, the shark can see a silhouette. And in stalking a big shark, silence is vital.

Mylar attached to the fly helps the shark locate the lure. Since it is also necessary for the angler to know the location of the fly, so he can keep it near the shark's eye, a fly with a dash of bright orange or red is helpful. I like a yellow-and-orange hackle streamer fly. Sharks take such a fly well, and you can easily see it, too. Sharks have powerful jaws and can crush a small hook easily. For sharks of more than 40 pounds, hooks in the 3/0 to 5/0 size are recommended. A fly that has taken many sharks, but is a little difficult for the angler keep track of, is a 5/0 hook with a dense wing of polar bear on top, and a few strands of Mylar added.

Sometimes, when stalking a shark you'll find that it is moving away at such a speed that you'll lose your chance for a cast. Stick the first 2 feet of the fly rod tip under the water and swish it rapidly back and forth. The vibrations may attract the shark, and it will often turn and approach the boat.

Another good trick is to catch a small fish of several pounds, tie it to a 20-foot length of heavy line, and allow the dead fish to drag along the bottom behind the boat as you move across the flat. Keep an eye on the bait, for sharks frequently will show up and try to seize it. Naturally, you should retrieve the bait and cast immediately to the aroused shark.

If you live in an area where the waters are slightly murky, or the water is deep enough that the sharks cannot be clearly seen, you can still take them on a fly. Establish your boat along a sod bank or other point sharks frequent. Set up a chum line of blood (hatcheries and slaughterhouses can supply it) or ground-fish chum. The sharks will often be attracted to within a few yards of the boat.

Once hooked, sharks can provide terrific excitement on a fly rod.

Big sharks like this will thrill any fly rodder. This fish was taken in Florida Bay near Flamingo. You need solid wire shock tippets and bright flies to con a shark like this into striking.

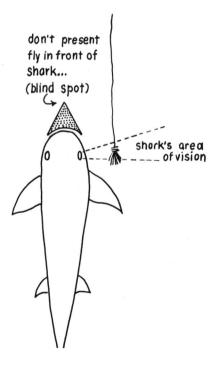

don't present fly in front of shark... (blind spot)

shark's area of vision

Fly must be within a few inches of shark's eye.

KING SALMON

I have never fished for king salmon, but Bob Edgely, Dan Blanton, and Lawrence Summers have sent me photos of giant kings, as well as a great deal of information about this magnificent fly-rod game fish. What follows is distiled from my correspondence with them.

Most of the regular fishermen that fly-fish for king salmon agree that the best time to fish the Pacific Northwest is the first week in November. This offers the best chance at a really big fish, though there are always fish in the river by the end of October.

The two best rivers to fly-fish for king salmon in the Pacific Northwest are the Smith River in northern California, near the Oregon border, and the Chetco, located near the Oregon-California border.

The Chetco River is a short coastal stream that has a good run of kings. The fishing starts a little earlier than on the Smith River. You can figure on taking fish around the beginning of the second week of October through November. The fish run a little smaller, but there seem to be more of them, maybe because of the salmon hatchery on the Chetco. Since the hatchery was built the run on this river has increased greatly.

The average salmon in the Chetco will range from 18 to 25 pounds, with a few fish running larger. A 65-pound fish was taken in 1971 on hardware, but this is an exception rather than a rule. Fishing with flies takes place from the mouth of the river to a point about five miles upstream. Most of the best fishing occurs within a mile of the river mouth. You fish from small, 8-foot prams, casting your flies in toward the shoreline from a point a short distance offshore. The flies drift with the tidal currents, and most strikes occur during the drift, rather than on the retrieve. The area between Highway 1 and the entrance to the harbor is a very good one. Cast your flies toward the harbor jetty wall.

There are a few holes upstream from the Highway 1 bridge. One is the Morrison Hole—large salmon hold well in this one.

The Smith is a beautiful river. The heavy annual rainfall is about 100 inches; the rains begin sometime in November. The stream has not been ruined by clear-cut logging or damming. One inch of rainfall in late October and November in a twenty-four-hour period and the river will be filled with king salmon. Give it maybe twenty-four more hours to clear and the river will be perfect for fly fishing.

King salmon usually enter the Smith during the bottom of the outgoing tide, when the current is at its strongest. The strong current helps the fish find their way over the bar and into the river mouth, but the kings won't come into the river if the surf is extremely rough. Once the fish are in the tidal lagoon area of the river they will mill around until the tide starts in, and then move upriver with the rising water. The river area that is called tidewater extends from the river mouth to the Woodruff's Hole—at least this is the water influenced by the tides.

The average size of the Smith River king salmon is between 25 and 35 pounds, with plenty of fish in the 25- to 45-pound class. There are some 50-pounders, too, but they're hard to nail.

The best holes to fish on the upper Smith River vary from year to year, but the most consistent ones are the Cable Hole, the Society Hole, and the Buck Early Hole.

The fly gear used for king salmon is the same as that used for West Coast steelhead fishing, and in some cases a little heavier. The rods must be able to handle a number 10 or 11 line, and 26 to 30 feet of 20-pound-test lead-core line that has been made into a shooting head.

These are big, strong fish, and it takes a good strong rod to tire them. Reels should be large, with ample line capacity, and a good drag, too. Tippets are generally 10-, 12-, or 15-pound test, and leaders run to about 9 feet.

A boat of some kind is needed for just about all the fly fishing with the exception of two holes. A moderate-sized powerboat will work, but a one-man boat is the only practical choice to use upriver. The boat should be stable enough for a man to stand up in; keep in mind that there are rapids to shoot and that currents can be strong.

Fly lines used in the tidewater are Hi-Density and fast-sinking shooting heads. The upriver fishing requires the use of a lead-core shooting head, since the holes are deep and swift and the lead is needed to get the fly down to the fish. Leaders can be shorter for upriver use, too. On the Chetco a lead-core shooting head is mandatory.

When fishing in tidewater you locate the fish holding in certain depressions or holes. You can often locate the salmon as they roll on the surface. Anchor your boat a long cast away from the fish. Never cross over the school with the boat or you'll scatter them. Cast your fly across the fish and let it sink close to the bottom; counting as the line sinks helps you find the level where the fish are holding. Retrieve the fly at various speeds until you find one that the fish seem to prefer. Bob, Dan, and Lawrence prefer an erratic retrieve.

Bob Edgely with a giant 50-pound king salmon he took in the Smith River. He and Dan Blanton fish together all the time; Blanton has taken a 54½-pounder from the Smith River on a fly.

The strike of king salmon is not spectacular; they just stop the fly. Salmon that are hooked fairly will rarely jump, but rather will take off on several long runs and fight deep. If a salmon jumps several times right after hook-up, or if it porpoises, it will, without a doubt, be foul-hooked and should be broken off. It's not legal to land a snagged fish. You can't help snagging an occasional fish if you are working a large school of kings, but breaking off the fly doesn't seem to bother them a bit.

Salmon prefer to hold in the deep slow pools and backwater eddies, rather than in the fast tail slick that steelheads prefer. They will mill around in the deep hole, sometimes 30 to 40 feet deep, waiting for the river to rise so they can continue upstream. The perfect situation is when enough rain has occurred to get the fish up to the pools, and then the river's dropped some, isolating them in their respective holes. The best way to fish these river pools is to fish your fly "down the shoot"; a shoot is a slot in which the fish are holding. You anchor above and cast a lead-core shooting taper almost straight downstream, then retrieve the fly straight up-current. Be sure the fly is near the bottom.

The two holes that you can fish by wading are the Cable Hole and the Water Gauge Riffle, but you must fish a lead-core shooting taper here. You can fish the Society Hole by standing on the rocks—which get crowded.

Bob, Lawrence, and Dan all find that two basic types of flies produce well on king salmon. Various shrimp patterns, tied on 3X strong hooks, number 2 in size, are effective. The shrimp are generally tied with brown bucktail for the tail, carried over the back to the head, with a body of silver Mylar. The head is brown tying thread, alone or with a tuft of bucktail.

A Comet series is also extremely effective. Bright colors are used, usually fluorescent. The tail is bright orange or sometimes black, either bucktail or calf tail. The body is Mylar, either silver or gold. A collar 1½ inches in diameter of yellow, yellow and red, or red is tied in palmer style right in front of the Mylar body. As on most West Coast flies, a bead-chain pair of eyes adorn the front of the pattern.

All king salmon flies are weighted to make them sink faster.

10 Deep-Water Fishing

The excitement and mystery of deep-water fishing make it a superb challenge to the salt-water fly fisherman rugged enough to lock his knees under the gunwale and versatile enough to present a fly to a host of species never before considered fly-rod fare. It is a true frontier, and there is more opportunity for the thinking fisherman to develop new techniques than in perhaps any other area of fresh- or saltwater fly fishing.

The sudden appearance of the huge body and dorsal fin of a fast-swimming sailfish a few feet behind the boat, ready to take on that long streamer fly, will make an angler's knees quiver and his heart beat at double speed. So will the location of a prowling school of savage blue-fish—jumbos tearing a frightened pod of baitfish to shreds. You know that the instant the fly hits the water, you're going to have a fish on, and you can bet you won't have an easy time landing it. And when a companion has teased a heavy-shouldered amberjack or husky cobia to boatside with a live bait and you're ready to drop a silver-dollar-sized popping bug to that wild-ly excited fish, the singular thrill is one that has to be lived to be completely understood.

Deep-water fishing should be defined as fly-rod fishing in water depths exceeding 12 feet. Much of this type of fly fishing is actually running the boat in search of fish or fighting dusty weather to come home. But when it's right, no other angling compares to it.

Unlike shallow-water fishing, where a silent approach is generally mandatory, and casting must be done with care, the emphasis in deep-water fishing is on locating the fish and then getting something in front of them that they will strike. Your lure can be a fly or popper dressed on any size hook—from a tiny number 4 to a huge 7/0. The length of the fly can range from a mere 2 inches, to 8 or 9, or even longer if you can cast it.

Deep-water fishes sought by fly fishermen can be divided roughly into two categories. The first are roamers; these fish, mostly pelagic, move great distances in a short time, working over bait today in one area, moving 20 or 50 miles away by the next day. This type of fish may be offshore in abundance for a few hours, a day, a week, even a month, and then suddenly have gone elsewhere. They are constantly on the move, searching for the right water temperatures and enough baitfish to feed upon. Temperature and availability of bait determine when these fish will move into your area, and when they will leave.

The second category includes the fishes that remain in a specific area for long periods of time. Such fish can often be located easily, and a scheme devised for duping them into taking a fly.

Huge schools of jack crevalle roam the deep waters near the coast of southern waters. Here a school of jacks tear into small sardines off Smith Shoal near Key West. These jacks average 10 to 18 pounds and put up a tremendous fight on a fly rod.

The roamers would be represented by such fishes as albacore, bluefish, oceanic and Atlantic bonito, cobia, dolphin, the jacks (crevalle, barjack, horse-eye), mackerels (cero, Spanish, Atlantic, Pacific, and king), marlins (blue, black, striped, and white), salmon, wahoo, sailfish (Atlantic and Pacific), yellowtail, false albacore or little tuna, and other tunas (blackfin, bluefin, Allison, Atlantic, and Pacific bigeye). These are only some of the major species available to fly fishermen who work deep water. Roosterfish and striped bass exist in deep water but are difficult to classify. The striped bass has been discussed with the shallow-water species.

Some of these species have yet to be caught on a fly rod, while others have been taken only in small numbers. There is still great room for experimentation.

The second group are homebodies. They sometimes appear in schools, but may also be solitary denizens, or accompanied by only a few companions. Among this notable group of fishes are African pompano, barracuda (Pacific and great), rockfish, grouper, amberjack, and snapper. This list does not seem nearly as long and impressive as the one for roamers—but remember that fifty-two species of rockfish occur in California waters, and that groupers and snappers are divided into several dozen subspecies. Not all rockfish are in water regarded as deep, but for practical purposes, the methods used to catch deep-water species will in most cases succeed for nearly all rockfish situations.

A world record jack crevalle, 19 pounds 2 ounces, taken by the author, holding fish, on six-pound test tippet.

FLY RODS

Two basic fly rods will form the nucleus of the offshore angler's tackle requirements. A rod that handles a weight-forward number 9 line is ideal for your light stick. This rod is great for salmon trolling on the West Coast and for casting to bonito, many jacks, mackerel (except king mackerel), yellowtail, false albacore and many other smaller open-water species. These fish are fast, capable of a 100- to 200-yard run, but do not dive deep and exert the tremendous strain on tackle that fish like amberjack, billfish, and larger tunas do.

The second rod is a fish-fighting tool first and foremost; as a casting implement it will always leave a little to be desired. Scientific Anglers has developed a rod that is superb for such work. Called a System 12, or Great Equalizer, it will actually handle any line size from 11 through 15 with ease. The rod is typical of the weapons that have been custom tailored to fight heavy fish, throw bulky flies, and do incredible work on fish that a few years ago were thought beyond the realm of fly fishing. The System 12 rod weighs 8⅜ ounces and is 9 feet long. Other companies are also manufacturing rods for heavyweight fly fishing. Fenwick has an FF 117, and Pflueger and Shakespeare have developed similar rods.

If you have always cast with a light rod, and considered a number 9 or 10 line heavy, you'll at first reject a rod like the System 12. But when you have a sailfish, amberjack, or roosterfish on a rod balanced with an 8 or 9 line, you'll suddenly become aware of the tremendous power of offshore fishes. You can actually feel the cork handle bend under the strain, and the rod no longer responds to your effort; it's bent into a deep inverted **U** by the fish's pressure. All you can do is hang on.

Should you ever hook a large fish on a light rod (accidentally, of course) you can add extra support to your rod by laying one hand under the rod approximately 18 inches from the front of the foregrip. When you lift the fish this hand helps change the basic fighting characteristics of the rod and assists in exerting force. Many heavy-duty rods, like the System 12, have a forward grip several inches in front of the foregrip. While this may seem like merely a commercial gimmick added to sell fish-fighting rods, it's really a good feature. Amberjack, roosterfish, big jacks, billfish, and others do not give up easily. It's not unusual to fight one of these giants for an hour, or even several hours. All of that time the fish will have the rod deeply bent, and without this forward grip your hand position on the glass shank of the rod can become very tiring.

FLY LINES

Lines for these rods will range in size from 9 through 15, with size 9 through 11 most frequently used. For general use, East and Gulf Coast fishermen prefer the size 9 weight-forward taper. This will accommodate most of their fishing where the quarry feeds on or near the surface. If the fish are very deep the angler will generally use Hi-D line.

West Coast fishermen use shooting heads. Commercial shooting heads average about 30 feet, while those made for personal use will vary a few feet from this, depending upon the caster's ability, his rod, and the line weight required to balance the tackle.

Shooting heads have never become popular on the East Coast, yet there are many places where eastern anglers could triple their catch if they would experiment with this system of fly fishing.

FLY REELS

No matter what type of rod and line you use, you must have a good reel. The Pflueger Medalist and the System reel made by Scientific Anglers are the only inexpensive reels I can recommend. The new Pflueger Supreme Model 578 and the Shakespeare Model 1896 are good medium-priced reels and will subdue almost any fish in existence. The Fin-Nor and the SeaMaster, both handmade, are the most highly regarded reels among topflight saltwater fly fishermen. You can fight any fish that can be taken on fly tackle with either of these two reels.

Captain Bob McChristian began making his famed SeaMaster about 1953. Veteran Florida Keys light-tackle guide George Hommell, who bought one of the first reels off the bench, says that he's taken more than 100 tarpon exceeding 100 pounds on that reel, plus thousands of other fish. It's never had to be repaired.

Captain Mac says that in the sixteen or so years he has been making the reel, he's never had one come back in need of repair. He inspects each one himself. Occasionally someone will send one back to have the drag renewed or to have it cleaned and checked out, but a SeaMaster is a lifetime buy.

The Fin-Nor, the forerunner of such reels, is another example of fine tackle; it is world-famous for its durability. This reel will hold approximately 300 yards of backing plus a full 90-foot fly line.

Most of the successful fly reels used in deep-water fishing have a stout spool and a strong reel frame and foot support, and are corrosion-resistant. They have another very important feature: the drag. Usually set at somewhere between 1 and 4 pounds, it must be smooth and remain stable, without loosening or tightening, throughout the battle. On the best fly reels, drag surfaces are relatively large and smooth, for heat buildup will often destroy small washers or cause them to malfunction. In the best reels there is some method of flashing off the heat; often the washers are mounted on brass or aluminum side plates that diffuse the heat rapidly.

The angler who runs to the blue water and knows nothing about fishing it will wonder how anyone can find fish in such vastness. Everything looks the same. Yet to the knowledgeable angler there are exact places to go, and definite procedures for finding these hot spots.

Birds can be a quick tip-off. Gulls, terns, and other water birds are—as described earlier—indicators of feeding fish; the man-o'-war or frigate bird is especially important when you're after larger fish.

Many species of fish will feed briefly at the surface, often for just a few minutes, then disappear, popping up somewhere else a few minutes later.

It pays to get to a feeding school of fish as quickly as possible, before the fish sound or the baitfish scatter. If you arrive late and see no fish activity, make several casts anyway. Often a few predators are still around.

Remember to approach a school from the upwind side, so you can throw your fly downwind. And *never* run the boat through a school of breaking fish.

Remember also that one of the greatest tricks the fly fisherman can learn about casting to breaking fish after a fast boat approach is how to hold and release his line. When the motor is moved rapidly toward the fish the fly rodder, if he casts with his right hand, should stand at the right rear quarter of the boat. The forward taper or belly section of the line, plus the leader and fly, is streamed out behind him in the boat's wake. When the boat reaches the fish and the motor is chopped, the fly rodder can make a quick forward cast.

If the boat is large, with spreading outriggers, the fly rodder should request that they be folded out of the way before the action begins. If that's not possible, a side cast can be made. But the angler should always remember those 'riggers and anything else that might be in the way.

When no birds are about, the surface of the ocean can often reveal your quarry. Schools of fish swimming just below the surface will often show color. Many skippers can tell the species of fish by the peculiar coloration of the water. Multicolored dolphins and rainbow runners are often a stirring sight as they swim in the clear waters of the sea.

Schools of baitfish are often revealed by the shimmering light reflected from their sides. Another tip-off is flying fish soaring quickly out of the water. When baitfish are under attack, the school will shower into the air, creating a stirring sight and sound. Sudden boiling of the water at the surface may indicate that a large fish just turned there. And nervous water may mean large fish swimming below.

Sails, marlin, and sharks often bask on the surface. Resting, maybe even sleeping, these big fish lie motionless so that their tail and backfins protrude above the water. In the Sea of Cortez and along the Pacific coast, there are numerous occasions when scores of striped marlin and sailfish can be seen basking on the surface. A very silent approach is necessary, for such fish are easily alarmed.

Floating weeds harbor myriads of tropical fishes 1 to 5 inches in length. Baby amberjacks, little bonito, and thousands of other tropical fishes rest and live in these floating weeds. Because of wind and current action, the weeds often form lines miles long. Weed lines are formed mostly during calm periods, since wave action tends to break them apart. In the Atlantic, the Gulf Stream's current forms the weeds in dense lines, especially when there is an easterly wind that gently blows them sideways to the current.

The first weed line encountered offshore is rarely the most productive. Unless you see visible fish action at the first line of weeds, it's a good idea to head farther offshore, looking for the next weed line.

Another method of locating offshore fishes is to look for floating debris—logs, sticks, boards, anything that offers shade. The Central and South American rivers spew millions of tree branches and whole trees down from the jungle forest to the sea. These provide a haven for dolphin and offer some of the finest dolphin fishing in the world. Wahoo frequently lie under such debris. I heard of one party that took seven wahoo and nineteen dolphin from under one huge tree using spinning tackle.

Frigate birds soaring above the surface are a tip-off to big fish feeding below.

When feeding under the surface, many fishes create a slick of the chopped bodies of the oily baitfish they are consuming. An oily slick on the water should definitely be investigated.

Saltwater fishermen should either know the bottom characteristics intimately or carry charts. Charts reveal the sudden drop-offs, ledges, bumps in the bottom, wrecks, and other fish-producing areas. Fish do not usually live on a plain bottom. They will generally be found where an upcropping of rocks occurs, or a shelf drops off to form a hiding place for the food that they prey upon. Studying a chart will reveal such places.

Marlin and other billfish often bask on the surface, as shown here.

Many years ago, one angler used to fish out of Ocean City, Maryland, and return later in the day with a spectacular catch of white marlin. No one could figure out how he did it. After following him one day they discovered his secret. About twenty-five miles offshore, this man had located an underwater plateau that rose from the ocean depths. The smaller fish the whites fed on lived along this uprising, drawing the marlin during the summer season to this particular area, now called the Jack Spot. Ocean City has now become the "White Marlin Capital of the World," and is vitally interested in pursuing a program of catch-and-release of these great billfish.

Well-marked charts will reveal many such uprisings, as well as drop-offs, where the bottom descends rapidly, forming vertical walls which accommodate the crabs and other crustacea, small fishes, and other foods that predatory fish feed upon. Vertical drop-offs are always prime fishing possibilities.

Perhaps most rewarding for offshore fly fishermen besides finding surface-feeding fish, is locating wrecks. Wrecks become underwater apartment houses. Many lie in water too deep to get a fly down to, but there are ways to bring these fish to you.

The easiest and fastest way to find a wreck is with a depth finder. Several types exist, but basically they can be divided into two groups: those that print an actual recording of the bottom on paper and those that emit flashes of light on an indicator dial at the depth beneath the finder at the moment. The type that paints the bottom on a chart is usually referred to as a recording-type depth finder.

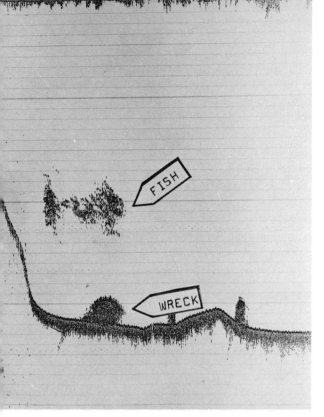

Use of a depth recorder to seek out wrecks and locate the schools of fish living on the wreck is a great asset to the fly fisherman. Here is the actual photo of a chart that shows the wreck on the bottom and a large school of fish above it.

Fishing around wrecks, either those that protrude above water or those on the deeper bottom, is always a good bet. Mark Sosin casts to a cruising cobia, often seen around such wrecks.

Flasher types are less expensive; you can buy good ones for from $100 to $200. However, they are limited in their usefulness. They indicate the depth under the hull at the moment, and in some situations, if you become skillful at using one, you may be able to determine whether the bottom beneath the hull is soft, hard, mud, or rock. The better ones will indicate any fish beneath the boat with weaker flashes, but the operator usually needs some skill and practice before he is aware of the fish sightings. And if he isn't watching the machine at the instant the flashes occur, he has no way of knowing that he has passed over fish.

The recorder types are far superior. The recorder actually paints the bottom on a moving chart, so you can see the profile of a ship's hulk on the bottom, or rock piles and other bottom configurations. But the recorder does more. It clearly paints on the chart the exact depth and size of the school of fish, and will even indicate a single large fish between the recorder and the bottom.

A 25-pound dolphin taken while fishing a weedline; yellow or red and yellow flies are particularly effective for dolphin.

If you drift or cruise slowly over a potential wreck site, a flasher type will indicate how deep the bottom is beneath the hull. But recorder models will furnish the exact and continuous outline of the bottom with all fish schools between you and the bottom, so that after you have made a pass across a wreck you can stop to examine the chart and see a photographic record of what is down there.

The compass and the depth finder are serious tools for the offshore fly fisherman.

The depth finder has the advantage of allowing you to return home in dense fog or low-visibility weather with comparative safety. Your charts tell you the water depths. As you return, the recorder can monitor the bottom, indicating where you are and preventing you from going ashore or crashing onto rocks. Many anglers, when moving slowly in deep water, run their recorders, hoping to pick up uncharted hot spots. Depth finders are useful in reading the bottom when you are approaching known good areas, too. If you are aware that a certain good drop-off occurs at 48 feet, with the recorder you can tell when this depth is reached.

Depth finders are now being rigged on many boats in 16-to-24-foot class. On these small boats they should be firmly installed to reduce vibrations, and an adequate cover should be maintained to keep salt spray from the sensitive working parts.

Once you have located fish you must either cast far enough to get a fly to them, or bring them to you. Naturally, when fish are crashing bait on the surface, the only problem is getting there while the action is still going on and tossing a fly into the feeding mass—a simple problem to solve.

Real problems occur when you know fish are nearby, maybe deep down, and you can't reach them. The lead-core line offers one solution. Make the longest possible cast and allow the super-fast sinking line to bomb right to the bottom. Count as the line sinks; note how long it takes the line on the first cast to get to the bottom. Lead-core lines can be fished well to a depth of 50 feet if there's no strong current. Once you are aware of that time span—let's say it took a count of 22—then make each succeeding cast at that count or just short of it if you want to work on or close to the bottom.

Myron Gregory, a West Coast saltwater fly-rod pioneer, has been the foremost advocate of the lead-core line technique. He began fishing with it in the 1950s, and it has become a standard procedure on the West Coast.

Several precautions should be mentioned, however. If the lead-core strikes the angler on either the back or forward cast, it can inflict a painful if not serious injury. I was struck once across the back when the wind caught one of my sloppy casts; I nearly leaped from the boat when the line hit me. It's also impossible to lift a lead-core line from the water with a normal pick-up. The best procedure is to strip all the monofilament shooting line inside the rod tip, along with 3 or 4 feet of the lead-core (you can leave the lead-core outside the tip as you become more proficient). Then you make a high roll cast with the rod at a vertical angle. This will roll the entire line from the water. Watch the leader. When the leader and fly rise from the water make an immediate backcast, and shoot a few feet of the lead-core line that was inside the rod tip top. Make another back and forward cast to establish the timing; then shoot the line, which will travel an incredible distance.

Details on which lead-core line is best, and how to make the lines and cast them, are given in other chapters.

The Salt Water Fly Rodders of America and most fishing clubs and organizations throughout the world consider it unethical to take a fish on fly tackle with a trolling technique. These organizations maintain that a fish is a legitimate catch only if the boat is dead in the water when the cast is made. Dead in the water is generally construed to mean that all forward power is off the motor. However, on the West Coast the anglers who pursue the silver and Pacific salmon, which take a fly readily, believe in trolling, and do it. They have experimented but so far have failed to find a successful conventional method of taking these fish in predictable numbers.

As a rule silver and Pacific salmon feed closer to the surface than the bigger king salmon. Yet even the silvers are generally at least 20 feet down. Salmon like a fly that moves rather fast, and casting to fish this deep from a dead boat is a real problem.

So the West Coast anglers troll a fly with a lead-core line at a speed from 4 to 7 miles per hour. The Pacific offers a lot of water to search for salmon. Fishermen who work the waters offshore from California look for "black water." From a high vantage point along the coast, the water often appears blue, green, and black. The salmon fishermen believe the black water is best; perhaps more food resides in these dark waters.

Once you have entered black water, stream out a lead-core line with a 4- to 6-inch streamer fly. Flies incorporating Mylar seem to work best. Silver salmon prefer bright colors, particularly orange, yellow, or a combination of the two.

Troll over an area suspected of holding salmon. If you don't get a strike, let out more line to allow the fly to ride deeper. Then make a return pass, continuing to maintain the 4-to-7-mile speed.

Fishing submerged wrecks is a totally different kind of deep-water fly fishing. Wrecks are always excellent places to fish. But if you find one in 80 to 100 feet of water, how can you bring these fish within reach of the fly? Perhaps one of the simplest methods of attracting snappers, cobia, and big amberjacks in tropical waters is to light several firecrackers and throw them overboard. The concussion never harms the fish, but the loud noise will often draw to the surface fish that will not respond to other techniques.

The most exciting method of luring fish topside from a wreck is with a teaser. Florida anglers have developed this technique in recent years to the state of a high art. Al Pflueger, Jr., was one of the pioneers. You obtain a number of baitfish before going to the wreck; blue runners are preferable since they're so lively and tough, but any fish of from 6 to 16 inches will suffice. Tie a short length—maybe 4 feet—of 50-to-60-pound-test monofilament to a gaff handle, heavy-duty rod, or pole, and attach a 4/0 to 6/0 hook to the other end of the line. Hook the baitfish in the center of the back, taking care not to strike its backbone and kill it.

Lower the teaser over the side and allow it to splash on the surface. If no larger fish appears within a few minutes, another angler can take a rod and violently swish it back and forth in the water. Apparently the vibrations set up by the rod and the swimming fish bring out the killer instinct in many fishes. Cobia, amberjack, dolphin, barracuda, big snappers, and other wreck-dwellers are drawn by such tactics. I have never met anyone who has tried this trick on roosterfish, but I'll bet it would work for them, too. Of course, sharks move in also.

Once the fish arrive on the scene you follow a prescribed routine. Swish the teaser back and forth right in front of the hungry fish. Sometimes the game fish become frantic and move so close to the boat that they charge, miss the bait, and actually run into the side of the boat. It's advisable when catching your bait to get an ample supply. When a dozen or more amberjacks and cobia are milling around the bait, you're going to lose baitfish. What usually occurs is that, while you're busy teasing the fish and keeping the bait away from several of them, a larger and wiser fish will sneak under the boat and ambush the teaser before you get a chance to yank it away.

Observe several rules for this type of fishing: a stout fly rod is mandatory; the lure that has performed consistently best in this situation is a huge, 1¼-inch across-the-face popping bug made of Styrofoam, with a well-sharpened 7/0 hook. Put just the leader and a few feet of fly line—rarely more than 7 or 8 feet—outside the rod tip.

I remember one day when my son, Larry, Jim Lopez—a great saltwater fly rodder—and I stopped alongside a black Key West harbor buoy to get blue runners for bait. We had thirty-one of them in the live well when Jim got the idea to go to a little-known wreck that lay more than 20 miles out in the Gulf of Mexico. He fired the engines and headed northwest. I complained that we should take time to get more bait; Jim felt we had more than enough. We found the wreck with no trouble. The Gulf was as flat and green as a pool table. Jim rigged 5 feet of 60-pound-test mono to a gaff handle and tied a 5/0 hook to the other end of the line. Larry rigged a stout fly rod with a number 12 line and a Styrofoam popping bug with a face the size of a half dollar.

I climbed to the bridge and took a light reading for my cameras, then nodded to Jim that I was ready. He dropped the teaser bait overboard and it began to struggle and fight. Within two minutes I began to see dark shapes emerging from the depths below. Up came more than a dozen big amberjacks and seven large cobia; all the cobia were more than 40 pounds. Within minutes Jim had lost four of the baits to the savage fish. Larry, casting like a madman as the fish swirled alongside the boat, hooked two in the next 20 minutes. Both fish wiped him out in the wreck more than 60 feet below. Both weighed well over 70 pounds, and despite the 12-pound-test tippet and heavy rod, Larry simply couldn't keep them out of the wreck. He handed the rod to Jim and began to tease the jacks and cobia.

Jim Lopez holds a stick that has suspended three feet below it a blue runner, a lively 12-inch bait. Larry Kreh, holding his fly rod, makes ready. Lopez is teasing amberjack and cobia by flopping the baitfish back and forth on the surface, attracting the fish and creating a frenzy among them.

Jim Lopez holds up a 48-pound amberjack taken on the fly rod and a popping bug. The fish was teased to the surface and held there by Larry Kreh.

Having done this many times before, Jim waited until the fish were about as excited as they were going to get, then dropped the line in and made several loud water-gulping whooshes with the bug. A good amberjack grabbed the bug and streaked into the wreck below. A large cobia repeated the trick a few minutes later. Jim managed to get a bug in front of the smallest amberjack in the pack. After a stirring battle I gaffed the fish for Jim. It weighed 48 pounds. Then I realized that we were out of baitfish. Those 31 blue runners had disappeared in less than an hour.

Offshore towers, like those on the Gulf coast and those offshore from the Carolinas, harbor big cudas and cobia, which can be lured with a teaser bait. Some of the fish that live around these towers become extremely smart and are difficult to fool with a fly. Norman Duncan has developed a technique for taking cudas after they have been excited by a teaser bait. Barracudas are incredibly swift and have keen eyesight. They quickly realize that a fly is just that—an artificial bait.

Norman teases the cuda until it takes a bite from the bait. He allows the bait to lie motionless in the water, then throws his fly right beside the mutilated bait. You must let the current sweep your fly without any manipulation by you—*the fly must float dead in the water.* Apparently the cuda thinks the fly is another hunk of the baitfish that is being swept away.

If you have no bait aboard, and you are over a wreck or near an obstruction that might harbor large fish, you can often tease them into striking a fly with the use of a "chugger" plug. This is a lure with a face that is deeply scooped to pick up gallons of water on a jerky retrieve by the angler. The lure carries no hooks. The chugger is cast out and brought back in swift jerks of the rod, causing the lure to make great gulping sounds, which attract many kinds of fish.

The lower artificial lure, with hooks, is a chugger that is cast on spinning or plug casting tackle and brought in with sweeps of the rod, creating loud, "blooping" sounds. The upper lure is the same, only the hooks have been removed. Such a lure can be used to tease fish to the fly; the upper lure was used one day in schools of surface feeding jack crevalle, who tore nearly all the paint from the lure.

As the chugger is worked rapidly through the water the fly rodder watches the lure intently. If any fish appear near the plug a cast is made so the fly falls near it—and it is almost always eagerly accepted by the stalking fish.

Sometimes the chugger is very effective around buoys and markers, as well as wrecks and towers. I remember fishing one day with my son, Larry. Returning from a good day offshore, we passed through the Key West harbor, and I mentioned that we should check some of the buoys for cobia. Larry didn't really think it would be worthwhile, but reluctantly agreed to try—just to please me. It was sundown and we had only a few minutes·to try. I stood on the casting deck of the 18-foot boat while Larry began to cast the chugger around the buoy. Suddenly, an amber shape arose and began to follow the plug. Larry jerked the plug away as it neared the boat and I asked him if he wanted to cast to the fish. He leaped to the platform and grabbed the rod. The cobia had dropped back into the channel depths but I was sure I could bring it back again. I cast and began to work the plug noisily. Larry saw the fish first. It was only 25 feet away, but Larry, a fine caster, was so excited that he had to make three casts before the fly plopped right in front of the fish. The fly was a 7-inch Lefty's Deceiver, which I have had great luck with when fishing cobia. The white hackles and Mylar inched along in front of the fish, which slowly moved up and inhaled the fly. Larry struck hard, and fifteen minutes later I gaffed a 37½-pound cobia for him.

Bob Stearns steers the boat at near top speed, while George Reiger holds the fly rod aloft. Trailing behind is the belly section of the line and fly. When the boat is stopped beside the feeding fish all George need do is flip the fly forward to the fish.

Kites provide a new and novel method of teasing fish into position where the fly rodder can make a cast. Though kites have been used in the South Pacific since before the time of Christ, Harlan Major is usually credited with establishing kite fishing in this country back in the 1930s. It died out as a fishing technique shortly after that, but in the past few years it has been revived and now promises to become more popular than ever.

The kite is flown from the boat by a special reel; the separate line allows the angler to put aloft a square kite that remains in a steady position. Dangling from the line near the kite is a clamp similar to a clothespin. Another reel is held by a companion, and from it the line runs up through the clamp and down to the surface beneath the kite. At the surface a live bait is dangled so it can splash and remain in one position on the water; naturally, this attracts any predator fish that is nearby.

In regular kite fishing, when the predator grabs the baitfish he pulls the line from the clamp, and the fisherman winds in the slack, strikes, and fights the fish. Fly fishermen employ the kite in a slightly different manner. The line holding the bait can be drawn through the clamp without falling from it—allowing the angler to adjust his bait to move it up or down in the air. Should a fish accidentally grab the bait, the line is secured to the clamp so the fish cannot pull the line free; when a fish is merely attracted to the bait, you can elevate the teaser quickly under the kite. The now-frantic fish will often accept a fly cast to the area where the baitfish disappeared.

A fishing kite can be used to hold aloft a line which has suspended from it a live baitfish, dancing about on the surface. When a fish arrives, the bait can be reeled high in the air under the kite and the caster can throw his fly to the now highly excited fish.

One of the truly pioneer fly-fishing experiments is the successful procedure for taking sailfish and marlin on a fly developed by Dr. Webster Robinson with his wife, Helen, and Captain Louis Schmidt, of Panama. Once these fish were considered beyond the realm of the fly fisherman.

Dr. Robinson was a man of great courage and perseverance. Doctors had told him he would be partially crippled all his life, yet through sheer willpower and exercise he went on to become one of this country's finest saltwater anglers. He caught more sailfish in five years than most serious anglers do in a lifetime. His score on black marlin, the strongest fighting fish in the sea, was 155. No other fisherman has caught even half that many.

His efforts to take blacks finally resulted in the plan to boat billfish on a fly. Fishing in Panama for black marlin, Doc became frustrated by the scores of sailfish that were attacking his baits and destroying them. In desperation he fashioned a wooden plug without hooks, which was trolled behind the boat near the larger marlin baits. It was hoped that the sailfish would attack the smaller lure, and they did. In fact, the sails were so aggressive that when the hookless wooden lure was reeled in, the fish would often continue to attack the lure. Sometimes they'd flee when they saw the stern of the boat, but often they were so intent upon killing and eating the wooden lure that they remained within a few feet of the transom.

Why not try for sails with a fly? Doc was not the kind to just fling a fly at a billfish. Instead, he went home to Key West, Florida, and devised a strategy.

Since he belonged to the famed Rod and Reel Club of Miami Beach, Doc determined to fish according to club regulations, which meant a leader with a breaking strength of 12 pounds, and a shock leader attached to the fly that did not exceed a foot in length. Knowing full well that sailfish often plunge to the depths then streak toward the sky in a leaping jump, Doc was aware of the terrific strain that would be placed against the leader as the fly line was dragged through the water. So he adopted a very old tactic, used by salmon and bass fishermen for many years, of cutting 30 feet of fly line from the back portion. This helped reduce the strain on the leader from line drag as the sailfish made its plunges.

He also studied the inside of the sailfish's mouth and found that it and other billfishes had a larger soft area in the upper jaw than they did in the lower. This meant he'd have a better chance of a hook-up if the hook point rode up.

On January 18, 1962, Doc stood on the deck of the *Caiman*, while his wife, Helen, held a trolling rod. Skipping in the wake behind the boat was a strip of bonito belly that had been cut and then sewn into a shape resembling a fish. The bait carried no hooks.

"Watch it!" screamed Captain Schmidt, as a sailfish rose behind the skipping lure and began to track the bait. Mrs. Robinson had already seen the fish; she was ready. The fish moved forward, then lunged and slapped at the bait with its bill. Mrs. Robinson fed a little line back and the sail got a good taste of the bait. Suddenly, she jerked the bait from the sail's mouth and reeled it closer to the boat. Enraged, the angry sail moved swiftly forward and again inhaled the bait. The whole act was repeated several times, until finally the fish was within casting range. Doc called out for Captain Schmidt to stop the boat dead (so that he could make a legal cast) and for Mrs. Robinson to remove the teaser bait. She snatched the bonito belly out of the water and Doc swept the 6-ounce rod forward with a muscular snap. The white popping bug fell ten feet to one side of the sail. The big popper swirled in the water; Doc popped the bug, and the sail moved toward the fly. No one on the boat was breathing as Doc gave the bug another gurgling pop. The fish hesitated, but its large dorsal fin was aglow with color. Doc raised the 9-foot rod a little, and the fly skittered on the surface. That was too much! The fish leaped forward and came hissing down through the air, the fly disappearing under that thrusting beak.

Dr. and Mrs. Web Robinson, shown here as a team, single-handedly developed the technique for teasing sailfish or marlin up behind a boat so the angler could stop the boat and cast to a now-excited fish. Helen is trolling a skip bait that has no hooks. Dr. Robinson stands ready for battle.

Here you can actually see the dark skipping bait, used as a teaser, moments before Helen flips the bait away. The white spot is a marlin intent on killing and eating that teaser. The boat has been stopped and you can see Dr. Robinson's popping bug in flight.

A right-angle retrieve, so the bill doesn't brush the popping bug away, is vital. Here you see perfect technique as Web swims the popper in front of the marlin.

Dr. Web Robinson *(left)* admires
his huge marlin held by Capt.
Lefty Reagan.

Dr. Robinson used a hook inverted in a popping bug so it would hook in the
upper portion of a billfish's mouth. Here you can see that his technique paid off
on this marlin.

Robinson struck, and the sail, less than 40 feet from the boat, skyrocketed out of the cobalt blue Pacific with a giant leap, then began greyhounding in and out of the water as it tore line from Doc's reel.

Screaming at Captain Schmidt to get the boat around and chase the sail, Doc watched his line almost disappear from the spool before the *Caiman* finally came around and began to pursue the fish. Finally the fish stopped running, changed tactics, and began circling the boat, leaping frequently. Rhythmically Doc pumped and wound, pumped and wound. After forty minutes of the most brutal fly rod punishment Doc had ever applied to a fish, the sail was ready to be boated.

Boating the sail was a problem that Doc had fretted about long before the trip. He realized that conventional boating would be out. Normally, the long leaders can be grasped by the mate and the fish controlled to some extent. With a little more than 12 inches of 12-pound-test leader, and a 10-inch wire shock leader, Doc knew that no one should grab the fly leader while boating a billfish. The fish was gaffed and heaved aboard.

The fish weighed 74½ pounds—not a big Pacific sailfish by Panama standards, but truly a prize. Doc had taken a billfish on a fly. He went on to capture 14 other Pacific sailfish during the next three years; his largest was 107½ pounds.

One factor in Doc's success was that he used bonito belly, rather than a wooden plug. After the sail had tasted the fresh belly bait (minus hooks, of course) it wanted more. Natural bait is far superior to an artificial teaser. Some modern anglers have forgotten Doc's basic lesson and are using artificial lures, which are probably not nearly as effective.

Successful with Pacific sailfish, Doc decided to try a bigger billfish. Blue and black marlin were certainly too large for any fly rod, and white marlin were not as big as the fish he had already caught. He finally decided upon striped marlin. They were bigger than sails, yet small enough to offer at least a fighting chance on fly gear. His tackle would be the same—12-pound-test tippet at least a foot long, no more than 12 inches of shock leader, and a 6-ounce fly rod.

He decided to test his ideas at Baja, California, where he knew that great concentration of striped marlin could be found. He took along his own captain from Key West, Lefty Reagan, one of the most experienced light-tackle skippers in the world.

They got a surprise on the first fish, and soon learned that marlin are considerably harder to excite with a teaser than sailfish. Once they're excited, it is difficult to get them to sustain their eagerness to get that teaser, even if they have tasted it. Once the marlin decided it liked the taste, however, it was an easy task to draw the fish to the boat.

"The first time I hooked a marlin," Doc said, "I remember telling myself I would be damned lucky if I managed to salvage any part of my equipment from the fly right down to the butt cap."

He fought the first marlin for two hours and lost it when the leader finally parted from fatigue. He then hooked four more. He worked one within gaffing range of the boat, only to lose it in the rough seas. Finally, one bright midday, he boated the first marlin ever taken on a fly rod, and rewrote the saltwater fly-fishing books. The giant billfish weighed 145 pounds.

During the next two weeks he fought many striped marlin on a fly. He lost count of the strikes he missed and the fish that threw hooks, but he knew that he lost 19 of those white popping bugs to striped marlin. He ran completely out of 12-pound-test leader material and used the next lightest material he had, 20-pound-test. With this leader, which is slightly higher than the weight acceptable for world records, Doc boated a 178-pound striped marlin. It's still the largest billfish ever taken on a fly rod.

Lee Cuddy, a close friend of the Robinsons, and one of the real pioneers in fly fishing, boated the first Atlantic sail ever taken on fly gear. Lee was fishing with Captain Bucky Stark out of Islamorada. He fought the fish in a terrible rain squall that saw one engine go out and everyone on board get drenched. His sail weighed 48 pounds.

Lee has since caught other sailfish, and Web Robinson, who started this exciting sport, has since passed away. Lee gives all the credit for his billfish to Doc, but Lee has, to my way of thinking, improved on Doc's technique.

Billie Pate, with one of four world record black marlin he and his wife, Laura, caught on a trip to Australia. This fish weighed 42 pounds 6 ounces and was captured on a 15-pound test tippet. Laura caught a world record on 12-pound tippet; Billy set records on 6-, 10- and 15-pound test tippets.

Doc would have his wife, Helen, troll the hookless teaser until a billfish attacked it, then she'd begin teasing the fish toward the boat. Doc had already determined that it was vital to cast the popping bug to one side of the billfish, so the fish would be forced to swing its head to the side to engulf the fly. Doc had seen how a fish that approached from directly behind the lure almost always pushed the fly away with its beak. He felt that casting directly in front of any billfish was wrong; but often when Helen had teased the fish to the boat Doc was forced to make the very cast he disliked.

Lee attaches a heavy bronzed snap to the outrigger and the teaser line is slipped through the snap. The line comes off the teaser, up through the snap suspended at right angles to the boat, and down to the rod held by the angler, who manipulates the teaser bait. As the fish is teased closer to the boat the angler continues to retrieve line. The outrigger allows the angler to draw the bait several feet closer to the boat than Helen could from her stern position, and most important, the line hanging down out of the outrigger places the bait 15 or so feet to the side of the boat, allowing Lee to make a perfect right-angle cast. Since his companion can lift the bait from the water by reeling toward the snap tied to the outrigger, he can make it disappear overhead—or drop it back to the surface again to infuriate the fish further.

One type of chum consists of ground, frozen pieces of fish in a sack with holes in it. The slowly melting block sets up a line.

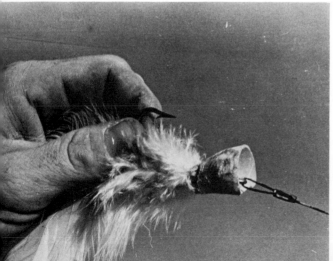

This is one of Dr. Web Robinson's striped marlin poppers. Note the hook is inverted and the face of the bug is scooped to make more noise.

Here are the basic techniques used to bait and catch a billfish:

Use fresh-cut, tough belly bait. Lefty Reagan, who did much experimentation with Doc, firmly believes that bonito belly is the best, but that dolphin belly is nearly as good; both are tough baits. Other kinds of belly bait will work in a pinch, but the numerous slashes inflicted on a bait by a billfish make toughness desirable.

Doc believed that popping bugs made with an upturned 7/0 hook (very sharp) were best. Chapter 6 describes one of his best lures.

Cutting back on the length of the fly line by removing 30 to 40 feet of running line will reduce line friction during the battle, and enable you to place more backing on the spool. Since casts to teased billfish are rarely more than 30 feet (including the leader) there really is no need for the long running line.

Doc used 20-pound-test backing, and since the leader tested at 12 pounds he found this ample. I, too, feel there is little need for 30-or-more-pound-test backing for fighting almost any saltwater fish.

Doc, Lee, and others who have taken billfish on a fly consider it is a waste of time to try unless there are many billfish in the area.

The captain is important, for he handles the boat. But the person teasing the billfish is just as important as the angler. If that person removes the bait too late, or too soon, the game is over. And if he fails to excite the fish properly, it will not strike. It did not take Doc and Helen Robinson long to determine that the person teasing the fish, not the angler, should say when the captain should bring the boat to a stop.

Doc liked the number 10 size line, feeling that heavier lines were not needed and would offer increased air and water resistance.

Subsequent trips by a number of fishermen have refined many minor techniques. It was soon determined that if a fly fisherman did his casting with his right hand he should stand in the right side of the stern. This facilitates casting. It is never a good idea to troll two teasers, since one of them always causes the angler trouble. Naturally, the person working the teaser bait should stand to the left side against the transom and out of the way of the fly caster. And the teaser bait should be approximately the size of the fly that is being used. Setting up the boat prior to putting out the teaser is vital. A spare fly rod, completely rigged, should be close at hand as a standby: a broken leader takes time to replace, and the angler can grab another outfit more quickly.

Wear proper boat shoes that have nonslip soles. Remove buckets and loose gear from the cockpit. If there is anything in the cockpit that might tangle the line and can't be removed, cover it with canvas or netting. Outriggers that are not being used should be folded out of the way if possible. Put masking tape over the cleats. Gaffs should be ready, but covered to prevent injury.

The process of teasing a billfish to the boat, successfully presenting a fly to it, and boating the billfish is a teamwork project. Everyone is vital to success, and it pays to rehearse exactly what each person will do when the moment of truth arrives.

Dolphin can be brought within range of the fly caster with a simple trick. One angler trolls a bait for dolphin (with a hook in the lure) and when he gets a strike, the fly fisherman gets ready. Bringing the hooked fish close to the boat, the fly rodder will see others closely following their hooked companion. Usually the school will remain near the hooked fish and allow the caster to take several on his fly.

There are other methods of bringing fish to the fly caster. Chumming is perhaps the oldest known method, and certainly one of the most effective. One firm rule of chumming is that once you have established a chum line you must keep it going. The fish that are actively feeding in the chum line will soon leave if the food supply is cut off.

Chumming for bluefish is an ancient art in the northeastern part of our country. The oily mossbunker (menhaden) is ground for chum and appeals to fish more than probably any other ground fish. Menhaden is so good for chumming that commercial outlets now sell half-gallon cans of it to southern anglers. The oily mess is mixed with seawater and dipped with a ladle. It spreads on the surface and particles begin to sink. Cutting up little fish to add to the chum slick makes it even more effective. Bluefish and many other species are attracted from a great distance to the origin of the chum. One of the best ways to take a big bluefish on a fly rod is to set up a proper chum line and have the fish come to you.

Other types of chum lines can be established. Coarse fish, or any type of fish not used in eating—scales, heads, everything—can be ground into small bits and frozen in half-gallon cardboard milk cartons. These can be kept aboard the boat in a hardened condition on ice. When needed, the chum is torn from the milk carton and deposited in an open mesh bag or old onion sack. It takes about an hour in a warm sea to melt a five-pound block. It's a good idea to give the sack an occasional yank as it hangs in the water.

If there are no fish where you set up a chum line and you decide to try another place, simply deposit the remaining frozen chum block in a bucket, then motor to another location.

If no chum is available, cutting the throats of fish already taken will produce blood which, added to water in a bucket, can be slowly fed overboard. Oatmeal is an old standby. It can be used alone, but is better when mixed with the existing chum slick.

One of the neatest tricks for chumming, which I have seen practiced only in Bermuda, is the open-end chum basket. A cage with four sides and a top is constructed of quarter-inch hardware cloth. The bottom is open, and a sinker is suspended beneath the bottom. The Bermudians fish on the Argus and Challenger Banks, where the water is well over 100 feet deep. They can bring fish right to the surface with a chum basket.

Here's how it works. The basket, approximately 6 inches long and 4 inches square, open on the bottom, is held upside down, and hog mouth fry (small baitfish) are packed into it. A 6- or 8-ounce sinker is attached to the open end of the basket. A cord, marked at 25-foot intervals, is tied to the upper or closed end. When the basket is full of little baitfish, it is turned over rapidly and allowed to plunge into the depths. Line is fed continuously as the basket descends. When the basket hits bottom, the mate pulls on the cord, flushing the contents. The swiftness of the descent keeps the bait within the basket. However, when the rope pulls the basket upward, all bait is flushed from the open bottom end. Naturally fish on the bottom congregate at the area where food has been dispensed. Another basket is filled and allowed to descend, but not as deep as the first one. It, too, is flushed. Then another basket is flushed even closer to the surface. Dumping each basket closer to the surface draws the fish from the depths to boatside. I've seen wahoo, blackfin tuna, even huge mackerel sharks, come right to the boat.

Once the fish are near the boat a steady feeding of either more small baitfish or ground chum will keep them within the fly caster's reach.

In the Gulf Coast areas and the lower Keys, as well as Mexican waters, the angler has a built-in chum supply. Shrimpers ply these waters at night, usually making three drags along the bottom. Naturally, they recover all sorts of fish life from the sea floor in addition to shrimp. Crabs, small fishes, and many other forms of fish food are piled on the deck during the night

In Bermuda they use this small cage open on one end. Small baitfish, usually hog mouth fry, are put into the container. Note that man on right holds two heavy sinkers that are attached to the cage bottom. The cage is turned over so that the open end is at the bottom. The sinkers cause the cage to descend to the bottom so quickly that no bait falls free. When the cage is jerked upward the bait is flushed from the box.

hours, where they're separated from the shrimp. At dawn the shrimpers shovel the collection overboard.

Often you can get permission to tie your boat to a shrimper who has anchored and is about to remove all this chum from his deck. Or you can carry a lightweight plastic garbage can, or even a large plastic garbage-can liner bag, and approach the shrimper. He has had a long, hot night of work, and for a six-pack of cool beer he'll load your boat to the gunwales with chum.

Aside from a bonanza of chum, you'll also have many fairly large, 3- to 8-inch fishes in the "gold" that the shrimper has deposited in your boat. Many fishes will respond to this type of chum. King mackerel especially like the larger tidbits. If you find kings in your chum line and are having trouble getting them to hit, there are several possible solutions. Often the bigger kings will be deeper. Then a sinking line must be used, and a cast made up-current and allowed to tumble back toward the chum line—it'll go deeper that way.

If you're chumming with large pieces, you'll probably get more strikes if you use a fly the approximate size of the chum, and if you allow the fly to drift dead in the current. Chum moves solely by current action and often a fly that is zipping along is ignored. Sometimes, when fish seem to get wise in a chum line, you can switch to a big, slurping popping bug, which makes a tremendous noise and can't be seen too well by the fish because of all the disturbance it makes.

How to make a strip bait for teasing billfish. A bonito belly is used here, but dolphin works well, too. Strip baits should be made from fish with a tough skin that won't shred when the fish strikes the bait. A cut is made along the line shown here.

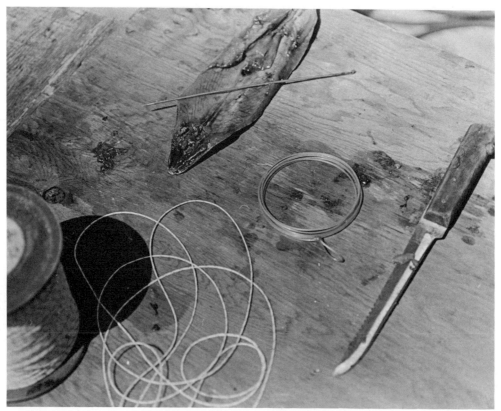

Materials needed to make a teaser strip bait: bonito or dolphin belly, needle, six to eight feet of 100-pound test monofilament, knife and some Dacron for sewing.

When pinched together it should look like this.

Excess meat is trimmed from each side.

Make a loop in the 100-pound test monofilament, lay it in as shown here, then bring sewing needle and Dacron through loop eye. This prevents monofilament leader from pulling free.

Make sure that you secure a firm knot.   Continue sewing the Dacron the length of the belly bait.

Stitch the entire length; the needle is then shoved up through the center and tied off.

Finished belly bait should look like this.

A strip bait is threaded through this snap, which is attached to the outrigger. This enables the man working a teaser bait for billfish to keep the bait away from the boat, enabling the angler to get a right angle retrieve on the fish. This technique was developed by Lee Cuddy.

The dead drift seems the best way to fool some fishes working a deep chum line. However, bonito, kingfish, albacore, and tuna often like a swiftly moving fly. Two retrieves will accomplish this. One is to point the rod tip directly toward where you think the fish may be. Then with a side-sweeping motion of the rod hand, and a fast strip with the other, you cause the fly to dart forward 8 or 9 feet. The fish will often strike such a fast-moving lure before it realizes the fly is a phony. Another fast retrieve can be maintained over a fairly long distance. Place the rod between the inside of both knees and use the knees to hold it there. Take both hands and one after another bring the line back in as fast as you can. This retrieve allows you to take fish that will only strike a fly that moves swiftly over a long distance.

Anyone who has fished from a California party boat knows about the 4- to 6-inch fish called anchovies that are carried aboard by the thousands for use as chum. Special live-bait tanks are used for such purposes. The boats head to sea, and often travel many hours before arriving at the yellowtail and albacore grounds. A mate is assigned to throw live anchovies overboard when fish are suspected of being nearby. This draws the yellowtail and albacore right to boatside. Special spinning rods with flexible tips are normally used to toss a baited hook at the frantic predatory fish. However, the fly caster can get off to himself and with a Hi-D or lead-core shooting line shoot a 5-inch streamer fly into the depths and hang these magnificent game fish. Trips on such boats can be made for a few dollars, and in addition to yellowtail and albacore the fly rodder can expect to find bonito, barracuda, and other fishes.

Using a similar trick, Mark Sosin, one of the great saltwater fly rodders, managed to land what I regard as one of the finest catches ever made in the salt with a fly rod. Mark was fishing on the edge of the Bermuda Challenger Bank with Captain Boyd Gibbons and Pete Perinchief. Mark waited anxiously as a school of Allison tuna were chummed up by the use of anchovies and hog-mouth fry, along with chunks of mackerel. He was using a 26-foot shooting head (floating line) with 100 feet of 50-pound monofilament backing; this was attached to nearly 300 yards of 30-pound Dacron. He used a polar-bear-hair and Mylar streamer fly that he and noted fly tier Bub Church had created for the situation, and a SeaMaster reel.

The Allisons were chummed right to the surface, where Mark made a 40-foot cast and hung one of the fish. After many long and scorching runs, and a problem with the line and anchor rope, Mark fought and landed one of the greatest catches ever taken from the sea on a fly rod—a 56-pound 6-ounce Allison tuna.

In 1973 Jim Lopez, a really fine saltwater fly fisherman, boated an 81-pound Allison on 15-pound-test line. Pete Perinchief, Bermuda fishing expert, claimed it was the best catch ever made on a fly rod.

Chumming and great rod handling were responsible for these world-record catches.

Another method of chumming is to toss, at regular intervals, small baitfish overboard. Two sizes of chum are being used here.

One of the greatest catches ever made on a fly rod, a 53 pound 6 ounce Allison tuna, taken by Mark Sosin, at left. Pete Perinchief, in charge of Bermuda sportfishing, can't help but grin at Mark's conquest.

11 Boats

Today most saltwater fly fishing is done from boats—ranging in size from 12-foot skiffs to 50-foot oceangoing craft. But for many years saltwater fly fishing was confined to inshore waters; rarely did anyone take a fly rod to sea. Twenty-five years ago J.T. Herrod, a Miami bonefish guide, had a skiff that was powered by two 25-horsepower motors. It was considered the hottest thing afloat, and the ultimate in a small, fast fishing boat.

In those days, if you decided to fish a particular area and found the fishing poor, you were struck with it. Today, a 14-to-18-foot outboard-powered skiff has a range of more than 150 miles and a speed in excess of 40; many go as fast as 50 mph, though for shallow-water fishing boats with a capability of more than 40 miles an hour are really not necessary.

Just as important to fly fishermen is that today's boat builders are finally designing and constructing boats for our needs. Protruding nails and screws, seats that trip anglers, gas tanks with entangling devices, and similar frustrations are gone. Now we have tanks that are hidden, and no visible cleats, nails, screws, or other gadgets. And the addition of a casting platform now makes it possible for the angler to stand and throw his fly comfortably.

Ample storage for tackle, food, extra gear, and ice are built-in refinements—and all out of the way. Rod-holders have reached a new pinnacle in design. Today the better 18-foot boats can carry four to six fly rods and as many as ten additional spin- and plug-casting outfits—ready to be cast.

Hull designs have improved radically. For the flats, there are boats like the Hewes Bonefisher, in which you can skim across a choppy bay at 35 to 40 mph in solid comfort. You can take them to sea in moderate weather; and they pole well in the shallows and give good gas economy. Usually made of glass, these boats are relatively maintenance-free, and carry a CB or other sophisticated radio, trim tabs, and a good depth finder. Good compasses, which stabilize well in rough water, are available.

Small boats should carry two anchors. One is light and used for holding in slow water, or when making a lunch stop. The other anchor should have plenty of holding power. Most of us now place 3 to 6 feet of rubber or plastic-coated chain in front of the anchor; the coating prevents rusting and the chain enables the anchor to grip better.

Always carry a release buoy. This float can be snapped to the anchor line so that, if a large fish is hooked, the anchor line will be loosened from the boat and the buoy will keep the line afloat while you chase the fish. A lobster pot float made from plastic foam is a perfect buoy.

Offshore fishing boats have evolved as well. Today the modern offshore boat carries an excellent depth recorder (not a flasher) and a multichannel radio. Radar, loran, and other navigational equipment is standard on many models. These hulls keep you dry and comfortable as you cruise at high speeds in relatively rough seas.

The angler who doesn't own a boat may still have to fish on a charter boat that is not designed for fly fishing in salt water (most of them are not). If it is a large oceangoing craft, you would be wise to mask off any cleats with masking tape; tape over anything that will catch the line. I also ask the captain to fold back the outrigger on the side where I plan to throw my backcast. It pays to take these precautions before you leave the dock. If the boat is small, netting can be thrown over the gas cans, seats, and other gear; line dropped in the netting hardly ever tangles.

A typical small boat now used for fly rodding in salt water. This boat is capable of 45 miles an hour with an 85 hp. motor and can navigate in fairly rough seas. The 30-gallon gas tank gives the boat a range of nearly 150 miles.

If you buy a small boat I suggest that you buy a small motor for emergency use. I spent two days on a sandy, mosquito-infested beach in the Everglades with Vic Dunaway and Nelson Bryant, and learned a number of vital lessons. One was to carry a small motor that is powerful enough to push your particular boat against the tide and wind.

And, think about survival gear, which can be stored in the kind of plastic battery cases used for storing batteries in the boat. They offer dry storage with ventilation. In those battery boxes I suggest carrying at least three suits of raingear—one for every passenger. A flashlight, with the batteries stored separately in sealed plastic bags, is good insurance. I carry a dozen packs of matches in a sealed glass jar, as well as a cigarette lighter and extra fluid.

Rod holders installed in the Bonefisher boat. Note that the shock cord can quickly free the rods and that the gunwale protects the rods from salt spray and angler's legs.

A small cooking pan is vital, as well as a pot to boil coffee or cocoa. Cans of potted meat, corned beef, and similar products need no refrigeration and can be stored indefinitely. I seal all cans in plastic bags with a rubberband closure to prevent rust. I don't worry about spare water; I always carry ice in the cooler.

The coast guard insist that you carry some basic equipment. You must have aboard a wearable device that will support an unconscious person upright in the water, one for every passenger. And you must have a throwable device immediately available. A seat cushion will answer for this—but it mustn't be stored; it must be immediately available.

An oar is required on many boats, and a horn or whistle in case you need to sound a distress signal. I carry a fire extinguisher, one that is actually overrated for my boat. Dry chemical is best but not always required by the coast guard. Don't forget to have several lines, one of at least 100 feet for anchoring in storms and in deep water, as well as several others, for which you will find many uses.

I lost a propeller one time and was lucky that it fell on white sand, where Mark Sosin dove in and retrieved it. However, I did not have a spare shear pin and washer, so I had to jury-rig the prop with a 9/0 hook and some leader wire to get us home. Now I carry the washers needed to fit the splined shaft, the nut, and shear pins—and a spare prop. An extra gas hose is also something you should never be without.

The best toolbox I've found is the battery box. Plastic tackle boxes and similar boxes seal in the moisture and cause your tools to rust. I simply spray all tools with a light coating of rust-preventive and, since I went to the battery box, my rust problems have ceased.

Plastic battery boxes are the perfect storage containers. They allow air to circulate through the box, but prevent rain and salt water from entering. I place a shock cord across it to prevent the lid from blowing loose. This box holds emergency food supplies.

This is a portable OMC compass. I carry it in this box (with a protective cover). If I go with someone who does not have a good compass, I can take mine along. Here Dennis Robinson takes a sighting.

There are a few first-aid items that should be carried aboard. The Johnson & Johnson kits are excellent. If you ever fish far from shore the cheapest and best insurance you can carry is a signal mirror. They are sold by army-navy stores, outlets that furnish pilots' gear, and some camping concerns.

With all these things it may sound as if you are overloading the boat—but each item is a mark of good seamanship.

Most saltwater fly rodders trail their boats to their fishing spot. Many of them violate rules of trailering, a practice that may endanger them, or at any rate cost them money.

Trailering is a science. Those who know the ropes make it look easy. It requires application at several times: before you go fishing, on the road, and at the dock when putting the trailer back on the boat. Then, when you return home there are additional procedures that should be followed for a maintenance-free boat and trailer.

To prevent accidents and get quickly and safely where you are going you should make a number of checks before leaving.

Carefully inspect your winch. Be sure the cable is not rusted or frayed. Tiny broken wires protruding from the cable can leave steel splinters in your hands, or cut deeply. If you use a rope, make sure it is not frayed; it could let go and hurt someone.

For several years some of the more expert tarpon fishermen have been using electric motors to approach schools of big tarpon. Here Bob Hewes, Miami boat builder, sneaks up on some tarpon in the lower Keys.

Gear teeth can be broken off, leaving you with a dangerous piece of equipment. Such gears should be replaced.

If you have an electrically driven winch, make certain all connections are free from corrosion. Make sure that they fit tightly, too. Have a manual handle, in case of power failure. Don't carry the handle on the winch, it may jiggle loose or be stolen.

You should carry a spare tire. Most anglers I know prefer to mount the tire right on the trailer. It must be locked to prevent theft. The most useful jack I've seen is one that resembles a half-moon gear, with a notch in one end that can be placed under the axle. When you use the jack, position a block of wood on the ground under it to prevent it from sinking into the soil. Place the jack under the axle and move the car slightly forward. The axle rides up on the half-circle jack, holding the wheel well off the ground. There are no moving parts to fail. When the tire has been replaced or repaired, the driver simply moves the car forward and the jack turns over and down, gently depositing the wheel on the ground. A hole can be drilled through one of the jack's supports and it can be bolted directly to the trailer frame.

Perhaps the most common offense against good trailering practice is tire abuse. Almost all fishermen disregard their trailer tires even though they support the entire rig. If they're low in pressure they flex violently on the road, building up tremendous heat that destroys the rubber. Bear in mind, too, that the smaller tires are traveling faster than your car's tires, since their diameter is less. Only in unusual circumstances should you trailer tires of 12 inches or less at more than 55 miles an hour for any length of time.

A typical Florida Keys bonefish or tarpon boat. The casting platforms are large, and free of obstructions. The guide is standing on the console to get better visibility. Ross Trimmer is in the bow waiting for bonefish to appear.

Most trailer tires take 50 or more pounds of air. Since few gas station attendants carry a gauge that reads that high, it's advisable to buy one that reads to 100 pounds. They're inexpensive and will save you money on the first set of tires.

Let's assume that your tires call for 65 pounds of pressure. *All tires should be checked cool, before running!* While your boat is still in the yard check the axle tires and the spare. If two tires read okay, and the third reads 45 pounds, that means it is 10 pounds below recommended tire pressure. Stop and check the tires! Let's say the tire pressure in that low one is now reading 59 pounds—you still add 11 pounds; so you add air until the gauge reads 70 pounds.

The boater who follows these rules will get several additional years of life from his tires. He'll also be a safer driver, his chance of a blow-out lessened.

Here is a manufacturers' chart giving recommended tire pressures.

	TIRE SIZE	PLY RATING	MAX LOAD	INFLATION PRESSURE
8-inch Tire	4.80/4.00	4	600	65
	5/70/5.00	4	710	50
12-inch Tire	4.80/4.00	4	790	65
		6	960	90
	6.90/6.00	4	1010	40
		6	1290	60

Most trailers carry a pair of safety chains that are hooked into holes drilled for that purpose in the trailer hitch. All states require that they be hooked up; this does *not* mean draping the chain across the ball. You can get a little more safety if you hook the right chain in the left hole and vice versa, forming an **X** directly below the trailer ball and tongue; should the trailer jump from the ball it will fall into the **X** cradle instead of onto the road.

Another piece of chain should be installed on all trailers. Your winch has a gear that prevents the boat from slipping backward off the trailer. Most trailers have only a rubber bumper to prevent the boat from moving forward onto your car in case of a sudden stop. You should install a short section of chain to the tongue of the trailer near the winch, with a stout eye that can be snapped to the front of the boat, immobilizing it. Properly positioned, the chain will come tight when the boat is correctly drawn up on the trailer.

Before you leave home you should tilt the motor slightly to prevent the lower unit from striking a curb or high spot in the road. One of the best devices for this is a half-inch commercial aluminum trailering brace. It costs less than $5 and fits most motors. When you are trailering it will hold the motor at a slight angle; when you fish it can be dropped flat against the transom.

If your trailer rig weighs more than half the weight of your car, the trailer should have its own brakes. Separate brakes will insure against many kinds of accidents, relieve your nerves, and prevent jack-knifing.

Load levelers are another important factor on heavy boats. These are mechanical devices that distribute the load throughout the trailer and car and are vital in pulling a really heavy boat.

Careful anglers always make sure that their straps lie tight against the boat before they leave the ramp. The straps really should have at least one twist in them on each side of the boat. Flat straps flutter badly in the wind, sometimes cutting through the metal holding-hook or eroding the strap. A twisted strap remains stationary.

The most frequent offense—next to disregard for proper tire pressure—by people trailering boats is committed at the launching ramp. Most ramps will accommodate one to three boats. Yet during a peak morning-hour rush more than one hundred boats will want to use the ramp. Don't tie up the ramp preparing to launch. Note the experienced fishermen. He'll stop a hundred yards back, load all his gear, remove his strap, put in the plug, and tilt the motor—he's ready and needs only a few minutes on the ramp surface.

There are some safe and practical hints about launching a boat. First, all your electrical fittings are designed primarily for automobiles. You certainly would not deliberately immerse your auto headlights in water, and you should not do it to your trailer lights, either. If you have trailed your boat a long distance, you'll have heated the grease and bearings in the wheels. When you back down the ramp, keep the rims and bearings out of the water. If those hot bearings hit cool salt water a vacuum will be created and water sucked right into the bearings. Only your tires won't rust—they're all that should go into the water.

Have your companion stand at the end of the runway, and when the boat nears the water ask him to spread his hands apart to indicate how far the wheels are from the water. This is a much better method than waving the driver toward the water, then suddenly saying Stop!

Put the car in park—and leave the driver's door open, in case you have to get back in quickly. Place a chock under the wheels to prevent the car from sliding into the sea. A strap on the chock allows your companion to pull it away quickly and easily as you drive off.

If the winch is manual be careful not to get hit by the whirling handle. I know of two people each of whom broke an arm that way. Attach a rope to the bow eye and as the boat slides back you'll have it under control.

Putting the boat back on the trailer at day's end can be accomplished easily with a little know-how. Attach a rope to the side of the boat from which the wind is coming. After the trailer has been positioned, the driver of the car can walk to the end of the trailer and connect the cable to the bow eye. His companion, with a rope for the front and one attached at the rear of the boat on the windward side, can control the boat's approach to the trailer. As soon as the boat is on the trailer, move off the ramp to give someone else a chance. Then at some practical distance you can attach straps, remove drain plugs, batten down, and be ready to roll homeward.

When you get home you'll wash the boat—and don't forget to wash the trailer, too. Both should be washed with warm soapy water. At most any hardware store you can buy an attachment that hooks to your garden hose. This dispenses soapy water or a fine, cutting rinse that will take all salt water from the boat and the trailer.

Get a can of touch-up paint and spot the areas where the paint has chipped. To prevent springs from rusting and to make them operate better, you can apply a solution of 50 percent STP and 50 percent kerosene. Take a paintbrush and sop the springs with the watery oil. It will penetrate between the springs. The kerosene will evaporate, leaving the STP to lubricate and protect the springs.

I carry a small jar of grease and a soldering brush (any small brush will do) and after I put the boat in the water I'll frequently dab grease on all my rollers. At the same time, I grease and oil the winch and gears.

Every fly fisherman must become familiar with charts. The first thing to learn is the difference between a chart and a map. A map tells you where to go on land—a chart tells you where not to go on the water.

Charts indicate surface and underwater hazards—shoals, wrecks, drop-offs, reefs, and flats. Properly used, a chart will tell you at any time during your trip exactly where you are.

Few books will give you half the information a chart can. Depths of water, heights of lights, unusual bottom contours, mouths of rivers, and other fish-producing bits of information are yours if you pour over charts.

With a good chart you can safely plot a course to unknown waters, having a thorough understanding of how to proceed and how long it will take you to get there. You can determine a good anchorage, and locate possible good places to fish—all before you leave home.

Charts are put out by two agencies: the National Ocean and Atmospheric Administration (called NOAA) and the Naval Oceanographic Office. Both offices are based in Washington, but the charts can be purchased at most major marine stores.

If you can't buy the chart you want at a local level, write the Distribution Center, C44, National Ocean Survey, Washington, D.C. 20235. Ask for their chart catalog if you aren't sure which chart number you want.

These charts are known as the "Small Craft Series" and if purchased in large numbers—perhaps for a club—they can be bought for a 20 percent discount.

Every angler should get "Chart Number One," which is not a chart at all, but a pamphlet that describes and illustrates all symbols and abbreviations listed on charts.

More than 1,000 charts are available, covering all shallow waters, including the Great Lakes. They are constantly being updated.

Don't depend on old charts. A recent wreck, dredging, or fill—even a channel—may be missing from older charts. The edition number, date, and date of most recent revision (as well as chart number and price) are listed in the lower left corner of most charts.

There are many kinds of charts. In the Small Craft Series, all charts are marked by SC following the number. These are for use on small boats; they are folded into small panels and enclosed in a protective jacket. A variety of reference information is printed on the jacket. Included are such items as service and repair facilities, marinas, and docks. Intercoastal Waterway Charts are being converted to the SC format, too.

Other conventional sheet charts include Harbor Charts, scale 1:50,000 or larger—intended for use by major ships as navigational tools. They indicate in detail many places for anglers to fish.

Weather is something every small-boat saltwater fly rodder must be aware of, alert to its changes. Here Mark Sosin and I are ready to run from a water spout, a dangerous cyclone over water.

The low black bottom on this heavy cloud formation indicates that a squall line is approaching. This usually brings strong winds and dangerous seas.

General Charts are large-scale charts 1:100,000 or more. The large areas these charts show will give you the overall picture. But for detailed study the average fly fisherman is better off with the SC charts.

NOAA shows the land on its charts as a buff color; water areas are blue-white. You should clearly determine when you look at the myriad numbers indicating water depths on a chart whether those figures refer to feet or fathoms. (Six feet is equal to one fathom.) Be sure to check your chart to determine which is being used.

If you have a depth sounder or recorder, and a working knowledge of a chart, you can discover new fishing areas. Use of the chart and a compass will allow you to return to any hot spot with a good chart.

Don't forget to replace old charts with new ones. You can also get from NOAA many very old, out-dated charts for wall displays. They may even have charts of your area that date back as far as the 1800s.

Learn to trust your chart and you'll catch more fish and get there safer and faster.

The datum plane, or reference point, in Atlantic and Gulf of Mexico waters is mean low water—an *average* of the two low tides. Half the time the depth of the water will be slightly lower than indicated. The Pacific Coast charts show the datum as mean *lower* low water—the average of the lower of the two daily tides, making these figures a little closer to the actual low tide. Always allow yourself a safety factor, for unusual local conditions could cause you to run aground.

Never mark a chart with a pen or marking pencil—unless the ink is permanent. At some time during their use all charts get water on them, and important chart notes could be marred. A number 2 lead pencil is good for such work.

Protect your charts from weather and water. Several containers work well. One of the handiest is an old rod case, especially the plastic tubes, which can be shortened with a hacksaw to the proper length. The charts are rolled and inserted into the tube. But store the tube off the deck, since most tubes allow some seepage.

Many fishermen spray their charts with acrylic plastic to give them a flexible clear plastic coating. Sheets of clear plastic can be purchased from upholstery firms. They can be cut slightly larger than the chart when it is flattened. Place a piece of plastic on either side of the chart. Fold a piece of aluminum foil over the outside edges. Then, with a warm iron, run along the edges, sealing the chart into a plastic envelope; be careful not to touch the plastic with the iron or it will melt. To save space, you can glue two charts back-to-back and seal them in a single envelope.

The Hewes Bonefisher is one of the new breed of boats designed for the fly fisherman. Rod holders under the gunwale carry the fly rods out of the way and protected from salt spray. Casting platforms front and back allow the fly rodder to work in confidence. The boat is devoid of entangling devices. The center console is a perfect storage compartment for radio and other important units that need to be kept dry. Note the depth recorder on top of console. Boats like this one, the Rabalo, the Mako, Aquasport, and several other models are the answer to the fly fisherman's dreams.

12 SWFRA—The Saltwater Fly Fisherman's Home

In 1964 a group of men met in Tom's River, New Jersey, to discuss the possibility of forming an organization of saltwater fly fishermen. Among others, Joe Brooks, Charley Waterman, Frank Woolner, Mark Sosin, and I listened intently to what was proposed. We all declared it a good idea. The following spring the group met again, this time more formally. It had grown. Fred Schrier, who had conceived the idea, saw his dream realized. The Salt Water Fly Rodders of America was born.

Some of the red-hot local fishermen, new to fly fishing in the salt but glowing with inner fire, aided immeasurably: George Cornish, Bub Church, Ken Smith, and particularly Cap Colvin, who runs a tackle shop near Tom's River.

The organization got off to a slow start, but within two years reams of copy had been devoted to it by writers from all parts of the country. The aim of the organization was to promote the sport of fly fishing; one of the most important steps taken was the formulation of a world's-record-keeping body, headed by Mark Sosin. This body has done a fantastic job of documenting catches.

The following are the official rules of the organiization:

CLASSES

There will be four separate and distinct classes based on breaking strength of the leader. (See the section on leaders in Chapter 5.)

TIME LIMITS

Claims for fish caught must be postmarked within 60 days of date of catch and received at SWFRA within 90 days of catch.

WEIGHT REQUIREMENTS

To replace an existing record for a fish weighing 25 pounds or more, the replacement must weigh at least one pound (16 ounces) *more* than the existing record. A catch exceeding

Salt Water Fly Rodders of America usually have an annual Get-Together to allow members of the organization to exchange ideas and to meet outstanding anglers in the field. Clinics are conducted. Here the author demonstrates casting, while Mark Sosin explains via a loudspeaker. Stu Apte, who also aided in the clinic, sits to the right.

the existing record by less than one pound will be considered a tie. Nothing less than the existing record will be considered a claim.

SCALES

Wherever possible a government-tested scale or one checked by a reputable fishing club or tournament committee should be used for weighing the fish. This scale should be operated by an accredited weighmaster.

In the event that the tested scale as outlined above is not available, testing the scale by weighing objects of known poundage is mandatory. A sworn affidavit must be effected in the presence of a person authorized to administer oaths, and the weight and exact measurements must be attested to by the angler and at least two witnesses.

No fish weighed at sea or on any vessel will be considered a claim.

At the time of weighing the actual tackle used must be submitted to the weighmaster.

PHOTOGRAPHS

Photographs of fish in all claims are encouraged, but are mandatory in the case of bonefish, bonito, channel bass, drum, jacks, kingfish, mackerels, marlins, permit, pompano, tunas, wahoo, and yellowtail.

It is important that photographs clearly show the fish in a horizontal position, and that all fins, swords or spear jaws, and markings be clearly visible. If possible a ruler or marked tape should be placed beside the fish.

GENERAL RULES

1. The angler must *cast,* hook, fight, and bring the fish to gaff unaided by any other person.

2. A gaff or net not exceeding 8 feet overall length may be used in boating a fish. Only a single or fixed prong may be used on a gaff. Flying gaffs are not permissible.

3. Fish must be hooked in the mouth. Foul hooking or snagging a fish is prohibited.

4. The use of any lure designed to entangle the fish is prohibited.

5. Once the fish is hooked, the tackle may not be altered in any way. This includes the insertion of rod stiffeners *or extension butts.*

6. Fish must be hooked on the lure in use. If a smaller fish takes the lure and a larger fish swallows the smaller fish, the catch will be disallowed.

7. The following acts or omissions will disqualify a catch:

a. Failure to comply with the rules or tackle specifications.

b. Splicing additional line or repairing a broken line during the playing of the fish.

c. Acts of persons other than the angler in adjusting reel drag or touching any part of the tackle during the playing of the fish, or giving aid other than taking the leader for gaffing purposes.

d. Shooting, harpooning, or lancing a fish, including sharks, at any stage of the catch.

e. Small superficial cuts, scratches, or healed scars and regeneration deformities shall not be considered disqualifying injuries. Injuries that affect a fish's ability to fight or its means of propulsion will disqualify the catch.

AFFIDAVITS

The angler is completely and solely responsible for filling in all items on the affidavits; obtaining the necessary signatures and photographs; enclosing the required samples of lines, leader, and lures; and insuring timely arrival at SWFRA headquarters.

RODS

Regardless of materials used or number of sections, rods must conform to generally accepted fly-fishing customs and practices. No rod shall measure less than 6 feet overall. Two-handed rods and rods with extension butts of over 6 inches are expressly prohibited. Any rod that gives the angler an unsporting advantage will disqualify the claim.

REELS

The reel must be designed expressly for fly fishing and cannot be used in casting the fly other than for storage of line. There are no restrictions on ratio of retrieve or type of drag employed except where the angler would gain an unfair advantage. Electric or electronic mechanisms are prohibited.

LINES

Any type of fly line and backing may be used. The breaking strength of the fly line and backing is not restricted.

LEADERS

Certain species of fish dictate the use of a shock tippet because of sharp teeth or gill plates. On the other hand, there are species for which the use of shock material is a disadvantage to the angler. For this reason, each leader class is based solely on the breaking strength of the leader tippet, and a shock leader may be added at the option of the angler.

1. LIGHT TIPPET CLASS (FLY LIGHT). Leaders must follow the accepted fly-fishing customs. Except for the tippet, the leader may be constructed of any material and there will be no restriction on length. The class tippet must be of *nonmetallic material* and attached either directly to the fly or to a shock tippet (which is then attached to the fly). The class tippet must be at least 12 inches long (measured inside any connecting knots) and not test more than 6 pounds breaking strength (wet test).

An additional shock tippet, not to exceed 12 inches, of any material and any test, may be added to the class tippet and attached to the lure. The length of the shock tippet is measured from the eye of the hook to the single strand of class tippet and includes any knots used to connect the shock tippet to the class tippet.

2. MEDIUM TIPPET CLASS (FLY MEDIUM). The same requirements as LIGHT TIPPET CLASS except that the tippet must be at least 12 inches long and not test more than 10 pounds.

3. LIGHT-HEAVY TIPPET CLASS (FLY LIGHT-HEAVY). The same requirements as LIGHT TIPPET CLASS except that the tippet must be at least 12 inches long and test no more than 12 pounds.

4. HEAVY TIPPET CLASS (FLY HEAVY). The same requirements as LIGHT TIPPET CLASS except that the tippet must be at least 12 inches long and test not more than 15 pounds.

LURES

The lure must be artifical of a type made specifically for fly casting and one which may be false cast in the generally accepted manner. Beaded chains, spinners, swivels, and similar devices are prohibited. In the case of weighted lures, the fact that they can be cast is not evidence, in itself, that the lure was designed for fly fishing. It must be light enough to permit repeated false casts without causing undue strain on the angler or his equipment.

CASTING

Casting and retrieving must be carried out in accordance with present and generally accepted customs. Trolling or drifting a lure behind a moving water craft is not permitted regardless of whether said water craft is being propelled, or is drifting with wind, tide, or current. The major criterion in determining proper casting is that the weight of the line carry the lure, rather than the weight of the lure carrying the line.

CLAIMS

No claims will be considered unless accompanied by the lure, entire tippet and leader, and one inch of the fly line beyond the attachment to the leader. These components should be sent intact and connected. The lure will be returned upon request.

WITNESSES

All catches must be witnessed. It is important that the witness attest to compliance with the rules and regulations as set forth above.

CORRESPONDENCE

Any and all correspondence about SWFRA or world fly records or the filing of claims should be addressed to SWFRA, Box 304, Cape May Court House, N.J. 08210.

INDEX

aircraft sight-hunting, 173
American Fishing Tackle Manufacturers' Association (AFTMA), 19,
   20
anchors, 110, *126*, 234
Andrewin, Phillip, 176-177
Apte, Stu, 63-64, *198*, *247*

backing, 18, 40
Barnes, Bill, *104-105*
barracudas, *172*
basking fish tip-offs, 208, *210*
beach fishing situation, *152*
billfish, 219, 222, 225. *See also*
   marlin; sailfish
"billing," *134*, 135
birds, as "signs" of fish, 146-147,
   148, 208, *209*
Blanton, Dan, 84, 155, 156, 201,
   202, 203
blind casting, 144
bluefish, 164-*165*
boat, bonefish or tarpon, *239*
boat, charter, 235
boat equipment, 236
boats, fishing from, 7, *9*, 106-112,
   146, *150*, 162, 184-185, 202,
   234-*235*
bonefish, *176-178*, 179-*183*, 184-
   185
bonito, 169-170
Brodney, Kay, 68
Brooks, Joe, 69, 70, 72, 95, 115,
   180, 185, *188*, *190*, 246
Brothers, Jack, 180
Bryant, Nelson, 235
buoy, 234
butts, extension, *23*

casting. *See* blind casting; fly casting
channel bass, 172-*174*, *175*
charts, 209, 210, *211*, 212, 242-
   245
chugger plug, *216-217*
chum basket (cage), 226, *227*
chumming, 115, 144, 163, 170,
   185, *224*, 226-227, 232, *233*
Church, Bub, 232, 246

clock system of communication, 106-
   107
cobia, *181*
Cochran, Cal, *6*, 59, *129*, 132
Colvin, Cap, 246
compass, 234, *237*
Coogler, Sid, 187
Cornish, George, 246
Crum, Paul, *142*
Cuddy, Lee, 223, 224, 225, 231
Curtis, Bill, 68, *150*, 178, *185*

Dane, Jeff, 164
dangers of handling fish, 136-*139*,
   140-141
deep-water fishing, 204-233
depth finder, 210, 211, 212-213,
   234
discolored water, 146
dolphin, *212*, 225
drag, 28-29, 117-118, 119
Dunaway, Vic, 177, 192, 235
Duncan, Norman, 64, 115, *194*,
   216
Dyer, Gary, 155

East Coast fishing, 11, 13, 63, 158-
   164, 166, 169, 172
Edgely, Bob, 84, 155, 156, *157*,
   201, *202*, 203
electric motors, use of, 238
Emery, John, 64, *194*

ferrules, stuck, *33-34*
fighting a fish, 7, 117-122, *123-
   130*
first aid equipment, 238
Flick, Art, 187
flies, saltwater, 34, 61-65, 66-72,
   88
fly casting, 90-94, 95-96, 97-99,
   100, *101-105*, 109, 112
fly lines, 44, 207
fly patterns, basic saltwater, 72-84
fly reels, 206-207
fly rods, 206-207
food supply container, *237*
Foth, Bart, 135-136, 178

gaffing, *6*, *129*, 131-*132*, *133*-135
Gibbons, Boyd, 232
Gilford, Jim, *6*
Green, Jim, 107, *139*, 163, 192,
   193
Green, Seth, 166
Gregory, Myron, 155, 213
guides (rod), 24-*26*
Gulf Coast, 13

Herrod, J.T., 234
Hewes, Bob, *238*
Hewes Bonefisher, *245*
hooks, 7, 84-85, *86-87*, 88

inshore fish, 144, 146-150
inshore fishing, 7, 144-203, *152*

jack crevalle, *205*
Jansen, Hal, 155
jetty fishing, 162-163
jumping fish, 118-119, *125*, 197
Kime, Harry, 60
king salmon, 201-*202*, 203
kite fishing, *218*
knots, 7, 35-36, 37-*39*, 40, *41-45*,
   47-*58*, 60
Knowles, Captain, 136
Kreh, Dick, *115*
Kreh, Larry, 67, 148, *174*, 214-
   215, 217
Kreh, Lefty, iv, *109-110*, *157*, 172,
   181, *206*, *247*
Kukonen, Paul, 165

ladyfish, *196*
landing fish, 131-141
launching a boat, 241
Lavenstein, Jerry, 178
Laws, Howard, *11*
lead-core lines, 18, 213, 214
leader spools, *58*
leaders, *46-47*, 54, *56-57*, *58-59*,
   60
line, correct use of, 108, *109-113*
line protection, 107-*108*
line selection, 114

line stripping, *124*
lines, 14-20, 30-31
Littleton, J.T., 172
Lohr, Dick, *165*
Lopez, Jim, 187, 214-*215, 216*

MaCathron, Joe, 72
McChristian, Bob, 207
McClellan, Bing, 70
mackerel, *168*
McNally, Tom, 95
Major, Harlan, 218
mangrove snapper, *195*
marlin, 219, 220, *221-223, 224*
marlin popper, *224*
Martuch, Leon, 149
"memory," 108-109
Metropolitan Miami Fishing Tour-
    nament, 136, 172, 178
monofilament, 17, 19, 38-40
Montgomery, Gene, *140*
mutton snapper, *190*
Mylar, 64, 67-68

National Oceanic and Atmospheric
    Administration (NOAA), 11, 12
navigational equipment, modern,
    235
"nervous water," 148, 180, 208
netting, 131
night fishing, 151, 162

offshore fish, 7, 206-210

Pate, Billie, 19, *223*
Pate, Laura, 19, 223
Perinchief, Pete, 69, 232, *233*
permit, *186*-187
Pfeiffer, Boyd, *166*
Pflueger, Al, Jr., 214
polarizing glasses, 106-107, 149,
    150, 179-180
popping bugs, 70-*71*
pumping, 118, *127, 128*

Reagan, Lefty, *221*, 222, 225
redfish. *See* channel bass
reels, 27-*28*, 29-*30*, 31-32
Reiger, George, *217*
releasing fish, 141-*142*
retrieve, the, 114-116
reviving fish, *141*
Ritz, Charles, 57
roamers, 204, 205
Robinson, Dennis, *237*
Robinson, Helen, 219-*220*, 224,
    225
Robinson, Web (Doc), 115, 219-
    220, 221, 222-225
rod handles, 24, *25*
rods, 20-24, 32-33
roosterfish, *195*
rules, fly-casting, 92-95
rules (SWFRA), 246-250

sailfish, 219-220, 222, 223
Salt Water Fly Rodders of America
    (SWFRA), 23, 46, 57, 132, 154,
    213, 246-250
saltwater vs. freshwater fishing, 2-
    10
Sanderson, Sandy, 62
Schmidt, Captain, 219, 222
school of fish, approach to, *160*
Schrier, Fred, 246
Scientific Anglers, 22
sea robin, *161*
sea trout, spotted, 170-*171*, 172
shad, 165-*166*, 167-169
shallow-water fishing, *144*
sharks, 199-*200*
sharpening tool, *85*
shock, 95
shooting basket, 154
shooting tapers, 16-*17*, 18
sight-fishing, 144, 173
sight-hunting, 173
"signs" for spotting fish, 146-150,
    208-209
sink rate, 63, 113
Smith, Ken, 246
snook, 187-*188*, 189-191
Sosin, Mark, *2*, 186-187, *211*, 232,
    233, 236, *243*, 246, *247*

specific-area fish (homebodies), 204,
    205
Splain, Dick, 72
spotting fish, 146-150
squall line, *244*
Stark, Bucky, 223
Stearns, Bob, *6*, 54, 176-177, 182,
    217
stingrays, 151, 153
striking fish, 116
strip bait for teasing, *228-231*
striped bass, 154-164
stripping basket, *153*
Summers, Lawrence, 201, 202, 203
survival gear, 235, 236
Swisher, Doug, *171*
Swope, Irv, 167, 169

Tabory, Lou, 69, *153*
tackle, offshore, 206-208
tackle, use and care of, 6-7, 8, 30-
    34
tarpon, 191-*193, 194*, 195-*198*
teasing, 214-*215*, 216-218, 224,
    225
tides, 10-13
tournament rules, 130
trailering, 238-241
Trimmer, Ross, *239*
tuna, *233*

vise, fly-tying, *62*, 72

wading, 151, 153-154, 184
Wadsworth, Dick, 156-157
water spout, *243*
Waterman, Charley, 135, 246
weakfish, 170-172
weed-line tip-offs, 209, 212
Weinstein, Rocky, *188*
West Coast fishing, 11, 13, 154-
    157, 166, 169, 213
Woolner, Frank, iv, 246
wrecks, 210, *211*, 214
Wulft, Lee, 67

Zimmer, Joe, 57, 58, 167, 169